Seasons of the Southwest

Country Cooking with Herbs

by Susan G. Stephens

Seasons of the Southwest

Country Cooking with Herbs

by Susan G. Stephens

HARBOR
HOUSE (WEST)
PUBLISHERS

Cover Photos: Bill Schlidge
Illustrations: Kathleen Jones
Book and cover design: Soozie Bing

Dedication

To my parents, Joseph Pascal and Catherine Honora Woolverton,
For the sweetness of childhood and the strength of my adult years

Many people offered support and invaluable assistance in this
endeavor. I am deeply grateful to the following friends:

To Irene Schaffer for convincing me I could write this book.

To Sheila Fox who helped me decide "when to hold 'em and when
to fold 'em" and was ever present with words of Irish wisdom.

To Madelyn Engel for her editing assistance and unwavering loyalty.

To Western Growers Association and especially former WGA
Governor John Powell for technical crop and product information.

Table of Contents

Cafe *This logo indicates recipe
favorites from Cafe Del Rey Moro*

Country Fresh
Products

"If we are in tune with Nature, all her music can find a way into the heart."

- Bolles

Have you ever stopped at a roadside produce stand? Then you've taken the first step toward cooking with the seasons! This book offers an immediate connection to the Earth's peaceful seasons amid the bustle of contemporary life. Cooking with the seasons renews our connection to the earth cycles. Learn how to grow your own herbs (see Spring Lore, page 19) and produce, or ask a farmer's leave to pick from his fields or orchards.

I find myself wondering about the journey food has taken from growth through harvest to my hands. It is enlightening to understand that journey. Buying from small local growers, neighborhood fruit stands, or farmers' markets offers this knowledge. I prefer to think of *people* processing my food rather than machines.

Not everyone has the space or time to grow food products, but you might experiment with some potted herbs or a tomato plant. Picking your own is amazingly satisfying, even if your bounty is just a sprig of parsley, basil or mint.

Seasons in the Southwest

Cooking with regional products automatically puts you in touch with seasonal cycles. The food that is freshly grown is the food that shows up in the smaller markets and stands. One of the most interesting food concepts I learned in Europe is that regional products have a natural affinity for each other and for the climate. For example, wine made from a particular region's grapes complements local cheeses and produce. This comes from perfect combinations nature makes through soil nutrients and climatic conditions. Explore these natural affinities, and you'll be pleasantly surprised.

Because we are fortunate to have a myriad of products available year round in our supermarkets, it's easy to lose touch with seasonal foods. To heighten awareness, I've included a Harvest Calendar at the end of the chapters for Spring, Summer, Autumn and Winter that lists seasonal product availability.

I also suggest you take the time to develop your own sources for fresh regional products. Here's some ideas to get you started.

Developing Sources

- *Contact the State Department of Agriculture or a County department to request a list of growers, markets and products in your area. If you are unsure who to contact, talk to your local librarian.*

- *Look in the Yellow Pages of your telephone directory to find certified farmers markets and local bazaars.*

- *Search for local produce stands or farmers markets. These are often open only one or two days a week. Ask people who work around food or cooking products if they know of any resources. Because I love to frequent local markets wherever I travel, I check with guidebooks, waiters, cabdrivers, and bellmen. Locals know when and where the markets occur. In other countries, markets are an ordinary part of life. The trend to smaller markets is now returning to more heavily populated areas in the Southwest.*

- *Rely on the old-fashioned barter system. Find out which of your friends and co-workers is interested in trading their fresh produce surplus for yours. If you have friends who make jams, jellies, condiments or canned produce, suggest trading these items also.*

- *Consider a thrifty ad in your neighborhood newspaper offering to buy local produce from small home or farm growers.*

- *Look on the neighborhood bulletin boards and newsletters, and post your own notices to buy or trade produce or herbs.*

- *Find out the schedule of your local church bazaars which may feature homemade product or fresh produce.*

- *Go into the wild woods. I add some caveats here:*
  Make certain the wild woods do not belong to someone else. If they do, get permission to gather. I have planted an entire parking strip in various types of rosemary. I would be happy to share, but I do resent the neighbors who sneak over to my garden and surreptitiously snatch herbs.
  Study botany so that you know what you are gathering. There are many good references on edible plants of the Southwest (See appendix). Sage and chamomile grow wild everywhere. I won't chance gathering any kind of wild mushroom or unidentified herb. Too scary!

- *Try going on early morning walks to see what nature has provided. Even in the middle of the city, I find seed pods, pine cones, and avocados lying in vacant lots or sidewalks.*

Traditional Southwestern Ingredients

Nowhere do the cooking traditions of the old world and the new combine so vibrantly as they do in Southwest cuisine. The Spanish and French introduced these old world ingredients as they colonized Mexico and the American Southwest:

black pepper	cinnamon	cloves	thyme
marjoram	bay leaves	wheat	chickpeas
melons	onions	grapes	sugar cane
radishes	beef	pork	chicken
mint	garlic	cilantro	

The indigenous Indian populations — Aztec, Mayan and Olemec had cultivated new world products for centuries. Native products include:

beans	peppers	squash	chiles
corn	avocados	coconuts	papayas
pineapples	prickly pears	tomatillos	peanuts
pumpkin seeds	turkey	mango	chocolate
vanilla	nopales or cactus pads		

Today, these traditional ingredients are being served in ever new combinations and form the basis of contemporary Southwestern cuisine.

Subtropical Fruits of the Southwest

Cactus Fruit or Prickly Pear. The "tuna," or fruit of the cactus, was appreciated by the early mining population of California. It has a pleasant acid flavor. To open the fruit and avoid the prickles, lay the pear on a plate; then, holding it firm by means of a fork, cut off both ends, slit the skin lengthwise and turn it back, thus exposing the flesh. It may be eaten thus with a fork, first squeezing lemon juice over it and sprinkling it with powdered sugar; or it may be sliced and served in fruit dishes.

The Carissa or Natal Plum, which is extremely decorative as a plant, bears a beautiful little fruit. The fruits - bright red, about the shape and size of a date - ripen almost continuously, but the chief crop comes in fall. Carissas have been used like cherries for pies, tarts and dumplings, first scalding them to take off the skin, then cutting them and removing the inner seedy pulp, the juice of which may be utilized. The result is delicious. Cooked with sugar, the little plums make a delicious sauce scarcely distinguishable from cranberry sauce. Carissas also make good jam, or they can be cut into thin, round sections and used with charming effect as a garnish for pear or pineapple salad.

Cherimoya or "Cherimoyer." Connoisseurs have pronounced the cherimoya fruits among the most delicious in the world. They are roughly heart-shaped and sometimes very large, their weight with us ranging from a few ounces to 2 or 3 pounds. The color is a soft green at maturity, changing to russet, brown and almost black, where the fruit is still edible, though not at its best. The flesh is a white custard with many large, black seeds. The best way to eat a cherimoya is to break the fruit, put a portion into a saucer, and dip the pulp from the thick skin with a spoon, rejecting the seeds as one does cherry stones. Or, if one has the patience to seed the pulp before serving, it makes a wonderful element in a fruit salad, being delicately sweet and spicy, with a trace of acid and what one can only call an exotic flavor. It is best as it comes fresh from the garden.

Guava. Two types of guava are grown in southern California; the strawberry guava, red as its name would imply, and the pineapple guava, lemon yellow in color. Within the waxed skin is a layer of firm flesh, then a central mass of seed and pulp. Sometimes the interior is pink and sometimes creamy white. Whatever the tint, the flavor may be either acid or quite sweet, and always highly — some would say obtrusively — aromatic. The firm, fleshy layer is used in preserves, becoming deep red, as pear or quince will, and very rich and tender. In California, where fruit salads are so popular, the fleshy part of the raw guava, peeled, cut small, and added to other fruits gives the palate a real thrill.

Flowering Apple, Plum, Quince, etc. A number of the ornamental fruit trees or shrubs grown solely for their blossoms produce, under favorable conditions, a crop of beautiful small fruits. These small fruits can be used for jelly and preserves with very good results.

Loquat, one of the most popular of ornamental fruiting trees, produces delicious as well as beautiful golden-yellow fruit in huge clusters. Fruits of the better varieties grow as large as eggs. In addition to being a delightful table fruit, and one that comes on earlier than most other fruits, the loquat makes excellent jams, jellies, and preserves.

Mango. The mango fruits are delicious things, though a novice must approach their flavor with some caution. Long ago, somebody described mangoes as like nothing so much as bunches of tow dipped in turpentine. It was high-flavored and juicy, mingling tart with sweet, and not especially fibrous, though the flesh clung fast to the big seed. The turpentine taste, so often referred to, is very noticeable in poor varieties; in really good ones it is absent, or remains only as a nutty, aromatic suggestion. Mangoes can be used just before they mature as a substitute for green apples in sauce and pies. When the ripe fruits are cooked they have more the texture and savor of stewed peaches, though they lose more than a peach in cooking. If you have access to a mango tree, it is best to let the fruit hang until it begins to soften, then carefully peel off the unpleasantly flavored rind, cut the flesh from the seed, and eat it at once. The richer ones are nice with Créme Fraiche and damara sugar, or try it with a squeeze of fresh lime.

Papaya or Melon Pawpaw or Melon Tree. The papaya is a tropical tree fruit which has many of the characteristics of a melon. The fruit is pear-shaped; the thick rind is green when immature, turning yellow as it ripens. The flesh is somewhat like the muskmelon in texture and its seed cavity and arrangement of the seeds. The papaya is ready to be eaten as soon as the impression of the thumb makes a dent in it. At this time, it should be placed in the refrigerator. Serve chilled with a squeeze of lime. After the fruit is cut, any unused portion may be returned to the refrigerator and kept for days.

Passion Fruit. The fruit of the passion vine is not only edible, but delicious indeed in flavor. About the size of a small hen's egg, the passion fruit when ripe is deep purple in color. Its thin, brittle, shell-like skin encloses a mass of small seeds covered with a brilliant yellow pulp. The juice of this fruit, which is on the market in bottled form, is a delicious addition to a number of fruit dishes. Sprinkled over fruits for salad, added to filling for lemon pie, added to fruit drinks, or used in various other ways, the distinctive flavor always excites the wonder and admiration of guests. The juice also makes excellent jam and jelly.

Wild Fruits of the Southwest

Beach Strawberry or Sea Fig. The good-sized fruit of Mesembryanthemum aequilaterale is gathered along the seashore. Its flavor remotely resembles that of the strawberry.

Buffalo Berry has small, edible acid fruits.

Blackberry or Dewberry. Use this as the tame fruit.

Crabapple. Small, acid fruit, used for jelly by pioneers.

Elderberries. These grow larger and juicer here in the West, and make delicious jam or jelly to serve with rich meats, such as pork. Combined with wild grapes for tartness, they make delicious pies also.

Huckleberries, juicy and delicious, are much used for canning and piemaking. The wild huckleberries are of several varieties, not all of them plentiful enough to be of commercial value.

Manzanita. The "little apple" of the Spaniards is a tiny, rather dry, and sub-acid fruit. It may be made into jelly before it is entirely ripe.

Wild Salal Berries. Too sweet to be pleasant by themselves, these combine deliciously with the grape in a mixture that is one-third salal and two-thirds grape juice.

Thimble Berry. A scarlet berry, related to the raspberry, and good to eat fresh.

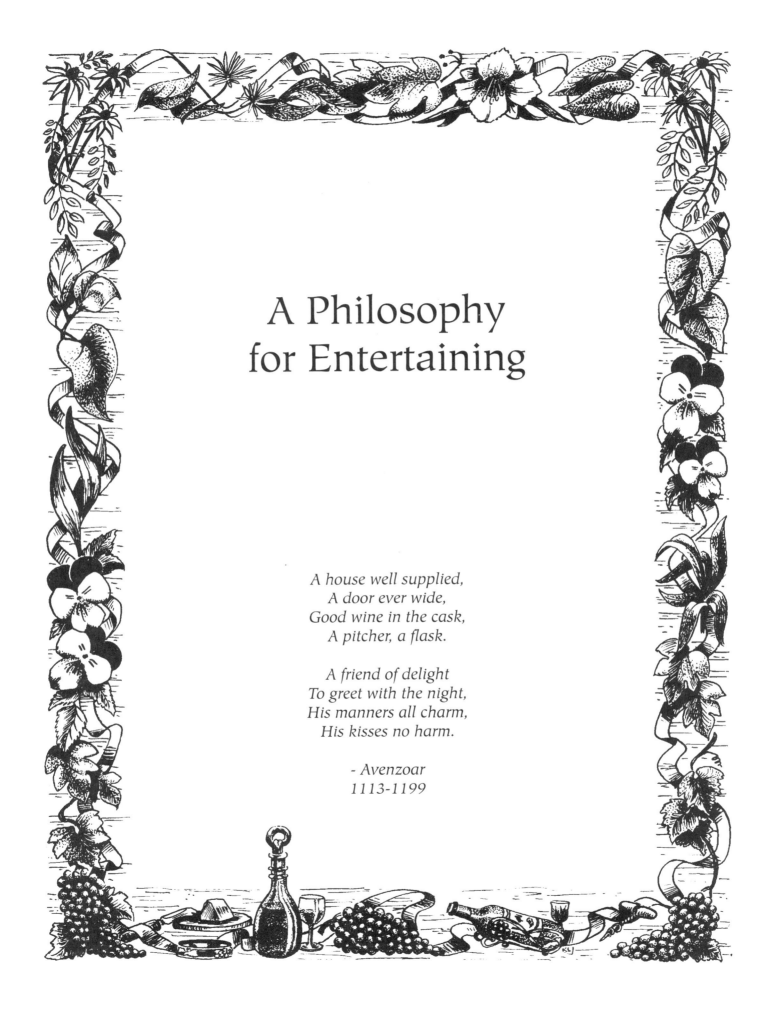

A Philosophy
for Entertaining

A house well supplied,
A door ever wide,
Good wine in the cask,
A pitcher, a flask.

A friend of delight
To greet with the night,
His manners all charm,
His kisses no harm.

- Avenzoar
1113-1199

Why are some events so memorable? Why do some homes seem so cozy? Why do we feel so welcomed by some hosts? I enjoy entertaining, and I often ponder these questions. In observing the hundreds of private parties I have planned for various clients or attended as a guest, I find that memorable events all have some points in common.

Nuture

Let your hospitality provide a special escape for your guests. Think of all the little things your guests may need or enjoy beyond basic food and beverage. Visualize your party or event. Will the day be sunny or wintry? How will guests arrive? Will they know each other? What will happen prior to your meal, during, after? This visualization exercise will give you valuable clues to anticipate your guests comfort level. How would you want to feel arriving at your party? What would **you** find disastrous or uncomfortable if you were experiencing your event as a guest.

Tips to Make Guest feel Welcome and At Ease

- *Send maps with invitations.*

- *Arrange valet parking for large groups.*

- *Hoist a colorful, decorative banner or flag at the front of your home to identify the party location for guests unfamiliar with your address.*

- *Provide a coat rack or umbrella stand.*

- *Hire a helpful "butler" to whisk away coats, purses, etc.*

- *Make name tags for large parties where many do not know each other.*

- *Break the ice by adding a symbol or key word under guests' names. Try a drawing of a suitcase, or a word like "Bali" under the name of a travel agent friend. This ploy gives guests a comfort level and makes them feel a part of the group.*

- *Will the day be blustery? How about a spiced cider, hot buttered rum or cocoa on arrival?*

- *Be available to greet guests. Plan to be and stay near the entry area for at least the first hour of arrivals.*

- *Always introduce guests to everyone at small events; to at least two other people at large events.*

- *What ever you do, make your guest feel as if you have taken the time to make him feel like a VIG (very important guest). If you convey this ego satisfying message well, you'll be a hero and a huge success.*

Amuse

Let your imagination run wild. You want your guests to have fun, so begin by having fun yourself.

How to Amuse Your Guests

- *Dress in a festive manner. Wear fishing lures as earrings to a fish fry. How about bells for holidays?*

- *Request in advance that everyone participate in a special dress or item of apparel; BUT keep it simple. Wear a crazy hat? Wear red for a Red Hot Evening? A Black and White Ball? Wear Gardening Clothes to my Garden Party? Come as your Favorite Fantasy? Come as your Favorite Hero? Come as You Are?*

- *Look for clever cocktail napkins.*

- *Give guests something to do besides talk.*

    - *Provide music or singers: carolers for the holidays, sea chanteys for a cruise or a fish fry, or a strolling guitarist to take requests.*

    - *Invite a palm reader to foresee the future.*

    - *Find a paper flower maker or craftsman to entertain. Give away the flowers or crafts as mementos.*

    - *Hire a costumed storyteller to spin wild yarns.*

    - *Rent a famous person look-alike, so your guests can talk to the stars.*

    - *Provide an astrologer for simple predictions (keep it light and general).*

    - *Offer a self-tour card pointing out items of interest, history and location:*
      — of your garden's rare plants, flowers or herbs
      — of your collection of art, antique boxes, needlepoint pillows, model trains,whatever
      — of your architecture if it's unusual or historical
      Keep the card simple, so guests won't feel obligated to march around, but will have the option to amuse themselves if they feel ill at ease mingling or chatting.

- *Arrange polaroid photo favors. Provide a special backdrop. Put the photos in folders available at photo supply stores. Personalize the folder to your party theme.*

Surprise

Have some fun and surprise your guests by doing unexpected things such as:

- *Putting a half moon on your bathroom door.*

- *Using raffia as napkin rings for a barn dance. Add a fresh daisy on top.*

- *Tucking paper fortunes into the meal napkin.*

- *Giving table favors.*

Surprise **and** amuse your guests with unusual centerpieces:

- *A Rooster alarm clock surrounded with square hard-boiled eggs. (Yes, they make square egg presses.)*

- *An edible centerpiece. (See section on edible centerpieces on page 13.)*

- *Centerpieces that include mini-gifts for the guest to select. For example: A miniature tree with victorian ornaments.*

- *Mass similar objects. For example: Large and small bunnies amid florists moss and potted violets on a mirrored runner.*

Be creative in your food presentations. You'll find many ideas and recipes in future chapters.

- *Add edible flower garnishes to any course.*

- *Use food art garnishes — make a radish, turnip, tomato, or onion flower.*

- *Freeze flowers or herbs in ice cubes for summer drinks.*

- *Use unusual containers: Hollow out a small loaf of bread or small squash to hold a cream soup or bisque. Use Ruffled clam shells for butter or condiments. Hollow cabbages or eggplants for dips. Make watermelon bowl baskets for fresh fruit displays.*

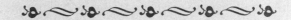

Table Favor Ideas

- *A tequila-lime sucker in the shape of a cactus*
- *A book mark*
- *A packet of herbs with a recipe*
- *Decorated sachets*
- *Miniature apothecary jars of tiny jelly beans*
- *Decorated gingerbread boys, girls, dogs, cats, bears, pigs, elephants, etc.*
- *Unusual votive candles at each place to light the table; then take home as a keepsake*
- *Miniature vases at each place to provide decor; then take home as a keepsake*
- *A spray of herbs or miniature nosegay tucked in napkins*
- *A basket, porcelain box or any unusual container filled with imported sweets*
- *An elegantly boxed individual truffle*
- *A cleverly decorated "grown-up" party favor sack filled with old-fashioned candies, streamers, noisemakers, gold chocolate coins, a fortune cookie, etc.*
- *Victorian Postcards*
- *French turn-of-the-century photographic postcards*
- *Miniature picture frames with a picture of your guest*
- *An unusual napkin ring to use; then take home as a keepsake*

Provide "Extra Something"

In Creole New Orleans, it's called a "Lagniappe" when you receive that "extra something". "Lagniappe" refers to the thirteenth cookie you receive when you buy a dozen or the colorful free wrap that comes with a shop purchase.

If you have used some of the suggestions above for nurturing, amusing, and surprising, chances are your guest already feels his entertainment experience has included an "Extra Something".

I often give a parting keepsake as well. These are kept in a big wicker basket by the door. These are usually edible or herbal—a small package of the cookies served with dessert, bath herbs, or the recipes served on 3" x 5" recipe cards and tied with a ribbon or raffia.

You'll find lots of ideas for parting keepsakes in the "Seasonal Gifts" section of each season chapter.

Make Guests Feel Paramount

For the few hours guests are with you, make them feel as if you totally focused on them. Be rested and relaxed. Do your food preparation and cooking ahead of time. If you do too much bustling around, guests will feel uncomfortable or downright harried. Plan your event well, and get an extra pair of hands if you need them. For help with a small group, ask one guest to tend bar, another to help clear. If you stay relaxed, so will your guests. Have fun, and your guests will too.

Recipes that Help

The recipes in this book are selected with guest delight in mind. An unusual presentation, use of special ingredients, a bit of history to go with the dish or ingredient are all sources of this delight. They are also designed to keep you relaxed and WITH your guests.

The entertainment menus and recipes in this book have the following points in common:

- *They can be prepared ahead.*

- *They require little or no time away from you guests if you are working as chef and server, as well as host, for the evening.*

- *All recipes list preparation time and cooking time; neither is excessive.*

- *For advance preparation, a "STOP and store" instruction is included in the recipes.*

- *The recipes allow an oven finish or a very brief final cooking period.*

"Mise en Place"

This is a French term that refers to having all ingredients available and ready in the shape called for by the recipe. You may wish to review recipes that will be used for an entire meal. Process all items that need slicing or mincing at one time. You will be surprised how much time you save by preparing your "Mise en place" before you begin cooking.

TARRAGON

Respect For Our Bounty

*"Although a lost work of art may be recreated,
or the phrases of a symphony reformed in a new melody, when
the last specimen of a plant or animal vanishes from
this planet, another heaven and another earth must come
to pass before such a thing can be again."*

Is the current emphasis on the "greening of America" new? Not really. Ever since we began seeing indications that nature's supplies may not be unlimited, people have expressed concern for our environment, for our natural resources and for diminishing plant and animal species. Today, when the quality of basic resources like air and water are threatened, living in harmony with our environment has assumed new importance.

Primitive people since the dawn of mankind placed great importance on using available resources as needed and without waste. Early settlers in the American Southwest practiced conservation by necessity because of limited supply and remote locations. Today, when the world's marketplace is a phone call or credit card away, is conservation relevant?

Yes!! By conserving, recycling and using fully what you have, you do contribute to the earth's balance.

Utilize All Available Product

In the restaurant industry, the best possible food cost does not come from purchasing at the lowest price. It is a result of utilizing everything you buy. In addition to offering superior flavors and freshness, cooking seasonally and using fresh available products saves on packaging and storing. The Gilroy Garlic Festival in California has proven one herb can provide an entire menu.

Do you have too much of a "good thing"? Sometimes, when produce comes into season, it does so with a vengeance, and you often have more than you can use. Consider a "tongue in cheek" approach to entertaining and celebrate your abundant harvest. For example, everyone knows that zucchinis are one of the most prolific vegetables in the garden. Here's a "Zucchini Harvest Menu" to start you thinking.

Zucchini Harvest Menu

Curried Zucchini Soup

Zucchini Parmigiana

Buttered Pasta with Herbs

Zucchini Pudding

Garlic Festival Menu

Roasted Garlic Spread with Toast Points

Capellini with Garlic and Herbs

Vegetables with Bacon and Garlic

Garlic Ice Cream

Use nature's available bounty as fully as possible, then preserve what is left by drying, canning or freezing. I have included a chart for freezing produce and fruit at the end of this chapter.

Give or trade surplus produce. The "gift ideas" section at the end of each season also offers ideas for preserving abundant supply.

Prior to 1900, when bread provided 80% of the French, English and American diet, recipes took advantage of "day old bread" in many ways. Pain Perdu (Lost Bread) is the French name for our "French Toast" and it really is better made with day old bread.

Fresh Bread Crumbs

Tear the bread slices into 1 inch pieces and grind them fine in batches in a food processor. The crumbs keep in an airtight container, chilled, for 2 weeks and frozen for 6 months.

Cheese Pudding and Trifle (Winter) and Summer Pudding (Summer) are delicious ways to make certain that no bread goes to waste. Make soup or snack croutons by slicing day-old baguettes or rolls, brushing lightly with olive oil and sprinkling with minced garlic or parmesan cheese. Toast in a 300 degree oven for 15 minutes.

Make salad croutons by removing crusts from day-old bread and cutting into 1/2" cubes. Saute 1 cup of cubed bread in 1 tablespoon olive oil and 1/4 teaspoon well-ground herbs of provence until cubes are coated. Then spread on baking sheet, and toast in a 300 degree oven for 15 minutes.

Make bread crumbs for use with Lamb with Herb Crust and Scallops Santiago (Spring). Store the remainder for future use.

Edible Centerpieces

As another clever approach to utilizing all available supply, make edible centerpieces.

This concept can be as simple as a woven basket cornucopia filled with rolls and breads of different shapes and colors tumbling out in profusion, and a shock of wheat tied with raffia or ribbon. Serve butter in a hollowed out squash or gourd.

What about a bowl of fresh and/or sugared fruits to be eaten with an assortment of cheeses for dessert (see Summer for fruit and cheese charts)? Or use one day's menu vegetables artfully arranged as the previous day's centerpiece. When massing fruits or vegetables in a centerpiece, you can add garden flowers or herb flowers in florist tubes throughout the arrangement for a touch of the unexpected.

In Springtime, I place giant ornamental kale in two terra cotta cachepots at either end of the dining room table. As I harvest lower leaves for garnishes or for salads, my table centerpiece slowly becomes more topiary in appearance until I have kale "trees". A large ceramic rabbit sits between the two cachepots.

Use reusable wooden forms as the base for edible centerpieces. Select a wooden cone or mill post with a circular top. Spray paint the wooden base forest green using non-toxic paint. Hammer in three to four inch finish nails evenly spaced all over the wooden form.

 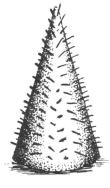 

Now cover the "tree" with fruits, mini-gingerbreads, vegetables, mini-muffins, or any edible product you can impale successfully. If you use vegetables, do them in designs.

OLIVES

BUTTON MUSHROOMS

BROCCOLI

CAULIFLOWER

With a little practice, you can do an hors d'oeuvres tree of salami cones with stuffed green olives.

1. Slice of Salami   *2. Folded in half*   *3. Rolled around olive*

An alternative base is a styrofoam cone covered with foil and studded with nails. This may work best for floppy items (like the salami cones) because you can pin them on instead of impaling them.

To wash finish nails for reuse, line the silver holder in your dishwasher with a piece of flexible plastic screen. Put in the nails, run dishwasher, and remove screen with the nails inside!

Recycle

In addition to composting and recycling in ordinary ways, be extraordinary and clever in your approach to recycling containers or glass.

I have always been fascinated by clear glass jars, bottles, canisters, and glasses. I collect them to reuse for my seasonal gifts. An empty container seems to have such great potential.

Bazaars, garage sales, antique shops and country markets are excellent sources. Glass can be sterilized and reused easily. Notice unusual shapes or attractive containers in your own cupboard and reuse them. Spray jar lids, if they need refreshing or purchase fresh cork stoppers. These recycled containers work for herbed oils, herbed vinegars, dried herb mixes, sauces, mustards, cordials and any other of the seasonal gifts.

Decorate the tops of filled gift containers with lace doilies or colorful fabric squares tied with ribbon or raffia. Add a sprig of dried herbs. Tie a card listing ingredients, recipe or serving suggestions to the gift. Search for old fashioned relish plates or cut glass bowls to combine with a bottle of homemade jelly, sauce, chutney, or mustard. Tie an antique teaspoon or pickle fork to your gift.

Buy old fashioned ribbons, laces or doilies to enhance your presentation. Metal containers can be refreshed using gold, silver or bronze florist spray. It is fast drying and waterproof. It won't survive dishwashers or heavy use, but it works wonders on packaging.

You can turn recycling into a creative adventure by looking at old containers in new ways. Here is an unusual approach to recycling.

To clear hard water marks from antique glass or crystal vases, use a denture cleaner. Fill container with water and add one or two tablets depending on volume.

Assembling a Victorian Basket

Victorians were hopeless romantics who made picnics as entertainment a popular pastime. Elaborate silver boxes held sterling utensils and containers for royalty. Common folk were content with everyday crockery, silver and linens packed up in a wicker hamper.

Find an old hamper or antique basket (they were heavy duty, sturdy affairs meant to carry heavy loads). Add an antique linen cloth and four napkins, matching or similar. Look for four old plates that needn't be matching, but look best if they have something in common, like size, color, color trim, or floral motif. Find four old goblets of a similar size and shape. Collect four silver sets of fork, knife and spoon. Try to match at least fork, knife and spoon, although having four different patterns in the basket adds interest.

Also look for four embroidered antique linen tea or hand towels. You need 8 grosgrain or white lace ribbons, 18 inches in length.

Now, line the basket with the folded tablecloth. Pack plates alternately with two of the tea towels to cushion china. Wrap each napkin around a goblet, tying with a ribbon. Tie a ribbon around each "set" of silver, and roll all four in a tea towel.

Before packing foods on top, cover bottom layer with the last tea towel. Your basket should now travel without breakage to that shady glen where you can read romantic sonnets, feast on gourmet delicacies or play croquet. Wear white and don a straw hat.

See the "Country Picnics" section in Summer for delectable menus and recipes.

Fruit Freezing Chart
(All fruits can be stored for 9-12 months)

FRUIT	PREPARATION	PACKING
Apples	Pare, core, slice and add ascorbic acid.	Pack dry with sugar for pies, or cook in light syrup 3 minutes, or cook until tender and puree.
Apricots	Scald, peel, halve and pit and add ascorbic acid.	Pack dry with sugar or cover with light or medium syrup.
Avocados	Peel, remove seed and puree.	Add an eighth teaspoon ascorbic acid or 1 cup sugar per quart of puree.
Blackberries	Pick over, wash in ice water, dry if necessary.	Freeze dry with or without sugar, or cover with light syrup.
Blueberries	Pick over, wash in ice water, dry if necessary.	Freeze dry with or without sugar, or cover with light syrup.
Cherries	Remove stems and wash; remove pits (optional) and add ascorbic acid.	Freeze dry with or without sugar, or cover with medium syrup.
Cranberries	Wash and dry.	Freeze dry without sugar.
Figs	Wash, halve, slice or leave whole and add ascorbic acid.	Cover with light or medium syrup.
Grapefruit; Oranges	Chill, peel, removing pith and cut in sections; add ascorbic acid.	Cover with light syrup.
Grapes	Wash and peel; remove seeds, if you like.	Cover with light syrup.
Melons	Cut in slices, cubes or balls.	Cover with light syrup.
Nectarines; Peaches	Scald, peel, halve and pit; slice (optional) and add ascorbic acid.	Cover with light or medium syrup.
Pears	Pare, core, slice and add ascorbic acid.	Cook in light syrup 2 minutes, or cook until tender and puree.
Pineapples	Remove skin and core, cut in slices.	Freeze dry without sugar, or cover with light or medium syrup.
Plums	Wash, halve and pit; add ascorbic acid.	Cover with light or medium syrup.
Raspberries	Pick over; wash only if necessary and dry.	Freeze dry with or without sugar.
Rhubarb	Wash and slice.	Freeze dry with or without sugar, or cover with light syrup.
Strawberries	Hull; wash in cold water only if necessary, leave whole or sliced.	Freeze dry with or without sugar, or cover with light or medium syrup.

For light syrup, allow 3/4 cup sugar to 2 cups water; for medium syrup, 2 cups sugar to 2 cups water. When packing dry with sugar, allow about 1 cup sugar for every quart fruit, depending on acidity.

Vegetable Freezing Chart

VEGETABLE	STORAGE TIME	PREPARATION	BLANCHING/COOKING TIME
Asparagus	9-12 months	Trim	2-4 minutes
Beans, Green	1 year	Top and tail, slice or leave whole	2 minutes, sliced; 3 minutes, whole
Beans, Lima	1 year	Shell	2-3 minutes
Beets (small)	6 months	Cook, peel, slice or dice	
Broccoli	1 year	Cut into 4 inch sprigs	3 minutes
Brussel Sprouts	1 year	Pick over and trim.	3-5 minutes
Cabbage	6-8 months	Shred.	1-1/2minutes; use only as a cooked vegetable
Carrots (small)	6 months	Scrape; slice or dice if large.	2-3 minutes
Cauliflower	6 months	Cut into florets.	3 minutes
Corn (ears)	1 year	Shuck and trim.	7-11 minutes if left on cob
Corn (kernels)	6 months	Stem; cook, then leave on cob or cut off.	4 minutes for kernels
Celery	6 months	Dice or slice.	3 minutes; use only as a cooked vegetable
Mushrooms	1 year	Wash in water with lemon juice, trim stems.	steam 3-5 minutes or fry in butter
Peas, Green	1 year	Shell	1-1/2 minutes
Peppers	1 year	Discard core and seeds, chop or finely slice.	1-2 minutes; use only as a cooked vegetable.
Pumpkin (puree)	6 months	Peel and cut in 1 inch cubes, cook and puree.	8 minutes or until tender
Spinach; Other Greens	1 year	Wash and dry.	1-3 minutes
Squash, Summer	9 months	Wash and slice.	3 minutes
Squash, Winter (puree)	6 months	Peel, cut in cubes, cook and puree.	8-10 minutes or until tender
Tomatoes (puree)	1 year	Scald, peel, remove seeds, cook, puree and sieve.	5 minutes
Tomatoes (quartered)	1 year	Scald, peel and cook.	10-20 minutes; use only as a cooked vegetable

Spring

"So the Spring days came and went, the sky grew clearer, the earth greener, the flowers were up fair and early . . ."

Alcott

The vernal equinox on March 21, marks the first day of Spring, a time of new beginnings. Bulbs sprout, plants begins to bloom again vigorously. The gray days of winter are behind us and brighter, warmer days are ahead. Little green shoots break expectantly through the soil and trees begin to blossom. As a child, we had an almond tree filled with white blossoms. I'd stand under it, while the spring breeze sent down showers of petals, and pretend I was a character in a toy snow scene.

In the Southwest, asparagus, artichokes, snap peas, grapefruits, avocados, peas, navel oranges, lemons, sweet corn, mushrooms, sorrel, carrots, baby lettuces, scallops, salmon, shrimp and seafood, fennel and sweet onions come into season.

Welcome the Spring by buying or growing armloads of bulb flowers. Fill your home and heart with daffodils, tulip, and hyacinths. Decorate with potted blooming plants. Cut branches of fruit tree blossoms and sprays of pussy willow. Clean and cull your herb gardens, adding new plants as needed.

Celebrate by preparing a traditional Spring feast, on March 21st. Have a sunrise picnic in a field of daisies overlooking the ocean, or in any other spot that inspires you. Visit the desert to view the year's new crop of wild flowers brought by winter rains.

In order to insure that your cupboards contain only the freshest seasonal food stuffs, welcome Spring by making certain winter's ingredients are used and stock up with Spring's bounty. Reserve an afternoon to gather and dry mint, rosemary and thyme. Make up herbal oils and vinegars, honey mustard, sun-dried tomato sauce, mint sauce, and herbal seasonings for your cupboard and to give as gifts.

Spring Lore
Herbs

My father was raised on a ranch in Nevada by my French grandmother. Herbs were gathered and used as a matter of course. The vegetable and flower gardens had herbs growing everywhere with the careless abandon of weeds. We also gathered wild herbs — squaw tea, wild sage, and watercress from the streams. In October, we picked our yearly supply of pinenuts from the piñon pines, a very sticky endeavor. It took almost as long to clean off the pitch as it did to pick the pine cones with their meaty nuts.

Stream fishing brought trout and salmon to the table. In the fall, hunting stocked the larder with pheasant, duck, quail, dove, partridge, and deer. We made a pact with nature never to take more than we could use, a legacy perhaps of the Piute Indian ranch hands.

Herbs have always been an important part of our cuisine. They were readily available and used to flavor everything. Surprisingly, I took this fresh, gourmet approach toward food completely for granted until I moved to southern California, where gourmet cuisine has reached cult status.

Grow Your Own

Even if you live in an apartment, try growing herbs. Most are hardy, easy to grow, and provide a great spark for seasonal cooking. I grow a full assortment of herbs, and most do grow like weeds. Try to plant those that prefer a drier soil in one area and those that love moisture in another. Below are some suggestions for laying out an herb garden of your own.

I also grow herbs, as my grandmother did, among my flowers. Mints and pennyroyal love the azalea bed. Lavender and thyme grow well with geraniums. I have an entire parking strip planted in three different types of upright and prostrate rosemary, with some decorative boulders and purple statice flowers. Herbs also act as a natural insecticide, and reduce plant pests for the flowers. Best herbs to reduce pests are marigolds, pennyroyal, nastursiums, garlic, chives, thyme, sage, lavender, and tansy.

Select a location that has good drainage for all herbs. Consider a raised bed bordered by railroad ties, so that you can add top soil and a high quality compost to provide the very best start for your garden. However, remember that too many nutrients will reduce the concentration of flavors in herbs. If possible, select a north/south alignment so that each side of the bed receives morning and afternoon sun.

For a sun herb garden, select a spot that receives full morning and afternoon sun, and no shade. Somewhat sandy soil conditions improve drainage, but may require more added nutrients. I water three times a week for five minutes with an automatic system. Use hay or straw to mulch. Avoid any mulch that is overly acidic. Sun loving herbs are rosemary, lavender, thyme, lemon thyme, cilantro, fennel, tarragon, marjoram, winter savory, summer savory, bay, chives, sage, basil and dill.

For herbs that enjoy more moisture, select a spot with some morning and afternoon shade to filter sunlight, and only about 5 hours of full sunlight. I water five times each week for 5 minutes, again with an automatic system. Again, use mulch to help retain moisture and soil nutrients. Herbs that enjoy a moist, loamy bed are mint, pennyroyal, French sorrel, parsley, chervil, viola, and tansy.

For ease of cutting, make beds about two feet deep. For accessibility, use stepping stones, gravel or flagstone paths to bisect wider beds. I use 12"x12" "adobe" pavers reinforced with concrete.

Culinary Herb Garden

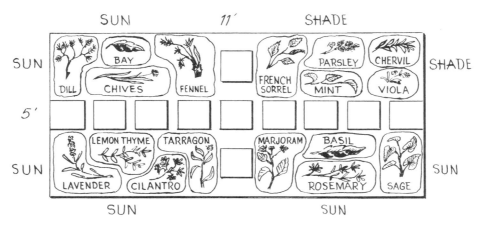

Picking and Drying Herbs

Home dried herbs are fresher and better than most store-bought products. Harvest in the early morning after the dew has dried, but before the heat of midday sun. Use kitchen shears and a basket for gathering. Shake the herbs thoroughly over the sink to dislodge any loose debris or wandering insects. If you feel the need, rinse in tepid water and spread over paper towels or cloths to air dry quickly in a warm place. I don't recommend the rinse, if the herbs are grown in a protected spot and only organic gardening methods have been used. Use your own judgment.

The air in my kitchen is warm and dry enough for drying herbs. You may need to find other locations. The ideal temperature is a dry 70°F. Just be certain to avoid direct sunlight and to select a location that offers good air circulation. Leafy sprays may be tied with raffia and hung in the kitchen as decor while drying. Broad leaf herbs like mint and basil are most easily dried on a plastic screen stretched over a wood frame.

Culinary Herbs

Herb	Uses	Herb	Uses
Basil	In pesto, with raw or cooked tomatoes, in Mediterranean cuisines and pastas	Marjoram	Bouquet garni; savory meat and vegetable dishes, desserts, beers
Bay Leaves	In bouquet garni; in soups, stocks, casseroles	Mint	Sauces, relishes, summer vegetables and fruit, teas and drinks
Chervil	Soups, casseroles, salads; egg dishes, omelets	Oregano	Savory meat and vegetable dishes; stuffings; pasta dishes
Chives	Salads, soups, savory butters, soft cheeses, egg dishes, sauces, grilled meats	Parsley	Savory food garnish; butters, sauces; salads; bouquet garni
Cilantro	Salads, garnish for curries, chutneys, oriental sauces	Rosemary	Lamb, pork, poultry; honey; fruit jellies; fruit juices, wine cups
Dill	Pickles, vinegars, salads, dressings, soft cheeses, fish	Sage	Rich meats, stuffings, sauces, sausages; cheeses; teas, apple juice, hot milk
Fennel	Fish, chicken, pork; stems placed under baking bread or grilling and roasting meats	Savory	Beans; cabbage, cauliflower; in crumbs and flour for coating; rich meats; eggs
Garlic	Everything! Salads, pastas, dressings, casseroles, butters, dips, pates, soups, bread mixes	Tarragon	Soups and salads; eggs; chicken, lamb; vinegars; sauces, butters; fish
Lemon Verbena	Cakes, fruit dishes, tea	Thyme	Savory dishes; bouquet garni; shellfish; preserves; lemons and oranges, cottage cheese

If you dry in small supply, an 18" x 18" frame is big enough and easily stored. This allows air circulation above and below. Most herbs dry in three to seven days.

If you have a ready supply, use herbs in their fresh state. If a recipe calls for an herb you don't have and must purchase, dry any overage. These can go into a small willow basket for a "kitchen bouquet". Keep adding various herbs, where they will dry and are conveniently available when you are in a hurry.

In today's health-conscious kitchen, herbs are a great alternative to salt products and introduce new flavor interest to most foods. Home dried herbs will look a lot like the fresh product, but weigh considerably less. Notice if the recipes calls for fresh or dried. You may use either but be certain to adjust quantities accordingly. Roll dried herbs between your palms or crush in a pestle to release flavors.

Use three times the amount of fresh herbs to dry herbs.

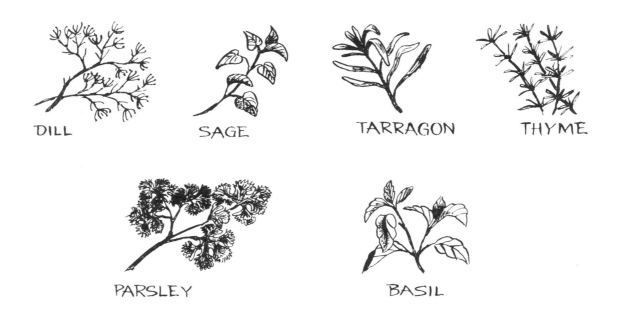

DILL   SAGE   TARRAGON   THYME

PARSLEY   BASIL

Spring Menus

∼ Brunch ∼
Fresh Fruit Compote with Créme Fraiche
Chicken and Wild Mushroom Crepes
Fresh Green Bean Salad with Balsamic Vinaigrette
Lemon Poppyseed Muffins

∼ Sunrise Picnic ∼
Thermos of Fresh Squeezed Orange Juice
Thermos of Cafe Canela
Mexican Sweet Onion and Chicken Quiche
Jalapeño Sausage with Honey Mustard
Blueberry Crumble

∼ Lunch ∼

Asparagus and Avocado with Tarragon Aoili	Curried Fresh Pea Soup
Chicken Babette	Scallops Dijon
Cilantro Garlic Potatoes	Lemon Fettucine with Pinenuts and Fresh Basil
Poached Leeks with Garlic Herb Dressing	Crusty Bread
Diplomat Pudding	Flan
	Hazelnut Cookies

∼ Dinner ∼

Mushroom Paté	Avocado, Orange, and Sweet Onion Salad with Poppy Seed Vinaigrette
Salmon Filet and Black Bean Salsa	Pollo Diablo
Lemon Thyme Rice	Roasted New Potatoes with Warm Bleu Cheese Dressing
Asparagus Almandine	White Corn with Scallions and Herbs
Strawberry and Cream Cheese Ring with Port	Mango Créme Brulé

May Wine Bowl
Spring Salad with Toasted Walnuts and Cheese
Roast Lamb in Herb Crust with Fresh Mint Sauce
Country-style New Potatoes with Sweet Onions
Dilled Carrots
Buttermilk Pie with Herbs and Fresh Berries

Spring Produce

Salads, Appetizers and Side Dishes

AVOCADO, ORANGE and SWEET ONION SALAD with POPPY SEED VINAIGRETTE

SERVES: 6
PREP TIME: 10 minutes
COOKING TIME: None
MAY BE PREPARED AHEAD: 2 hours

INGREDIENTS:

6 cups butter lettuce, washed
3 navel oranges, sliced
1/2 Imperial sweet onion, thinly sliced,
    rings separated
1 avocado, thinly sliced into rings
    (slice in bite-sized pieces widthwise
    to remove pit)
1/2 cup Poppy Seed Vinaigrette
    (see page 128)

PREPARATION:

Place 1 cup butter lettuce on each plate.

Top with sliced oranges and single onion rings, in that order.

If preparing ahead, STOP. Cover and refrigerate for up to 2 hours.

Add avocado rings, and top with 1-1/2 tbsp. Poppy Seed Vinaigrette (see page 128).

FRESH BABY LETTUCE with PECANS and ASIAGO CHEESE VINAIGRETTE

SERVES: 6
PREP TIME: 15 minutes
COOKING TIME: 15 minutes
MAY BE PREPARED AHEAD: 24 hours

INGREDIENTS:

2 Tbsp. butter
1 tbsp. brown sugar
1/4 tsp. chili colorado powder
1 cup pecans
6 cups mixed winter greens (endive,
    radicchio, mache, argula, spinach,
    butter or red leaf lettuces)
1 cup grated asiago cheese
1/2 cup Dijon Vinaigrette
    (see page 58)

PREPARATION:

Spray baking sheet with non-stick oil.

Melt butter in small saucepan, and then add sugar and chili. Mix well. Add nuts and toss well to coat.

Arrange in single layer on baking sheet.

TO COOK:

Toast in 350 degree oven for 15 minutes and reserve.

If preparing ahead, STOP. Nuts may be stored in tightly covered container for 24 hours.

TO SERVE:

Arrange salad on individual plates and sprinkle with toasted nuts and Asiago cheese. Drizzle with vinaigrette.

FRESH GREEN BEAN SALAD with BALSAMIC VINAIGRETTE

SERVES: 4
PREP TIME: 10 minutes
COOKING TIME: 6 - 8 minutes
MAY BE PREPARED AHEAD: 24 hours

INGREDIENTS:

1 lb. green beans
1/4 cup olive oil
2 tsp. balsamic vinegar
2 tsp. fresh lemon juice
1/4 tsp. coarse (kosher) salt
freshly ground pepper to taste
3 radishes, thinly sliced
1/3 cup finely chopped red onion
2 tbsp. minced parsley
1-1/2 tsp. drained capers

PREPARATION:

Wash beans, removing ends and "string."

Bring a large saucepan of salted water to boil. Add the green beans and cook until crisp-tender, 6 to 8 minutes.

Meanwhile, in a small bowl, whisk together the oil, vinegar, lemon juice and salt. Season with pepper to taste.

Drain the beans in a colander, rinse briefly with cold water and pat dry.

If preparing ahead, STOP. Cover and refrigerate up to 24 hours.

TO SERVE:

Arrange the beans on a serving platter, or on individual salad plates, and sprinkle with the radishes, onion, parsley and capers.

Spoon the dressing over the salad.

FRESH GREEN PEAS with BIBB LETTUCE

SERVES: 6
PREP TIME: Mise en place
COOKING TIME: 10 minutes
MAY BE PREPARED AHEAD:
    Not recommended

INGREDIENTS:

2 cups shelled green peas
1 tbsp. unsalted butter
2 small heads Bibb lettuce, cut into
    fine julienne strips
1 tsp. sugar
salt and pepper to taste

PREPARATION: Mise en place

TO COOK:

In medium saucepan, simmer peas in a small amount of water until just tender, approximately 5 to 10 minutes.

Melt butter in small skillet, add lettuce and cook briefly over low heat until just wilted. Sprinkle with sugar, salt and pepper. Add peas and toss salad. Serve while still hot.

SPRING SALAD with TOASTED WALNUTS and CHEESE

SERVES: 6
PREP TIME: 10 minutes
MAY BE PREPARED AHEAD: Dressing
    may be stored up to 1 week

INGREDIENTS:

1/2 cup vegetable oil, such as safflower
1/4 cup walnut oil
1/3 cup raspberry vinegar
1 tbsp. dijon mustard
Salt and pepper to taste
1/2 cup toasted walnut halves
1/2 cup shredded English cheddar cheese
4 to 5 small heads (or 2 medium heads) lettuce

PREPARATION:

Combine oil, vinegar, walnut oil, dijon
mustard, salt and pepper in bowl and
mix until creamy; a hand held mixer may
be used.

Add walnuts and cheese and toss
with dressing.

TO SERVE:

Divide lettuce into six portions, and place
on individual salad plates.

Drizzle with dressing and serve.

TO TOAST WALNUTS

Rinse well. Bake on an
oiled baking sheet at
375 degrees for 15 minutes.

WARM WALNUT LAMB SALAD

You may use left over roast lamb for this.
Just reduce saute time.

SERVES: 6
PREP TIME: 20 minutes
COOKING TIME: none
MAY BE PREPARED AHEAD:
    Not recommended

INGREDIENTS:

1 lb., 2 oz. leg of lamb, cooked,
    cut in 1" strips
2 tbsp. walnut oil
2 tsp. green peppercorns, rinsed, drained
12 oz. snow peas, lightly steamed
2 oz. orange juice
2 tsp. lemon juice
1/4 tsp. black pepper
1/4 tsp. rosemary, ground
1/4 tsp. salt
6 oz. mandarin orange slices, drained
12 oz. apples, chopped
4 oz. walnuts, chopped
2 oz. raisins
6 cups mixed leafy greens

PREPARATION:

Lightly saute lamb in walnut oil. Add
peppercorns, snow peas, orange and
lemon juices, pepper, rosemary, and salt;
heat thoroughly.

Combine and toss together orange slices,
apples, walnuts and raisins.

Mix fruit mixture with lamb mixture.
Serve on a bed of mixed greens.

ASPARAGUS and AVOCADO with TARRAGON AOILI

SERVES: 6
PREP TIME: 10 minutes
COOKING TIME: 7 minutes
MAY BE PREPARED AHEAD:
    2 hours refrigerated

INGREDIENTS:

24 asparagus spears, cooked
2 avocados
6 tbsp. tarragon aoili (recipe follows)
6 cherry tomato "roses" for garnish

PREPARATION:

Cook asparagus spears in boiling water for
7 minutes until just tender. Drain and chill.

Peel each avocado; remove pit and cut
lengthwise in half. Cut each half into 6 slices
lengthwise for a total of 12 per avocado.

TO ASSEMBLE:

Place 4 asparagus spears in center of plate.
Surround asparagus with 4 slices of avocado, 2 on each side.

Spoon a line of aioli across the middle of
the asparagus and avocado. Garnish with
tomato rose.

CHERRY TOMATO ROSES

Make a half inch spiral cut 1/2 inch
wide and 1/4 inch deep with a
sharp knife to produce a continuing
spiral tomato strip. Form the
strip into a circular rose pattern.

AIOLI (Garlic Mayonnaise)

SERVES: 8 - 12
PREP TIME: 5 minutes
COOKING TIME: None
MAY BE PREPARED AHEAD: 5 days

INGREDIENTS:

1/4 cup fresh bread crumbs
1 tbsp. lemon juice
6 cloves garlic, peeled
1/4 tsp. salt
2 cups oil
5 egg yolks
1 whole egg
2 tsp. dijon mustard
freshly cracked pepper to taste (1/4-1/2 tsp.)

PREPARATION:

Soak the bread crumbs in the lemon juice.
Squeeze dry.

Chop garlic in a food processor. Add bread
crumbs, 1/4 tsp. salt and few drops of oil,
until a smooth paste is formed. Beat in
the egg yolks and the whole egg. Gradually
beat in the oil until a thick mayonnaise is
formed.Add mustard, correct seasoning and
refrigerate until needed. (Can be thinned
with a little hot water.)

If preparing ahead, STOP. Cover and refrigerate.

Tapenade Variation
Add 2 tsp. anchovy paste and 1/2 cup
chopped black olives to ingredients.

Tarragon Variation
Add 1-1/2 tsp. dried tarragon or 1-1/2 tbsp.
fresh chopped tarragon to ingredients.

SERVING SUGGESTIONS:

Spread on bread as an hors d'oeuvre,
especially the tapenade variation.

Use as a condiment with cold meats.

Dot on grilled fish or chicken.

Use as a dip or sauce with fresh vegetables.

FRESH FRUIT COMPOTE with CRÉME FRAICHE

Serve a selection of fresh fruits cut in chunks, topped with Créme Fraiche and a light sprinkle of demara sugar as a garnish.

CRÉME FRAICHE

I wanted to include this recipe early in the book because I use Créme Fraiche in soups, over black beans, and in endless combinations.

SERVES: 1 cup
PREP TIME: 1 minute
COOKING TIME: none
MAY BE PREPARED AHEAD: 4-6 weeks

INGREDIENTS:

1 cup heavy cream
1 tbsp. buttermilk

PREPARATION:

In a jar, combine the cream and the buttermilk; cover the jar tightly, and shake the mixture for at least one minute.

Let the mixture stand at room temperature for at least eight hours, or until it is thick.

If preparing ahead, STOP. The Créme Fraiche keeps, chilled, for 4-6 weeks.

EASY CRÉME FRAICHE DESIGNS

If you are using Créme Fraiche as a soup or sauce garnish, put creme in a plastic squeeze bottle, like those used for condiments, and draw borders or designs in the soup or sauce. (See below.)

Clover

Southwest

Spiderweb

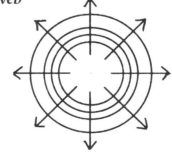

Make 3 concentric circles. Draw a knife from center outward like spokes on a wheel, and violá — a spiderweb!

CURRIED FRESH PEA SOUP

A great make-ahead soup.
Perfect for picnic or alfresco luncheons.

SERVES: 6
PREP TIME: Mise en place
COOKING TIME: 45 Minutes
MAY BE PREPARED AHEAD: 1 Day

INGREDIENTS:

1 cup shelled fresh peas
1 medium potato, peeled and sliced
1 medium onion, sliced
1 small carrot, sliced
1 tsp. salt
1 clove garlic
1 tsp. curry powder
1 stalk celery with leaves, sliced
2 cups chicken stock
1 cup milk
3 tsp. chopped chives for garnish

PREPARATION: Mise en place

TO COOK:

Place all ingredients except 1 cup of the
chicken stock and milk in a heavy saucepan
and bring to a boil.

Reduce heat and simmer, covered, for
15 minutes, stirring occasionally.

Remove from heat, pour into a blender
or food processor, and puree.

Add remaining chicken stock and milk.
Mix well.

*If preparing ahead, STOP. Cover container
and store in refrigerator.*

TO SERVE:

Either reheat or serve chilled. Garnish
with chopped chives, black pepper and
a cloverleaf of Créme Fraiche.

MUSHROOM PATÉ

Very popular with my vegetarian friends.

SERVES: 8 - 12
PREP TIME: 15 minutes
COOKING TIME: None
MAY BE PREPARED AHEAD: 3 days

INGREDIENTS:

1 lb. mushrooms
1/4 cup butter
1 tbsp. lemon juice
1/8 tsp. cayenne
12 tsp. freshly cracked pepper
1/4 tsp. tarragon vinegar
1/2 cup butter, room temperature
2 eggs, scrambled in butter
4 tbsp. parmesan cheese

PREPARATION:

Slice mushrooms and saute in 1/4 cup butter.

Add lemon juice and cook for 5 minutes,
shaking pan often.

Puree mushrooms and their juice in a
blender or food processor. Cool slightly.

Add seasonings, vinegar and softened
cube of butter. Transfer to a bowl.

Add the scrambled eggs and parmesan
cheese, and mix well.

Put in a crock and refrigerate.

*If preparing ahead, STOP. May be stored in
refrigerator for up to 3 days.*

TO SERVE:

Serve on Melba toast rounds or toast points.

VARIATIONS:

For an exotic flavor variation, substitute
up to 8 oz. of wild mushrooms for domestic.

ASPARAGUS ALMANDINE

Asparagus is a favorite vegetable when I serve "American style" and arrange plates in the kitchen to serve at the table. It stays in one spot on the plate and doesn't "run" into other foods or sauces, making a more artful presentation than some other vegetables.

SERVES: 6
PREP TIME: Mise en place
COOKING TIME: 7-10 minutes
MAY BE PREPARED AHEAD:
   Not recommended

INGREDIENTS:

18-24 stalks asparagus, ends trimmed
salt to taste
2 cubes chicken bouillon
2 tbsp. butter
1/4 cup sliced almonds

PREPARATION: Mise en place

TO COOK:

Fill saucepan with enough water to cover asparagus, add salt and bouillon, bring to boil.

Add asparagus and cook 7 - 10 minutes, or until tender.

Remove asparagus to serving plate.

Top with butter and sliced almonds.

DILLED CARROTS

SERVES: 4
PREP TIME: Mise en place
COOKING TIME: 15 minutes
MAY BE PREPARED AHEAD: 24 hours
   if necessary; not recommended

INGREDIENTS:

12 oz. baby carrots
salt to taste
2 cubes chicken bouillon
2 tbsp. butter
1/2 tsp. dill

PREPARATION: Mise en place

TO COOK:

Fill saucepan with enough water to cover carrots, add salt and bouillon cubes.

Bring to boil.

Add carrots and cook about 15 minutes, until tender.

Drain carrots and place in serving dish.

Add butter and dill and toss well.

If preparing ahead, STOP. Cover and refrigerate for up to 24 hours (not recommended). Reheat in microwave for 3 minutes on medium, or until hot.

DILL

WHITE CORN with SCALLIONS and HERBS

White corn is very sweet. Don't overcook this; it is best slightly crunchy.

SERVES: 6
PREP TIME: Mise en place
COOKING TIME: 10 minutes
MAY BE PREPARED AHEAD:
    Not recommended

INGREDIENTS:

2 cups water
pinch of salt
6 ears white corn, cut from cob
1 tbsp. butter
6 scallions, thinly sliced
    (include green part)
1/2 tsp. dill
1/2 tsp. tarragon

PREPARATION: Mise en place

TO COOK:

Boil water with salt and cook corn until tender, 7 to 10 minutes. Do not overcook.

Drain and immediately add butter, scallions, dill and tarragon.

COUNTRY STYLE NEW POTATOES with SWEET ONIONS

SERVES: 8
PREP TIME: 5 minutes
COOKING TIME: 1 hour
MAY BE PREPARED AHEAD: 4 hours

INGREDIENTS:

4 tbsp. bacon drippings or unsalted butter
(Bacon gives better flavor)
6 medium red potatoes, thinly sliced
11 medium sweet onions, thinly sliced
tsp. salt
1/2 tsp. freshly cracked pepper
1/4 cup fresh parsley, finely chopped

PREPARATION:

Preheat oven to 350 degrees.

Put bacon drippings or butter in an 8" x 12" glass baking dish and melt in a 350 degree oven (or microwave).

Put the rest of the ingredients in baking pan and mix well. (It may be easiest to do this with your hands) until all potatoes are coated with drippings.

If preparing ahead, STOP. Cover and refrigerate for up to 4 hours.

For instant plastic gloves, slip
your hands into biodegradable
disposable sandwich bags.
Toss when done.

BABY NEW POTATOES with HERBS of PROVENCE

SERVES: 6
PREP TIME: 5 minutes
COOKING TIME: 45 minutes
MAY BE PREPARED AHEAD: 8 hours

INGREDIENTS:

12 - 18 baby new potatoes,
    depending on size
2 tbsp. olive oil
1-1/2 tsp. Herbs of Provence (see page 61)

PREPARATION:

Preheat oven to 350 degrees.

Wash and clean potatoes, removing eyes
or discolorations.

Prick each potato with fork.

Place on 18" foil paper.

Sprinkle with oil, rubbing oil liberally
over potatoes to coat well.

Sprinkle with Herbs of Provence.

Seal foil and place packet on baking sheet.

*If preparing ahead, STOP. Store packet
in a cool place up to 8 hours.*

TO COOK:

Bake at 350 degrees for 45 minutes.

When scrubbing potatoes, remove
"eyes" or bruises easily with a
small melon baller. It's easier and
quicker than a knife or peeler.

LEMON FETTUCINE with PINENUTS and FRESH BASIL

This recipe provides a unique flavor
combination with very simple ingredients.

SERVES: 4-6 as a side dish
PREP TIME: Mise en place
COOKING TIME: 15 minutes
MAY BE PREPARED AHEAD:
    Not recommended

INGREDIENTS:

8 oz. lemon pepper fettucine
    (available from fresh pasta sources)
2 tbsp. extra virgin olive oil
1/4 cup fresh basil, minced
1/4 cup pinenuts

PREPARATION: Mise en place

TO COOK:

Cook fettucine in boiling water until al dente,
approximately 15 minutes. Drain and rinse.

Immediately add the rest of the ingredients,
and mix well. Serve immediately.

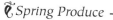

CILANTRO GARLIC POTATOES

SERVES: 6-8
PREP TIME: 10 minutes
COOKING TIME: 25 minutes
MAY BE PREPARED AHEAD: 2 hours

INGREDIENTS:

6 large russet potatoes, peeled
1/4 cup sour cream
1/2 tsp. salt
3 tbsp. melted butter
6 cloves garlic
1/4 cup cilantro, chopped

PREPARATION:

Boil potatoes until cooked in boiling, salted water, about 25 minutes.

Meanwhile, brush garlic cloves with oil, and roast for 25 minutes in a 350 degree oven.

Puree garlic in food processor. Add sour cream and melted butter.

When potatoes are done, mash well. (I use a hand held mixer.)

Add sour cream mixture to potatoes and mix until smooth with spoon. Add chopped cilantro and mix well.

If preparing ahead, STOP. Place in a buttered baking dish and reserve in a warm oven (250 degrees) for up to 2 hours.

LEMON THYME RICE

SERVES: 6
PREP TIME: Mise en place
COOKING TIME: 30 minutes
MAY BE PREPARED AHEAD: Not
   recommended, but 2 hours if necessary

INGREDIENTS:

1 cup long grain white rice
2-1/2 cups water
1/2 tsp. salt
1 tbsp. unsalted butter
1 tbsp. fresh lemon juice
1/2 tsp. lemon zest
1-1/2 tsp. lemon thyme

PREPARATION: Mise en place

TO COOK:

Add rice to boiling, salted water, cover, and reduce heat. After 15 minutes, add butter, lemon juice, zest and thyme. Continue cooking until all water is absorbed, about 15 minutes.

If preparing ahead, STOP. Set aside and keep covered for up to 2 hours. Add 3 tbsp. hot water and reheat, stirring constantly.

THYME

Spring

Fish and Shellfish

SHRIMP in GARLIC, WINE and THYME SAUCE

SERVES: 4
PREP TIME: Mise en place
COOKING TIME: 5 minutes
MAY BE PREPARED AHEAD: No need

INGREDIENTS:

6 oz. butter
20 shrimp
4 medium garlic cloves, chopped
1 cup Chardonnay wine
8 sprigs of fresh thyme
1 cup heavy cream
salt and pepper to taste

PREPARATION: Mise en place

TO COOK:

In saute pan, melt butter. Add shrimp and cook for 1 minute. Add garlic, wine and 4 sprigs of thyme stripped from stem. Cook for 1 more minute. Add cream and salt and pepper to taste.

Cook until sauce starts to thicken and bubble.

TO SERVE:

Arrange shrimp on plate in pool of sauce. Garnish with additional sprig of fresh thyme.

SHRIMP CARDINALLI

This recipe is deceptively simple. Unless you tell guests, they will guess the sauce is far more complex than it is. Incidentally, the recipe doesn't work with butter.

SERVES: 6
PREP TIME: 15 minutes
COOKING TIME: 12-15 minutes
MAY BE PREPARED AHEAD: 4 hours

INGREDIENTS:

36 medium shrimp, uncooked in shell
1-1/2 cup good quality margarine
12 cloves garlic
salt and pepper to taste.

PREPARATION:

Wash shrimp well and remove any visible vein and legs.

Melt margarine in shallow saucepan with garlic. Add shrimp, laying on side, and salt and pepper.

If preparing ahead, STOP. Cover and refrigerate for up to 4 hours.

TO COOK:

Bake together for 12-15 minutes at 350 degrees. (If refrigerated and margarine is hard, add 5 minutes baking time.) Remove garlic.

TO SERVE:

Serve over linguini with garnish of chopped parsley, scallions, and red and green tomatoes.
OR
Serve in a large rimmed soup bowl with mounds of crusty french bread to dip.

To easily peel garlic, place under flat side of butcher knife blade and strike top sharply.

SCALLOPS SANTIAGO

This is an old recipe said to originate in Santiago De Compostela in northern Spain. This town was a destination of medieval pilgrims traveling to worship relics of St. James. In France, this dish is known as "Coquille Saint Jacques".

SERVES: 6
PREP TIME: 30 minutes
COOKING TIME: 10 minutes
MAY BE PREPARED AHEAD: 24 hours

INGREDIENTS:

2 cups dry white wine
4 sprigs parsley
1 sprig thyme
1 bay leaf
2 lbs. scallops
1/2 tsp. salt
1/2 lb. sliced mushrooms
1 tbsp. minced parsley
1/4 cup minced onion
3 tbsp. butter
2 tbsp. water
1 tsp. lemon juice
1/4 cup butter
1/4 cup flour
2 egg yolks
1/4 cup cream
3/4 cup bread crumbs

PREPARATION:

Heat two cups dry white wine in saucepan with a bouquet garni of 4 sprigs parsley, 1 sprig thyme, and 1 bay leaf tied with a string.

Wash and quarter 2 lbs. scallops and add them to the wine along with 1/2 tsp. salt. Cover and simmer until tender (about 10 minutes). Remove the scallops and bouquet garni; save the wine.

In another saucepan, cover and simmer together the mushrooms, 1 tbsp. parsley, minced onion, butter, water and lemon juice for 10 minutes.

In another saucepan, make a roux by blending 1/4 cup butter with 1/4 cup flour. When mixture bubbles, slowly add wine mixture and cook over low heat until mixture thickens. Remove from heat and rapidly stir in 2 egg yolks and 1/4 cup cream. Add scallops, mushrooms, and onions. Mix well.

If preparing ahead, STOP. Cover shells with plastic wrap and store in refrigerator.

TO COOK:

Fill six scallop shells with the mixture and top with buttered dry bread crumbs. Place in oven to brown for 8 to 10 minutes at 450 degrees. Serve immediately.

SCALLOPS DIJON

SERVES: 4
PREP TIME: 15 minutes
COOKING TIME: 5-10 minutes
MAY BE PREPARED AHEAD: 6 hours

INGREDIENTS:

1 avocado, sliced lengthwise in 12 pieces
4 large scallop shells
24 scallops
3 cups dry white wine
1 bouquet garni
4 tbsp. butter
4 tbsp. prepared Dijon mustard
1/2 cup grated Swiss cheese

PREPARATION:

Arrange 3 slices of avocado around perimeter of each shell.

In a saucepan, poach scallops in 2 cups white wine with bouquet garni for 6 minutes; remove scallops to center of baking shells.

In a saute pan, add butter and dijon to 1 cup wine and cook together for 10 minutes, until slightly reduced. Pour over scallops and top with grated Swiss cheese.

If preparing ahead, STOP. Baking shells may be covered with plastic wrap and stored in refrigerator for 6 hours.

TO COOK:

Brown in oven for 5-7 minutes at 400 degrees, until cheese is melted.

To make a bouquet garni, wrap sprig of thyme and a bay leaf in the center of parsley stems. Wrap string around herbs, and tie.

BRANDY SCALLOPS

One of our perennial best sellers from the restaurant. Serve with sourdough bread to dip.

SERVES: 4
PREP TIME: Mise en place
COOKING TIME: 15 minutes
MAY BE PREPARED AHEAD: NO

INGREDIENTS:

2 lbs. raw scallops
2 oz. butter
12 oz. fresh sliced mushrooms
2 oz. scallions
2 oz. brandy
8 oz. beef stock
6 oz. whipped butter
4 sprigs chopped parsley for garnish

PREPARATION: Mise en place

TO COOK:

Saute scallops in 2 oz. butter in skillet until they are cooked half-way through (about 5 minutes). Add mushrooms, scallions, brandy and beef stock. Mix thoroughly and cook an additional 5 minutes.

Place contents in serving casserole dish. Top with whipped butter and brown under broiler. Garnish with parsley.

FISH "EN CAMISA" with PEPPERS, TOMATOES, GARLIC & CILANTRO

"En Camisa" literally translates "with a shirt on" and refers to cooking in parchment or foil, wherein the paper is sealed to keep in juices and flavor. It is an easy and elegant way to prepare fish. I usually cut parchment or foil in a heart shape and then fold it over, so the finished product is shaped like half a heart. This shape seem to seal better than a half circle.

SERVES: 6
PREP TIME: 10 minutes
COOKING TIME: 10 minutes
MAY BE PREPARED AHEAD: 6 hours

INGREDIENTS:

6 sheets parchment or foil
6 6-oz. filets of fresh sea bass, sole,
    halibut, or snapper
salt and pepper to taste
6 tbsp. melted butter
1 large onion, peeled and sliced
2 cloves garlic, peeled and minced
3 medium tomatoes, cut in chunks
1 large bell pepper, cut in chunks
1/2 cup chopped cilantro

PREPARATION:

Preheat oven to 450 degrees.

Fold parchment or foil in half and place fish filet on bottom half next to fold.

Season lightly with salt and pepper.

Top fish with 1 tbsp. melted butter, and 1/6 portion onion, garlic, tomato, pepper and cilantro.

Seal parchment or foil by folding and crimping edges, starting at rounded end.

If preparing ahead, STOP. Refrigerate for up to 6 hours if desired.

Place packages on baking sheet. If using parchment, spray with olive oil mist.

TO COOK:

Bake for 8-10 minutes until packages are puffed.

TO SERVE:

Place parchment or foil packages directly on plate and cut cross in paper. Be careful of steam being released.

If desired, you may remove fish completely from paper with spatula, taking care that peppers remain on top as garnish. More juices remain, if fish is left "en camisa".

FISH "EN CAMISA" with SWEET PEPPERS, DIJON & BASIL

SERVES: 6
PREP TIME: 10 minutes
COOKING TIME: 10 minutes
MAY BE PREPARED AHEAD: 6 hours

INGREDIENTS:

6 sheets parchment or foil
6 - 6 oz. filets of fresh sea bass, sole,
    halibut, or snapper
salt and pepper to taste
2 large shallots peeled
2 cloves garlic peeled
1/2 cup olive oil
3 tbsp. Dijon Mustard
2 tsp. lemon juice
1 tbsp. fresh basil
1 large red bell pepper sliced
    into 2" x 1/8" julienne pieces
1 large yellow pepper sliced into
    2" x 1/8" julienne pieces

PREPARATION:

Preheat oven to 450 degrees.

Fold parchment or foil in half and place
fish filet on bottom half next to fold.

Season lightly with salt and pepper.

Process shallots, garlic, oil, mustard, lemon
juice and basil in food processor to form
thick sauce.

Spread sauce over fillet and top with
julienne pepper strips.

Seal parchment or foil by folding and
crimping edges, starting at rounded end.

*If preparing ahead, STOP. Refrigerate for
up to 6 hours if desired.*

Place packages on backing sheet. If using
parchment, spray with olive oil mist.

TO COOK:

Bake for 8-10 minutes until packages
are puffed.

TO SERVE:

Place parchment or foil packages directly
on plate and cut cross in paper. Be careful
of steam being released.

If desired, you may remove fish completely
from paper with spatula, taking care that
peppers remain on top as garnish. More
juices remain, if fish is left "en camisa"

SALMON FILET and BLACK BEAN TEQUILA SALSA

SERVES: 4
PREP TIME: 5 minutes
COOKING TIME: 7 - 10 minutes
MAY BE PREPARED AHEAD:
    Salmon - No;
    Honey - 1 week

INGREDIENTS:

4 8-oz. salmon filets
sea salt to taste
8 tbsp. red chili honey
black bean tequila salsa (see page 133)

PREPARATION:

Preheat oven to 450 degrees.

Lightly salt both sides of each filet.

TO COOK:

In a large saute pan or oven pan placed
in the oven, sear filets for 2 minutes
on one side.

Before turning over, brush each filet with
1 tbsp. honey on the uppermost side.
Cook the other side for 5 minutes, brushing
the tops with another tbsp. of honey.

TO SERVE:

Place a serving of black bean salsa on each
plate, top with salmon and serve immediately.

RED CHILI HONEY

Blend 1/2 cup wildflower honey with
a large pinch of red chili powder
and 1/4 tsp. crushed garlic.

*If preparing ahead, STOP. Cover and
refrigerate for up to 1 week.*

SALMON MOUSSE

SERVES: 8 for appetizer;
      16 for hors d'oeuvres
PREP TIME: 10 minutes
COOKING TIME: none
MAY BE PREPARED AHEAD: 24 hours

INGREDIENTS:

1 pkg. Knox gelatin
2 tbsp. lemon juice
1 small onion, grated
1/2 cup boiling water
1/2 cup mayonnaise
1 small pkg. cream cheese
1/4 tsp. paprika
2 tsp. dried dill
1 pound cooked red salmon
      (canned may be used)
1 cup heavy cream

PREPARATION:

In blender, put gelatin, lemon juice, onion, and boiling water; blend at high for 40 seconds.

Add mayonnaise, cream cheese, paprika, dill, and salmon; blend briefly and add heavy cream slowly.

Pour mixture in large or individual molds that have been sprayed with a non-stick oil or oil substitute.

Refrigerate for 2 hours before serving.

TO SERVE:

For hors d'oeuvres, serve on platter surrounded by toast rounds. Garnish with fresh dill.

For appetizer course, unmold on red leaf lettuce. Garnish with dill. Serve with three toast points or rounds.

DILL DIP

I use this instead of tartar sauce with fish. It is also an excellent dip for fresh spring vegetables.

SERVES: 8 - 10
PREP TIME: 10 minutes
COOKING TIME: None
MUST BE PREPARED AHEAD: 24 hours

INGREDIENTS:

1 cup light mayonnaise
1 cup light sour cream
2 tbsp. parsley, finely chopped
1-1/2 tsp. celery salt or
      Beau Monde seasoning
1 tbsp. freshly squeezed lemon juice
1/4 cup chopped scallions
1-1/2 tsp. dried dill

PREPARATION:

Combine all ingredients well.

Refrigerate overnight.

DILL

Spring

Meat and Poultry

CHICKEN BABETTE

Babette was a charming Frenchwoman who married a wealthy Moroccan businessman and lived in palatial splendor in Rabat. In spite of having a competent kitchen staff to prepare more complicated cuisine, her favorite dish was a country bistro basic — a simple roasted chicken with herbs. Whenever she came to visit, she fixed it for me.

Energy Saver: Roast the carrots and potatoes with the chicken to cook all items with the energy of one dish.

SERVES: 4
PREP TIME: 2 minutes
COOKING TIME: 45 minutes
MAY BE PREPARED AHEAD: 24 hours

INGREDIENTS:

1/4 cup butter
1 tsp. tarragon
1 clove garlic, minced
2 tsp. parsley
1/4 tsp. onion powder
1/2 tsp. oregano
1 2-1/2-lb. Roasting chicken

PREPARATION:

Melt butter for 1 minute in microwave, medium heat.

Add tarragon, garlic, parsley, onion powder, and oregano and microwave for an additional minute.

TO COOK:

Bake chicken at 350 degrees for 45 minutes, basting with butter/herb mixture every 10 minutes.

If preparing ahead, STOP. Cover and refrigerate.

TO SERVE:

Serve with roasted carrots and potatoes.

Serve cold as excellent picnic fare.

CHICKEN and WILD MUSHROOM CREPES

These crepes are a perfect party dish, and may be served buffet style or on indivudual plates.

SERVES: 6
PREP TIME: 20 minutes
COOKING TIME: 25-30 minutes
MAY BE PREPARED AHEAD: 6 hours

INGREDIENTS:

1/4 cup Shitaki mushrooms
3/4 cup sliced mushrooms
1 cup sliced scallions
5 tbsp. butter
2 tbsp. finely milled flour
2 cup milk
2 tsp. seasoned chicken stock, condensed
3 cups shredded cooked chicken
1/4 cup sherry
3/4 cup gruyere cheese, grated
12 crepes

PREPARATION:

Saute mushrooms and scallions in 3 tbsp. butter until soft.

Melt 2 tbsp. butter in a saucepan; mix in 2 tbsp. finely milled flour to make a smooth roux; add milk slowly stirring constantly to maintain smooth consistency.

Add condensed chicken stock.

Allow roux to thicken slowly, by cooking over low heat for 15 minutes.

Add mushrooms, scallions, chicken, and sherry.

Fill crepes and roll; secure with toothpick.

If preparing ahead, STOP. Cover and refrigerate.

TO COOK:

Grate Gruyere over top and heat at 300 degrees for 20-30 minutes.

MEXICAN SWEET ONION and CHICKEN QUICHE

This is chocked full of flavorful ingredients and is more a meat pie than a quiche. Perfect to carry along on a picnic; it's great warm or at room temperature.

SERVES: 6
PREP TIME: 10 minutes
COOKING TIME: 30 minutes
MAY BE PREPARED AHEAD: 2 days

INGREDIENTS:

7 cups sweet onions, chopped
1/2 cup sweet red pepper, diced
3 tbsp. green chilies, diced
4 tbsp. butter
1 tbsp. oil
1/2 cup flour
1 cup chicken, cooked and diced
2 eggs
1/2 cup cream
1 tsp. salt
pepper to taste
3/4 tsp. cumin
1/2 cup jack cheese, grated
1/2 cup cheddar cheese, grated
1 8-in. pie shell, baked
6 sprigs cilantro

PREPARATION:

Saute vegetables in 3 tbsp. butter and oil until al dente; sprinkle with 1/4 cup flour and continue cooking, stirring constantly for 2-3 minutes.

Cool; then add chicken.

Combine eggs, cream, seasonings, and cheeses.

Place onion-chicken mix in pie shell; top with liquid.

Dot with 1 tbsp. butter.

TO COOK:

Bake at 375 degrees about 30 minutes or until golden.

If preparing ahead, STOP. Cover with plastic wrap and store in refrigerator for up to 48 hours.

TO SERVE:

Reheat for 15 minutes at 350 from chilled state, if stored in refrigerator.

Cut into 6 pieces and top with a sprig of cilantro to garnish.

POLLO DIABLO

A simple recipe with complex flavor nuances. It has remained a favorite on the restaurant "gourmet" menu. This dish has saved my face on many occasions when I have guests arriving, and I am running late.

SERVES: 6
PREP TIME: Mise en place
COOKING TIME: 20 minutes
MAY BE PREPARED AHEAD: 1 hour

INGREDIENTS:

1/2 cup scallions, finely sliced
2 tbsp. butter
2 tbsp. olive oil
6 chicken breast halves, flattened
1/4 cup rough grain mustard
1/2 cup sherry

PREPARATION: Mise en place

TO COOK:

Saute scallions in oil and butter.

Add chicken breasts; saute on both sides for 5 to 7 minutes until done.

Mix mustard and sherry together, and add mixture to chicken breasts.

Stir and deglaze pan.

Simmer for 12 to 15 minutes until sauce is slightly reduced and thickened.

If preparing ahead, STOP. Place in hot glass pan. Cover tightly in foil. Keep warm in oven.

TO SERVE:

Serve with sauce over chicken.

Garnish with green herb (parsley, rosemary, or thyme).

Serve with buttered linguini and chopped parsley.

ROAST LAMB in an HERB CRUST

SERVES: 8
PREP TIME: 15
COOKING TIME: 1 3/4 - 2 1/2 Hours
MAY BE PREPARED AHEAD: 6 hours

Energy Saver: Roast carrots and baby new potatoes with the lamb to cook all items with the energy of one dish.

INGREDIENTS:

large bunch fresh parsley
4-5 sprigs fresh rosemary
1 sprig fresh mint
1-1/2 cups fresh breadcrumbs
1/4 tsp. cumin
black pepper to taste
6 oz. butter
4 lbs. leg of lamb
8 garlic cloves, peeled and halved

PREPARATION:

Process the parsley, 3 of the sprigs of rosemary, the mint, and then mix with the breadcrumbs, cumin and black pepper in food processor.

Melt butter, stir it into the breadcrumb mixture, and let it absorb and expand for a few minutes.

Wipe the leg of lamb with a damp cloth, and put it on a trivet over a baking tray. Prick lamb with knife 16 times and insert 1/2 cloves of garlic.

Cover with breadcrumb paste, pressing it firmly into the meat, first on the underside and then on the top.

If preparing ahead, STOP. Cover and refrigerate for up to 6 hours.

TO COOK:

Give it a good 15 minute blast in a 475 degree oven. Turn the oven down to 350 degrees and bake for 1-1/2 to 2 hours depending on oven and desired degree of doneness.

TO SERVE:

Slice lamb. Put the remaining sprigs of rosemary of top.

Serve with carrots and roast potatoes.

HERBED LAMB with SWEET POTATO & ROASTED ONION SAUCE

SERVES: 6
PREP TIME: 30 minutes
COOKING TIME: 1 hour 10 minutes for
    Sauce and Potatoes; 30 minutes
    for lamb and sauce finish
MAY BE PREPARED AHEAD: 24 hours
    (Sauce and Potatoes)

INGREDIENTS:

3 sprigs of fresh rosemary
3 sprigs of fresh thyme
6 boneless loin lamb chops
1/4 cup olive oil
1 head garlic
1 medium yellow onion
2 tbsp. butter
6 small sweet potatoes
2 cups rich chicken stock
1 chipotle chili
1 tbsp. lime juice
1/2 cup heavy cream
1 tsp. coarse cracked pepper
1 tsp. salt
6 additional sprigs of rosemary
    or thyme for garnish

PREPARATION:

Preparing the Lamb
Finely mince the rosemary and thyme.
Rub the lamb chops with the olive oil
and coat with minced herbs.

Allow to marinate for a few hours or
overnight.

Preparing the Sauce and Potatoes
Remove the cloves of garlic from the head.
Do not peel. Peel the onion and slice into
1/4 inch slices.

Butter the bottom of the roasting pan. Cover
the bottom of the pan with onion slices and
the garlic cloves. Quarter the sweet potatoes.
Place the sweet potato quarters, skin side
down, over the onions and garlic.

Roast the ingredients in a 350 degree oven
for approximately 1 hour or until the sweet
potato is done. Baste the sweet potato with
the butter and juices in the roasting pan
every 15 to 20 minutes.

Remove the sweet potato from the roasting
pan and keep warm. When the garlic cloves
are cool enough to handle, remove the
skins. They should just pop out.

Transfer the roasted onions, garlic and any
juices from the roasting pan to the blender
or use hand held blender. Add the chicken
stock and chipotle chile and puree until
smooth. The sauce should be creamy.

*If preparing ahead, STOP. Cover and
refrigerate. May be stored for 24 hours. Reheat
Potatoes and continue with sauce preparation.*

Pour the puree into a sauce pan and bring
to a boil. Add the lime juice and cream
and reduce the heat immediately to simmer
the sauce. If the sauce is too thick, add
some chicken stock or water to thin the
sauce to the desired consistency. Salt and
pepper to taste.

TO COOK:

Cooking the Lamb
Heat a tablespoon of olive oil in a skillet
over medium heat. Saute the lamb loins
until lightly browned.

Transfer the loins to a 300 degree oven and
roast for approximately 15 minutes or until
the loins are medium rare.

TO SERVE:

Wait 5 minutes before carving. With a very
sharp knife, slice the loins across the grain
into 1/8 inch slices.

Fan the slices out on dinner plates. Spoon
some of the roasted onion sauce over the
lamb slices. Garnish with the roasted sweet
potatoes and rosemary or thyme sprigs.

ROSEMARY PORK MEDALLIONS

SERVES: 6
PREP TIME: 10 minutes
COOKING TIME: 6-8 minutes
MAY BE PREPARED AHEAD: 1 hour

INGREDIENTS:

1 1/2 lb. pork tenderloin cut to
    1-inch medallions
1 cup flour
3 eggs
pinch of salt
2 tbsp. water
2 cups plain dry bread crumbs
3 tbsp. fresh rosemary, chopped
1 tbsp. fresh sage, chopped
salt and pepper to taste
vegetable oil

PREPARATION:

Cut pork into 1 inch medallions. Place each piece between sheets of plastic wrap or waxed paper, and flatten with a meat pounder until thin.

Place flour in a plastic bag. In a flat dish beat the eggs with the salt and water until mixed.

In a second flat dish, combine the dry bread crumbs, rosemary, sage, salt and pepper.

Lightly dust each piece of pork with flour, shaking off excess. Dip the pork into the egg mixture, then place in the seasoned bread crumbs, turning to coat completely. Place the breaded pork in a single layer between sheets of waxed paper. Repeat. Chill for a few minutes to set the crumbs.

TO COOK:

Place 1/4 inch vegetable oil in a large saute pan. Heat to medium high. Add the breaded pork, and saute 3 to 4 minutes on each side until lightly browned.

Drain on paper towel. Repeat with remaining breaded pork, adding more oil as necessary.

If preparing ahead, STOP. The cooked pork medallions can be kept covered in a warm oven (200 degrees) for up to 1 hour.

Serve with warm fresh pear and red pepper chutney. (See Autumn, page 208.)
OR
Serve on a pool of Madiera Sauce
(See Autumn, page 172.)

SAGE

Spring

Desserts

BUTTERMILK COUNTRY HERB PIE

Top slices of this pie with the first fruits of Spring. Any of the berries work especially well.

SERVES: 8
PREP TIME: 10
COOKING TIME: 35-40 minutes
MAY BE PREPARED AHEAD: 6 hours

INGREDIENTS:

2 eggs, separated
1 cup sugar
1/4 tsp. salt
3 tbsp. flour
2 cups buttermilk
1/2 cup melted butter
1 tsp. vanilla
1 tsp. dried basil
1/2 tsp. dried thyme
1 tbsp. grated lemon peel
1 9-in. unbaked pie shell*

*May use cream cheese pie shell.
(See Winter, page 276.)

PREPARATION:

Beat egg yolks and set aside.

In a large bowl, combine sugar, salt and flour. Blend in buttermilk, melted butter, egg yolks, and vanilla.

Add herbs and lemon peel.

Beat egg whites until stiff but not dry and gently fold into mixture. Pour into pie shell.

TO COOK:

Bake in preheated 325 degree oven for 35-40 minutes. Pie should be relatively firm in center when done.

If preparing ahead, STOP. Cover and refrigerate for up to 6 hours.

TO SERVE:

Serve with fresh fruit.

STRAWBERRY and CREAM CHEESE RING with PORT

This is a showy dessert item for buffets or sideboard display during sit down dinners.

SERVES: 8
PREP TIME: 1 hour marinade,
    plus 15 minutes
COOKING TIME: none
MAY BE PREPARED AHEAD: 24 hours

INGREDIENTS:

1 qt. strawberries, washed and hulled
1/2 cup sugar
16 oz. cream cheese, softened
1/2 cup port wine
3 tsp. vanilla
4 tbsp. confectioner's sugar
1/2 cup heavy cream
Mint sprig garnish

PREPARATION:

Slice two cups strawberries, leaving two cups whole.

Add sugar and port wine to sliced strawberries; let stand at least one hour at room temperature. Do not chill.

Beat cream cheese, vanilla, confectioner's sugar, and heavy cream until light and fluffy, or use a food processor.

Pack into 1-pint ring mold, which has been lined with cheesecloth; chill at least three hours.

Unmold onto serving plate; fill center with the two cups of whole strawberries.

Garnish edge with a few whole strawberries and mint sprigs, if desired.

Serve with the sliced strawberries in port wine.

FLAN

For flan connoisseurs, this most closely follows the Mexican flan recipes that use goat's milk or unpasteurized milk.

SERVES: 8
PREP TIME: 15 minutes
COOKING TIME: 45 minutes
MAY BE PREPARED AHEAD: 3 days

INGREDIENTS:

3/4 cup sugar
5 whole eggs
1/8 tsp. salt
1 quart evaporated milk
1 tbsp. vanilla flavoring
1/8 cup brown sugar
8 sprigs fresh mint

PREPARATION:

Mix eggs, sugar and salt in mixing bowl at high speed for one minute; add milk and vanilla and mix for 1/2 minute at high speed.

Melt brown sugar in saucepan until sugar melts and caramelizes. Pour 1 teaspoon in bottom of each ramekin; then fill up the cups with the flan mixture.

TO COOK:

Place ramekins in baking pan with water halfway up ramekins. Bake for 45 minutes at 300 degrees.

TO SERVE:

Chill for 2 hours.

If preparing ahead, STOP. Keep in refrigerator for up to 3 days.

To unmold, run knife around sides of ramekins, and invert on serving plate. Garnish with sprig of mint.

MANGO CRÉME BRULÉ

One of the best selling desserts in my restaurant. You may also use raspberries or passion fruit in place of the mango.

Serves: 8
Prep Time: 15 minutes
Cooking Time: 45 minutes
May Be Prepared Ahead: 3 days

INGREDIENTS:

1 cup sugar
10 egg yolks
1 quart heavy cream
1/2 oz. vanilla flavoring
16 slices fresh (or canned) mangos
16 tbsp. brown sugar for topping

PREPARATION:

Mix egg yolks and sugar in a bowl; mix until creamed. Add cream and vanilla.

Put two slices of mangos in each ramikin, and pour in mixture of yolks and cream. Place into a pan filled with enough water to go up halfway on the baking cups.

TO COOK:

Bake for 45 minutes at 300 degrees. Cool.

If preparing ahead, STOP. Store in refrigerator.

TO SERVE:

Before serving, apply a thin layer of brown sugar (2 tablespoons) on surface of custard and place under broiler until sugar carmelizes, about 3 minutes. Serve warm.

FIVE-MINUTE MOUSSE

Super easy, Super rich, Super gourmet.

SERVES: 6
PREP TIME: 5 minutes
COOKING TIME: none
MAY BE PREPARED AHEAD: 24 hours

INGREDIENTS:

6 oz. semi-sweet chocolate chips
2 tbsp. Kahlua, or any coffee liqueur
2 tbsp. Cointreau
2 egg yolks
1 tsp. vanilla
1/4 cup sugar
1 cup heavy cream
chocolate shavings or fresh violets or
    violas for garnish

PREPARATION:

Melt chocolate chips in Kahlua
and Cointreau in small saucepan in
350 degree oven.

Put yolks in blender with vanilla and sugar;
blend two minutes at medium high.
Add cream and blend for 30 seconds. Add
chocolate/liqueur mixture, and stir
to mix thoroughly.

Pour into footed sherbet dishes or goblets.
Chill for 2 hours before serving.

*If preparing ahead, STOP. Store in refrigerator
for up to 24 hours*

Garnish with shaved chocolate or fresh
violets or violas.

DIPLOMAT

This is called "Diplomat" because it
is a variation of trifle brought to the
Mediterranean countries by diplomats.
I was given this recipe by a Spanish chef
born in Fez. The use of grapes gives it
an unusual twist.

SERVES: 6
PREP TIME: 15 minutes
COOKING TIME: 40 mintes
MAY BE PREPARED AHEAD: 24 hours

INGREDIENTS:

1 pint milk
5 eggs
1/2 cup sugar
1/2 tsp. vanilla extract
1 tbsp. dark rum
1/4 cup seedless grapes, green or red
3/4 cup mixed candied
    (or fresh/canned*) fruits
2 sponge cake layers, broken up

PREPARATION:

Boil milk. Mix eggs with sugar and pour
boiling milk over, beating well. Add vanilla
and rum. Put through a sieve.

Mix grapes with candied
(or fresh/canned) fruit.

In a 6 cup cylindrical buttered mold,
place layers of cake, custard, and fruit
mixture, ending with cake.

TO COOK:

Bake in a pan of hot water in a
350 degree oven for 40 minutes.

Cool; chill if desired and unmold to serve.

*If preparing ahead, STOP. May be stored
in refrigerator for up to 24 hours.*

*Fresh or canned fruits such as peaches,
apricots, strawberries, raspberries, or
mixed fruit cocktail may be used instead
of candied fruit.

BLUEBERRY CRUMBLE

An old favorite. The Créme Fraiche is a different finish.

SERVES: 8
PREP TIME: 5 minutes
COOKING TIME: 40 minutes
MAY BE PREPARED AHEAD: 24 hours

INGREDIENTS:

2 cups blueberries, washed and culled
1 tbsp. lemon juice
1/4 tsp. ground cinnamon
1/4 tsp. ground allspice
1/2 cup butter, softened, cut into pieces
1 cup all purpose flour
1 cup white sugar
1 cup sour cream or Créme Fraiche

PREPARATION:

Preheat oven to 375 degrees. Spray shallow baking dish with non-stick oil (like Pam) and Place blueberries in baking dish. Sprinkle with lemon juice and spices.

Cut butter into flour, using fingers if necessary. Stir in the sugar, and spread the mixture over the blueberries.

TO COOK:

Bake for 40 minutes, or until topping is crisp and golden.

If preparing ahead, STOP. Cover and store in cool place for up to 24 hours.

TO SERVE:

Serve hot or cold with sour cream or Créme Fraiche.

HAZELNUT COOKIES

SERVES: 48 cookies
PREP TIME: 10 minutes
COOKING TIME: 15-20 minutes
MAY BE PREPARED AHEAD: 1 week,
    or 1 month frozen

INGREDIENTS:

1/2 cup butter
1/2 cup powdered sugar
2 egg yolks
1-1/4 cup flour
1/2 tsp. salt
1/4 cup chopped hazelnuts
1 tsp. vanilla

PREPARATION:

Cream butter and sugar.

Add egg yolks.

Sift in flour and salt; add hazelnuts and vanilla. Mix well.

Make into small balls, roll in powdered sugar, and press flat. Use decorative press if desired.

TO COOK:

Bake 15 to 20 minutes at 325 degrees.

If preparing ahead, STOP. Store in an airtight container for up to 1 week, or in freezer for up to 1 month.

Spring

Seasonal Gifts

Dressings

I prefer vinaigrettes to all other dressings because I believe a dressing should enhance, not mask, the delicate flavors of fresh greens and produce. These sections on salad/vegetable dressings are a springboard for your creativity. Each recipe includes one serving suggestion. Use your imagination for other uses! All recipes may be refrigerated for up to one week.

Dressings make excellent seasonal gifts in a decorative decanter. Include a card with recipe, service ideas and refrigeration instructions.

ALL VINAIGRETTES

SERVES: 1 cup
PREP TIME: 5 minutes
COOKING TIME: None
MAY BE PREPARED AHEAD:
    1 week refrigerated

Basic Vinaigrette
Made with white wine vinegar

INGREDIENTS:

1/4 cup white wine vinegar
salt and white pepper to taste
3/4 cup olive oil

PREPARATION:

Mix white wine vinegar, salt and pepper in a bowl.

Add oil and whisk until well blended and slightly thickened.

If preparing ahead, STOP. Keep in a well sealed dressing bottle for up to 1 week.

VARIATIONS:

Caper Vinaigrette

Whisk 1 tsp. finely chopped scallions, 1 tbsp. capers, and 2 tbsp. parsley into basic vinaigrette.

Salad Idea: Serve with sliced grilled chicken over a bed of mixed greens.

Creamy Vinaigrette

Beat together one egg yolk and 1/2 cup heavy cream.

Whisk in basic vinaigrette, drop by drop.

Season with 2 tbsp. herbs of your choice. For example, 1/4 tsp. tarragon, 1/2 tsp. dill, 1/2 tsp. chervil and 1/2 tsp. parsley.

Salad Idea: Serve over sliced cooked carrots and pea pods that have been cooked and chilled.

Garlic Vinaigrette

Add one clove of minced garlic into basic vinaigrette.

Service Idea: A great pre-barbecue marinade for chicken or lamb.

Guacamole Vinaigrette

In a blender, puree 2 avocados with 2 cloves minced garlic, 3 tbsp. white wine vinegar, 1 tbsp. cilantro, a dash cayenne, and salt and pepper to taste.

Salad Idea: Serve over butter lettuce and radicchio salad, topped with baby black beans and fresh corn kernels.

Basic Vinaigrette
Made with red wine vinegar

INGREDIENTS:

1/4 cup red wine vinegar
salt and white pepper to taste
3/4 cup olive oil

PREPARATION:

Mix red wine vinegar, salt and pepper
in a bowl.

Add oil and whisk until well blended
and slightly thickened.

*If preparing ahead, STOP. Keep in a well
sealed dressing bottle for up to 1 week.*

VARIATIONS:

Blue Cheese Dressing

Blend 2 minced cloves of garlic with 1/4 cup
olive oil, 3 tbsp. red wine vinegar, 1/2 cup sour
cream, 2 tbsp. milk and 4 ounces crumbled
blue cheese. Season with salt and pepper.

Warm Blue Cheese Dressing

Soften 2 minced cloves of garlic in 1/4 cup
olive oil. Add 3 tbsp. red wine vinegar and
2/3 cup heavy cream. Bring to a boil.

When mixture separates, remove from heat.
Stir in 4 ounces crumbled blue cheese until
it melts. Season with salt and pepper.

*Service Idea: Serve warm over halved roasted
new potatoes.*

Roquefort Dressing

Follow either of the Blue Cheese Dressings,
but substitute 2 tbsp. lemon juice for 1 tbsp.
of the vinegar, and use Roquefort cheese
instead of blue cheese.

Caesar Dressing

Whisk yolk of 1 soft cooked egg with 1 clove
crushed garlic, 2 minced anchovies and
1 tsp. Dijon mustard until lightly thickened.

Add 1 tbsp. red wine vinegar, juice of
1/2 a lemon, and 2 tsp. Worcestershire
sauce. Blend.

In a slow, steady stream, whisk in 6 tbsp.
olive oil blended with 6 tbsp. vegetable oil.
Season with salt and pepper.

Salad Idea: Serve over hearts of romaine.

Tonnato Caesar

Prepare the Caesar Dressing, adding
2 ounces canned oil-packed tuna with
the Worcestershire sauce.

*Salad Idea: Serve over mixed greens with
chopped tomatoes, bell peppers and olives
for a Salad Nicoise.*

Creamy Rosemary Dressing

In a small bowl, bruise 2 tsp. fresh rosemary
leaves with back of wooden spoon. Add
1 small clove minced garlic, 1 tsp. Dijon
mustard, and 1 large egg yolk. Whisk until
lightly thickened.

Add 2 tbsp. red wine vinegar and 6 tbsp.
peanut oil in a slow, steady stream,
whisking continuously. When oil has been
incorporated, season with salt and pepper.

*Salad Idea: Serve over greens topped with
cooked julienne strips of lamb.*

Creamy Orange Fennel Dressing

Follow Creamy Rosemary Dressing, but use
1/4 cup minced fresh fennel instead of
rosemary and 3 tbsp. orange juice in place
of half the vinegar.

*Salad Idea: Toss with cooked salad macaroni
and serve as a chilled appetizer. Garnish with
a feathery sprig of fennel leaf.*

Mom's French Dressing

Whisk together 1/4 cup red wine vinegar, 1 tsp. sugar, 1/2 tsp. salt, 1/4 tsp. paprika, 2 tbsp. catsup, 1 clove garlic, and 1/2 cup oil.

Salad Idea: Serve on avocado or seafood salads or try filling the hole in half an avocado for a quick, no-fuss salad.

Garlic Herb Dressing

Mince 2 large cloves of garlic.

Whisk with 1/4 cup red wine vinegar, 3/4 cup olive oil, 1/2 tsp. salt, freshly ground pepper to taste, 1 tbsp. minced parsley and 2 tsp. dried herbs (basil, dill, oregano, chervil, tarragon, etc.).

Service Idea: Serve over leeks cooked until tender, quartered lengthwise and chilled.

Creamy Italian

Whisk 2 tbsp. mayonnaise in Garlic Herb Dressing.

Salad Idea: Serve over an antipasto salad: mixed greens with julienne salami and mozzarella strips.

Hot Pepper Vinaigrette

Add 1 tbsp. crushed red pepper flakes to basic vinaigrette.

Salad Idea: Serve with mixed greens, shredded red cabbage, shredded carrots, kidney beans and grated cheddar cheese.

Lime Vinaigrette

Whisk together 3/4 cup olive oil, 1/4 cup red wine vinegar, finely grated zest and juice of 1 large lime, salt and pepper to taste.

Service Idea: Serve over sliced cucumbers - regular and lemon cucumber if possible.

Creamy Avocado Dressing

Add 1 pureed, pitted and peeled ripe avocado to Lime Vinaigrette. Season with dash of hot pepper sauce.

Service Idea: Serve over chilled asparagus spears.

Nicoise Vinaigrette

Add 2 cloves minced garlic and 1/4 cup finely chopped oil-cured black olives to Basic Red Wine Vinaigrette.

Salad Idea: Serve over sliced tomatoes and sweet onions.

Pesto Vinaigrette

In a food processor, puree 1 cup basil leaves with 1 clove garlic and 1/4 cup pine nuts.

Add 2 tbsp. red wine vinegar and 1/3 cup virgin olive oil and process. Season with salt and pepper and with 1 tbsp. freshly grated Parmesan cheese.

Service Idea: Use as a dip for foccacio or Italian bread.

Sweet Pepper Vinaigrette

Finely dice 2 roasted red bell peppers (available in grocery stores).

Combine peppers in heavy saucepan with 2 cloves minced garlic1/4 cup sugar, 3/4 cup red wine vinegar, an1/4 cup walnut oil. Season with salt and pepper.

Service Idea: Serve over chilled angel hair pasta as an appetizer.

Made with Balsamic Vinegar

Basic Balsamic Vinaigrette

Whisk togethe1/4 cup balsamic vinegar, 1 clove garlic, minced, 1/2 cup olive oil, dash of cayenne, 3 tbsp. lemon juice, and salt and freshly ground pepper to taste.

Service Idea: Serve over sliced beef steak tomatoes with buffalo mozzarella.

Dijon Vinaigrette

In a mixing bowl, combine 1 clove minced garlic, 2 tbsp. Dijon mustard and 3 tbsp. balsamic vinegar.

In a slow steady stream, whisk in 1/3 cup each peanut oil and olive oil. Season to taste with salt and pepper.

Salad Idea: Serve with Fresh Baby Lettuce with Pecan and Asiago Salad.

Tarragon Dijon Vinaigrette

Add 2 tbsp. fresh tarragon leaves to Dijon Vinaigrette.

Salad Idea: Serve over butter lettuce, fresh mushrooms and thin, thin slices of asiago cheese.

Sun-Dried Tomato Vinaigrette

Follow basic vinaigrette recipe, using the oil from oil-cured sun-dried tomatoes instead of bottled olive oil. Add 6 minced sun-dried tomatoes.

Service Idea: Serve with chilled penne pasta as an appetizer.

Sweet Balsamic Dressing

Combine 2 tbsp. balsamic vinegar and 2 tbsp. red wine vinegar, 2 tbsp. apple juice and 2 tbsp. honey.

Whisk in 1/2 cup olive oil in a slow steady stream. Add 1 clove minced garlic and salt and pepper to taste.

Salad Idea: Serve over a bed of mixed Winter greens with warm grilled veal sausage sliced over the top.

Using Cider Vinegar

Apple Cider Dressing

Combine 1/4 cup cider vinegar with 2 tbsp. minced onion, 2 tbsp. apple juice and 2 tbsp. honey.

Whisk in 1/2 cup safflower oil in a slow steady stream. Season with salt and pepper.

Salad Idea: Mix with shredded carrots and dried currants; serve on a lettuce cup.

Clear Coleslaw Dressing

Mix 6 tbsp. vegetable oil, 6 tbsp. cider vinegar, 1/2 tsp. sugar and 2 tsp. caraway seed. Season liberally with salt and pepper.

Salad Idea: Serve with shredded red cabbage and lettuce with a little (1/4 cup) shredded coconut.

Poppy Seed Dressing

Use 2 tbsp. poppy seeds instead of caraway seeds in the recipe for Clear Coleslaw Dressing.

Salad Idea: Serve with Avocado, Orange and Sweet Onion Salad.

Garlic Ranch Dressing

Blend 1/4 cup mayonnaise with 1 tsp. cider vinegar, 3 tbsp. buttermilk, 1 tsp. seasoning salt (or salt-free seasoning blend), 1/2 tsp. onion powder, 2 cloves minced garlic and pepper to taste.

Service Idea: Use as a dip for fresh vegetables.

Basil Ranch Dressing

Add 1/4 cup finely chopped fresh basil leaves to the Garlic Ranch Dressing.

Service Idea: Use over cold, cooked asparagus spears.

Yogurt Ranch Dressing

Follow Garlic Ranch Dressing, but substitute 1/4 tsp. garlic powder for minced garlic, and 3 tbsp. yogurt for buttermilk.

Service Idea: Serve with baked potatoes in place of butter.

Green Goddess Ranch

Blend 1/4 cup mayonnaise with 1 tsp. cider vinegar, 3 tbsp. buttermilk, 1 tsp. seasoning salt 1-1/2 tsp. onion powder, 1 clove minced garlic, 1 minced anchovy filet, 1 tbsp. minced parsley, tbsp. of an other green herb (basil, tarragon or chervil), and pepper to taste.

Salad Idea: Serve with a bed of baby greens topped with grilled tuna.

Salsa Vinaigrette

Place 1 clove garlic, 4 or 5 seeded and stemmed pickled jalapeno peppers, 2 stemmed tomatoes, 1/4 cup olive oil and 1 tbsp. cider vinegar in a blender or food processor. Process until finely chopped.

Salad Idea: Serve over mixed greens topped with smoked chicken and sliced tomatoes.

Sweet Mustard Dressing

Whisk 2 egg yolks with 2 tsp. prepared mustard until yolks are pale.

Mix in 1/4 cup cider vinegar, 1 tbsp. apple juice and 1 tbsp. honey. Whisk in 1-1/2 cups vegetable oil in a slow, steady stream. Season with salt and pepper.

Service Idea: Serve with quartered cooked baby new potatoes, sliced scallions, and 1/4 tsp. chopped lavender leaves for an unusual potato salad.

Warm Bacon Dressing

In a deep skillet, soften 1 minced large red onion and 1 large clove minced garlic in rendered fat of 3 bacon slices. (Save bacon for another use.)

Add 1/2 cup apple cider vinegar, 2 tbsp. sugar, 1 tbsp. ketchup, salt and pepper to taste.

Salad Idea: While still hot, toss with strong-tasting greens such as escarole, chicory, endive or spinach.
OR
Serve warm with 4 large potatoes cooked and sliced for a warm "German-Style" Potato Salad.

Speciality Vinaigrettes

Raspberry Vinaigrette

In small bowl, whisk together 1/4 cup raspberry vinegar, 1/2 cup almond or walnut oil, a pinch of cayenne and salt to taste.

Toss with 1/4 cup fresh or unsweetened frozen raspberries.

Salad Ideas: Use with delicate greens, chicken or fruit salad.

Sherry Vinaigrette

In small bowl, whisk together 1/4 cup sherry vinegar, 1/2 cup almond or walnut oil, a pinch of cayenne and salt to taste.

Toss with 2 tbsp. minced raisins soaked in dry sherry.

Salad Ideas: Use with delicate greens, chicken or fruit salad.

Spicy Ginger Vinaigrette

Combine 1/4 cup peanut oil with 1/4 cup sesame oil, 2 tbsp. rice wine vinegar, juice of 1 lemon, 1 clove minced garlic, 1/2 tsp. crushed red pepper flakes, 1 tbsp. finely shredded ginger, and salt and pepper to taste.

Salad Idea: Serve with shredded carrots and cold grilled shrimp for an unusual salad.

Tarragon Vinaigrette

Prepare basic white wine vinaigrette using tarragon vinegar instead of white wine vinegar.

Add one tbsp. fresh, minced tarragon.

Salad Idea: Serve with baby greens topped with warm bratwurst sliced diagonally.

HERB VINEGAR

SERVES: 1 quart
PREP TIME: 5 minutes
COOKING TIME: None
MUST BE PREPARED AHEAD: 2 weeks

INGREDIENTS:

4 cups fresh herbs - Use rosemary, thyme,
    tarragon, basil, etc.
1 quart boiling white wine, cider or
    rice vinegar

PREPARATION:

Rinse herbs thoroughly, pat dry, and place in
two 1-pint wide-mouth sterilized canning jars.

Bruise leaves with wooden spoon (or pestle
for rosemary).

Add boiling vinegar and cool to
room temperature.

Seal jar and store 2 weeks in cool
dark place. Do not refrigerate. Shake
jar gently daily.

When flavoring period is complete (the
longer the storage period, the stronger
the flavor), strain through fine sieve
or cheese cloth.

Pour into sterilized decorative gift bottles.

Add 1 sprig fresh washed herb as garnish,
and seal tightly.

SUGGESTED COMBINATIONS:

Basil with red wine vinegar

*Tarragon, parsley, or lavendar with white
wine vinegar*

Basil and oregano with red wine vinegar

Rosemary with either type of vinegar

Star anise with rice vinegar for Oriental vinegar

Red chili and cilantro with red wine vinegar

SANTA FE OIL

Use in stirfrys or as a meat
marinade before grilling.

SERVES: 1 quart
PREP TIME: 5 minutes + 2 weeks
    storing time
COOKING TIME: None
MAY BE PREPARED AHEAD: 2 months

INGREDIENTS:

1 quart olive oil
3 tbsp. chopped cilantro
3 pico de pájaro chiles, dried
4 sprigs Mexican oregano
2 large garlic cloves
1 tsp. cumin seeds

PREPARATION:

Add all ingredients to oil and shake well.

Put in cupboard for two weeks, shaking
daily to mix flavors.

Rebottle oil in sterilized decorative jars,
dividing garlic, chiles, and herbs equally.

HONEY MUSTARD

Makes a good sandwich spread or an accompaniment to meats and chicken. Try it with hot or cold jalapeño sausage.

SERVES: 4 1/2-cup jars
PREP TIME: 10 minutes
COOKING TIME: None
MAY BE PREPARED AHEAD: 1 month

INGREDIENTS:

1 cup honey
6 tbsp. red wine vinegar
1/2 cup dijon mustard
salt, pepper, nutmeg to taste

PREPARATION:

Stir together honey, vinegar and mustard. Add salt, pepper and nutmeg to taste.

Fill gift jars and label. Refrigerate.

If preparing ahead, STOP. Gift jars may be refrigerated for up to 1 month.

"HERBS OF PROVENCE" SPICE MIX

SERVES: 2 cups
PREP TIME: 5 minutes
COOKING TIME: None
MAY BE PREPARED AHEAD: 1 year

INGREDIENTS:

1/2 cup dried marjoram
1/2 cup dried thyme
1/2 cup dried savory
4 tbsp. dried basil
1 tbsp. dried rosemary
2 tsp. dried sage
2 tsp. fennel seeds
1 tsp. lavendar buds

PREPARATION:

Mix well and spoon into small jars.

USES:

Crumble between your fingers to sprinkle over meat or poultry before roasting.

Season stuffings and vegetables.

BASIL

SAVORY HERB SEASONING

To enhance any savory dish, especially meats and stews. Use sparingly.

SERVES: 1/2 cup
PREP TIME: 10 minutes
COOKING TIME: None
MAY BE PREPARED AHEAD: 1 year

INGREDIENTS:

1 tsp. ground nutmeg
1 tsp. ground mace
1/2 tsp. ground cloves
2 tsp. peppercorns
1 tsp. dried bay leaves
3 tsp. basil
3 tsp. marjoram
2 tsp. savory
3 tsp. thyme
1/2 tsp. cayenne pepper
1/2 tsp. grated lemon
1 clove garlic, minced

PREPARATION:

Mix ingredients together in a bowl, process in coffee mill, and pour into sterlized bottle.

MINT SAUCE

Serve as sauce with roast lamb or pork, or grilled lamb chops.

SERVES: 1 cup
PREP TIME: 15 minutes
COOKING TIME: none
MAY BE PREPARED AHEAD: 3 days

INGREDIENTS:

1/2 cup fresh mint leaves, tightly packed
6 tbsp. sugar
1/4 cup boiling water
wine vinegar to taste
pinch of salt

PREPARATION:

Strip mint leaves from stem, chop finely, and pound with sugar in pestle until smooth.

Add boiling water to improve color and melt sugar. Add wine vinegar to taste and season with salt.

Mint sauce should be bright green, smooth, and pulpy; not liquid.

THYME

MAY WINE

Springtime often is celebrated with traditional May Wine, a legacy of German immigrants. Be aware that woodruff only develops its unique scent as it dries—it has the fragrance of new-mown hay and vanilla. If using as a gift, take May Wine bottled without the fruit, or transport fruit separately.

SERVES: 3 bottles, approximately 24 ounces each or 24 punch servings
PREP TIME: 10 minutes + 1 hour
    (fresh woodruff) or 2 hour
    (dried woodruff) marinade
COOKING TIME: None
MAY BE PREPARED AHEAD: 6 hours

INGREDIENTS:

1 large bunch fresh woodruff or 1/2 cup
    dried woodruff
1/2 cup sugar
3 bottles Moselle wine, well chilled
24 strawberries or 12 unpeeled
    orange slices, halved

PREPARATION:

Wash fresh woodruff and pick off dead leaves.

Marinate woodruff with sugar and one bottle of wine in refrigerator - 1 hour for fresh woodruff; 2 hours for dried.

If preparing ahead, STOP. Keep wine refrigerated for up to 6 hours.

Pour into sterilized bottles and seal tightly.

TO SERVE:

Pour into a glass punch bowl and add fruits just before serving.

Ladle into punch cups and garnish each with fruit.

VARIATIONS:

To make a sparkling May Wine, substitute 1 bottle well-chilled dry champagne for 1 bottle of Moselle.

CAFE CANELA

My favorite morning coffee. Many Mexican households begin the day with a variation of this drink. You may make up jars of the ground coffee and cinnamon premixed for gifts.

SERVES: 8 cups
PREP TIME: 5 minutes
COOKING TIME: None
MAY BE PREPARED AHEAD: No.
    Gift jars will stay fresh in refrigerator
    for up to 1 month.

INGREDIENTS:

1/3 cup Arabica coffee beans
1/2 tsp. ground cinnamon
8 cups water

PREPARATION:

Fresh grind arabica beans or other rich, dark blend. Place grounds in coffee maker, top with cinnamon, and make coffee as you normally do.

TO MAKE FOR GIFTS:

INGREDIENTS:

1 lb. ground Arabica coffee beans
4 tbsp. ground cinnamon

PREPARATION:

Mix ingredients well, put in sterilized jars, and seal well.

If preparing ahead, STOP. Keep in refrigerator for up to 1 month.

HERB PILLOWS

Herb pillows are said to reduce stress and aid in sleep. Different herbalists make different claims. Roses relax and reduce headache. Lavender promotes general good health. Rosemary energizes. With new research in aromatherapy, we may find that the benefits of herb pillows have a basis in fact.

You may make herb pillows in any size or shape. Lay the herb pillow on top of your regular pillow to scent your linens during the day and your dreams at night. This gift item is not edible.

PREPARATION:

Use any dried herb mixture you find pleasing. My favorites are lavendar, rose petals, rosemary, lemon geranium, rose geranium, lemon verbena.

Make a pillow case out of a quilted fabric to cushion the lumps caused by herbs. A floral chintz or regimental print helps minimize any visual irregularity.

Fill casing about half full with pillow stuffing of your choice.

Add layer of herbs and stitch the pillow closed.

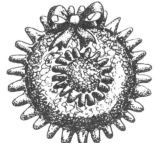

SPRING HARVEST CALENDAR

SOUTHERN CALIFORNIA[1]

FRUITS AND VEGETABLES

apples, artichokes, asparagus, avocados, beans, beets, broccoli, cabbage, carrots, cauliflower, celery, cucumbers, grapefruits, green onions, lemons, lettuce and greens, mushrooms, navel oranges, nectarines, onions, peas, potatoes, radishes, rhubarb, snap peas, spinach, squash, strawberries, sweet corn, sweet onions, sweet potatoes, tangelos, tomatoes, turnips, Valencia oranges, zucchini

OTHER PRODUCTS

bay scallops, dried fruit and nuts, eggs, farm fresh scallops, honey

NEW MEXICO[2]

FRUITS AND VEGETABLES

asparagus, cabbage, lettuce, onions

ARIZONA[3]

FRUITS AND VEGETABLES

artichokes, beets, broad bean, broccoli, brussel sprouts, cabbage, cardoon, carrots, cauliflower, celeriac, celery, chard, Chinese cabbage, collard, endive, Florence fennel, green onions, horseradish, kale, kohlrabi, lettuce, mustard, onions, parsley, parsnip, peas, potatoes, radishes, rutabaga, sorrel, spinach, turnip

[1]From the Cooperative Extension Service, University of San Diego, the Produce Marketing Association's Produce Availability and Merchandising Guide, and Western Growers Association's 1992 Export Directory.

[2]From the Cooperative Extension Service, New Mexico State University and the Produce Marketing Association's 1992 Produce Availability and Merchandising Guide.

[3]From the Cooperative Extension Service, University of Ariziona, the Produce Marketing Associations's Produce Availability and Merchandising Guide, and Western Growers Association's 1992 Export Directory.

Summer

"I only know that Summer sang in me."

Millay

Memories of lazy summer days come drifting back from my childhood. Warmer days meant wading in streams, lying in wildflower filled meadows, picking (and eating) berries warm from the woods, lying in the shade of fragrant plum trees with sweet, fruity aromas filling the warm air. Summer meant wearing fewer clothes, and long hours to fill with adventures and fantasies. It meant picnics at the lake or at evening concerts in the park. The warm languid days drifted along, filled with good foods, day-long adventures, and family gatherings.

I've always believed that one of the particularly civilized customs in France is the August exodus from cities to the country. How wonderful to be able to close down your business and escape for four weeks of relaxation and rejuvenation. It is one of those goals I've yet to achieve, but still a goal. While it is difficult to escape for an entire month, I compromise by welcoming summer with a suspension of ordinary schedules, and try to recapture the lazy summer days of memory by "playing hooky" from my serious grown-up life-style.

How to Recapture Lazy Summer Days

- *Eat outside whenever you can, in your garden, on your balcony, in the park.*
- *Pick your own produce. I select the most fragrant produce I can, so that the gathering turns into a sensual experience of warm sun, fragrant fruit and wonderful tastes.*
- *Take the time to wade in a creek, in the surf, at the lakeshore.*
- *Take advantage of daylight evening hours and plan evening picnics, beach parties, outdoor concerts theater or star-gazing.*
- *Walk along a country road.*
- *Pick wildflowers.*
- *Lie in a meadow. Make daisies chains, or braid lake grass. Pluck petals from a daisy to find out if "he loves you or not"*
- *Sit in the sun or shade and just listen to the birds singing, the hum of summer insects, the sounds of nature. Amazingly, sitting and listening is one of the hardest things for me to do in my hustle-bustle life.*
- *Buy an ice-cream cone.*
- *Cook outside on the grill.*
- *Picnic every chance you get. Keep your picnic basket stocked with supplies, so all you need to add is the food.*

The summer recipe ideas that follow will help you pursue those lazy summer days. Eat lighter and more informally. Avoid time spent in a hot kitchen. Chilled Soups, entree salads, and summer grills all help to keep your days carefree. Buy or outfit a picnic basket with supplies.

We recently stopped at a local winery to picnic, and as fellow picnickers passed us, they remarked about how we were "much more gourmet" than they. I was puzzled, since none of the people passing knew what we were eating. Then I realized that the setting and supplies made us appear well organized. After all, who would enjoy a "gourmet" setting without food to match? I keep my picnic basket packed to save preparation time, but it does assure us of a gracious setting without extra fuss. Who knows, maybe the food is more tasty in gracious surroundings.

Enjoy *your* lazy summer days!

Country Picnics

Picnics are a great escape any time of the year, but the gorgeous weather and lazy days of summer seem especially good for impromptu excursions. Even in the middle of a city, picnics offer a taste of the country before a summer symphony, or in a tiny park. Picnics are the perfect respite from the hustle-bustle of daily life.

Consider picnic breakfasts, or dinners as well as midday repasts. While, this may be considered "overkill", I often include some type of centerpiece—A hurricane candle, a bowl of fruit, or a bud vase. When my children were young, one of our favorite picnic entertainments was finding a "centerpiece". At the beach, we looked for shells; in autumn, we collected natures' palette of fallen leaves and seed pods; in a woodland setting, we gathered pinecones, mossy twigs, brightly colored birdfeathers or wildflowers. (Be certain you are there are no laws that prohibit your gathering.)

To Keep Things Simple

I keep a heavy duty plastic fold-up picnic table complete with benches that seats four in the trunk of my car. The folded size is 14" x 34" and this table is easily carried up mountains, down river banks, or to the beach. I also keep a picnic basket packed with supplies, so all I ever need to add is food.

Boutiques and food shops offer a variety of outfitted hampers, some elaborately fitted with china and crystal. (See Chapter 3, for "Assembling a Victorian Picnic Hamper). Mine has four place mats, four napkins, heavy duty flatware for four, four heavy plastic champagne flutes, four mugs, and four plates.

Having the table and supplies ready to go encourages me to make more "spur-of-the-moment" escapes. Sometimes, my lunch hour picnics come totally from the local deli: paté, cheese, wine, a baguette, and fruit. If you keep it simple, you'll do it more often.

Summer Lore

Fruits and Flowers

Use edible flowers in a variety of dishes for flavor, appearance, and your guest's delight. Summer is the perfect season to experiment with a full range of flowers as foods. Grow your own, using organic gardening methods and no pesticides. Gather in the cool of the morning. Float them in a bowl of water to drown any visiting insects. They may be patted dry and stored in the refrigerator for a few hours.

Creative Ways to Use Flowers

- *Freeze ice cubes with miniature roses or pansies. Use them in ice tea, lemonade or sparkling sodas.*

- *For punch bowls, use a ring mold filled with flower and fern garlands. Larger blocks of ice are always better for punches. They last longer and dilute less.*

- *For a unique bottle chiller, cut the top from a half-gallon milk carton and place an empty wine bottle inside. Fill space between the bottle and carton with flowers and crushed ice, then refreeze, until ready to serve. Peel sides of carton from ice block, and remove the empty wine bottle by pouring in warm water. Insert your chilled bottle of wine. Place block of ice on a napkin in a shallow plate or coaster with a rim, to avoid puddling the table as your wine chiller melts. This will usually last at least 2 hours, or throughout the meal.*

- *Press fresh flowers and fern between two glass plates, and set table with the flower plates for the first course. My clear glass plate set is 9", and works well as an underliner for chilled soups, fruit compotes, or as salad plates. This is a wonderful delight for guests, and a good conversation piece as guests are being seated.*

- *If you are serving cold canapes, consider using a bamboo tray covered with smooth black river stones (available at a florist supply or garden shop) with a unique flower lying on the stones. The canapes go on top of the stones. Select your cold canapes with bright color and harmony in mind. The rocks can be washed in the silver basket of your dishwasher.*

- *Sprinkle confectioners sugar and rose petals over a clear glass plate used as an underliner for summer sorbets or fruit compotes. Encourage guests to taste the petals.*

- *Use nasturtiums, pansies, or chive flowers mixed with baby greens for a unique salad.*

- *Garnish with flowers: Top a chocolate mousse with a violet or viola. Use lavender rosemary flowers on cold curried pea soup. Top an herb grilled chicken with chive flowers. Use fresh flowers as a plate garnish instead of an herb or watercress.*

- *Collect miniature bud vases and use them for mini-bouquets at each place setting; on breakfast or hors d'oeuvres trays.*

- *Glue a fresh flower on place cards or menus. (These flowers don't need to be edible).*

- *Tuck a sprig of lavender or any other garden flower into a napkin tied with a matching ribbon.*

- *Make mini-nosegays and put them at each place setting, or on service trays.*

- *Use flowers as an accent and with a light touch, unless they are an integral recipe ingredient. Too many can be overwhelming and ruin the effect.*

Directory of Edible Flowers

FLOWER	USES	FLOWER	USES
Bachelor Buttons	Garnish	Nasturtiums	Salads, Sandwiches, Herb Cheeses
Calendula	Salads, Rice, Soups, Herb Butters, Desserts	Pansies	Salads, Garnish, Desserts, Cold Soups, Tea
Chive Flowers	Soups, Salads, Fish, Chicken, Omelets, Garnish	Primroses	Tea, Jams, Crystallize to Decorate Cakes
Chrysanthemums	Tea, Soups, Salads, Sandwiches, Eggs	Rosemary Flowers	Green or Fruit Salads
Cosmos	Garnish	Roses	Desserts, Fruit Salads, Jams, Vinegars, Syrups, Sorbets
Fuchsias	Garnish		
Gilly Flowers (Carnations/Pinks)	Desserts, Salads, Vinegars, Jams, Syrups	Snapdragons	Garnish, Salads
Lavenders	Tisanes, Potato Salad, Grilled Meats, Honey, Fruit Compotes, Vinegar, Jellies	Sweet Williams	Cold Soups, Desserts
		Viola (Johnny Jump-ups)	Salads, Garnish, Desserts, Cold Soups, Tea
Marguerite (English Daisies)	Garnish, Float in Punches	Violets	Crystallize to Decorate Desserts
Marigolds	Salads, Rice Soups, Herb Butters, Desserts	Zinnias	Herb Cheeses, Omelets, Salads, Garnish

Abundant Fruits and Vegetables

Use seasonal fruits and vegetables in every way you can. One of the pluses of cooking with the seasons is to recognize the abundance of whatever food is in season, and use it!

Use fruits in the appetizer course as soups, salads, compotes. Use them in the main course as side dishes or in entree salads. Use fruit for desserts, alone, with an assortment of cheeses, in tarts, crumbles, crisps, and puddings.

Use vegetables in soups, salads, side dishes and vegetarian entrees. Make zucchini bread, stuffed zucchini, zucchini pickles. Prepare tomato soup, tomato salad, grilled tomatoes, tomato salsas, tomato sauces for pasta, and tomato cake.

Summer is the season when you are most likely to have an over abundance of produce. Preserve whatever you cannot use by freezing. I freeze overages of fresh produce, and find that this preserves fresh taste better than canning. Freezing also encourages you to use your larder more rapidly. See Chapter 3 for freezing instructions for fruits and vegetables.

Summer Menus

∽ Lunch ∽

Berry Bois Soup
Grilled Chicken Salad
with Spicy Peanut Vinaigrette
Corn Muffins
Plum Tarte

Chilled Fallbrook Soup
Southwestern Pasta Salad
with Smoked Chicken and Sundried Tomato
Sourdough Bread
Summer Pudding

County Cream of Cherry Soup
Shrimp Salad Cardinale
Mini Croissant and Strawberry Butter
Champagne Sorbet
with Lemon Almond Butter Cookies

Small Melons with Port
Aztec Pork Salad
Indian Fry Bread (Winter)
with Strawberry Honey Butter
Blueberry Tarte

∽ Dinner ∽

Margarita Punch
Tri-Color Peppers Stuffed with Goat Cheese
Grilled Chicken with Cilantro Pecan Pesto
in Sweet Pepper Coulis
Broccoli with Herb Garden Butter
Mushroom Scallion Rice
Peaches in Red Wine

Summer Garden Salad with
Goat Cheese Dressing
Grilled Lamb Chops with
Tomato-Mint Coulis
French Green Beans with
Bacon & Onions
Cous Cous with Lemon & Tomato
Snow Bluff with
Black Currant Sauce

Herb Dip with Flower Petals
Angel Hair Pasta with
Herbed Tomato Vinaigrette
Grilled Fresh Fish with Herb Butters
Bulgar with Lemon & Parsley
Roasted Plum Tomatoes
Orange Flower Creme

Blueberry Bleu Salad
Santa Fe Top Sirloin
Southwestern Corn Slaw
New Potatoes with
Herbs of Provence (Spring)
Hearts of Cream

∼ Country Picnics ∼

Gazpacho
Black Bean and Corn Salad with Chili Cured Chicken
Blueberry Muffins (Winter)
Fresh Fruit Slices with Honey Lime Dip
Sangria

Berry Bois Soup
Grilled Sausages with Sweet & Sour Mustard and Black Bean Tequila Salsa
New Potato Salad Vinaigrette
Olives with Herbs
Mexican Wedding Cookies

Raw Carrots and Asparagus with Aioli
Goat Cheese and Tomato Tart
Marinated Mushrooms
Mini Croissants with Honey Butter
Orange Cinnamon Ice Tea
Chocolate Cherry Cake with Fresh Mint Cream

Guacamole and Chips
Game Hens with Herbs of Provence
Valencia Salad
Spicy Ratatouille
Pink Lemonade with Mint
Plum Tarte

Country Sausage Paté
Assorted Mustards and Spiced Pickles
Pasta Salad with Tuna
Strawberries with Brown Sugar and Créme Fraiche
Lemon Bars

Summer

Chilled Soups and Appetizers

COUNTRY CREAM of CHERRY SOUP

SERVES: 6
PREP TIME: 20 minutes
COOKING TIME: 15 minutes
MAY BE PREPARED AHEAD: 24 hours

INGREDIENTS:

2 lbs. fresh cherries* (a mixture of sweet and
    sour), washed, stems and stones removed
4 cups water
1 stick cinnamon (optional)
1/2 cup sugar, or to taste
4 tbsp. flour
1/2 cup cold water
1 cup sweet or sour cream
1 cup dry red wine (optional)

*Pared and diced apples, stoned and halved
ripe plums, peaches, or nectarines may replace
cherries in above recipe. Adjust sugar as
necessary and flavor with red or white wine.

TO COOK:

Cook cherries in 4 cups water with the
stick of cinnamon for about 10 minutes
or until they are soft. Remove cinnamon,
and add sugar to taste. (Practically no
sugar will be needed if frozen cherries are
used as they will already be sweetened.)

Combine flour and 1/2 cup cold water
in a screw-top jar. Close tightly and
shake vigorously until flour and water are
smoothly blended. Pour into hot cherry
soup and stir. Bring to a boil and simmer
for 3 to 4 minutes.

Chill thoroughly, preferably overnight.

Stir in sweet cream or beat in sour cream
and flavor with red wine, if desired, just
before serving.

SWEDISH CHERRY SOUP

A smoother more refined version.

After cooking cherries, puree
through a sieve.

Thicken soup with 2 tbsp. cornstarch
dissolved in water instead of flour.
Flavor with dry white wine instead
of red wine.

Instead of adding cream to soup,
garnish each serving with a dab of
Créme Fraiche or sour cream and a few
uncooked, stoned cherries.

BERRY BOIS SOUP

"Bois" means woodland, and this soup was originally made from small intensely flavored wild berries.

SERVES: 4
PREP TIME: 10 minutes
COOKING TIME: None
MAY BE PREPARED AHEAD: 8 hours

INGREDIENTS:

1 cup strawberries
1 cup raspberries
1/3 cup sugar
1/2 cup sour cream
1/2 cup heavy cream
1-1/2 cups water
1/2 cup rose or beaujolais wine

PREPARATION:

Place berries and sugar in a blender and puree. Pour into a pitcher and stir in creams until well blended. Add water and wine; chill.

If preparing ahead, STOP. Cover and refrigerate for up to 8 hours.

CHILLED SHRIMP and JICAMA SOUP

This soup has a refreshing crunchy texture.

SERVES: 6
PREP TIME: 30 minutes
COOKING TIME: Soup - None;
    Shrimp - 2 to 3 minutes
MAY BE PREPARED AHEAD: 8 hours

INGREDIENTS:

1 medium red bell pepper
1 medium yellow bell pepper
1 medium cucumber, peeled, seeded
1 large jicama (about 1-1/2 lbs.), peeled,
    cut into julienne strips
1/4 cup raspberry vinegar
2 tsp. sugar
2 tsp. salt
1/2 lb. small shrimp (about 15),
    shelled and deveined
1/4 tsp. cayenne pepper
2 tbsp. olive oil
2 cups cultured buttermilk
1 cup heavy cream
1 cup sour cream
1 cup (packed) chopped fresh basil

PREPARATION:

Roast red and yellow bell peppers directly over a gas flame or under a broiler as close to the heat as possible, turning frequently until charred all over. Put the peppers in a paper or plastic bag, seal and let steam until cool.

Peel the peppers and discard the cores, seeds and ribs. Cut the peppers into 1 by 1/4-in. strips and set aside.

In a food processor, puree the cucumber until smooth. Pour the puree into a large bowl and add the jicama. Mix in the vinegar, sugar and 1 tsp. salt; set aside.

Sprinkle the shrimp with 1 tsp. salt and the cayenne. In a large skillet, heat the olive oil over high heat until lightly smoking. Add the shrimp and saute until they turn pink, about 2 minutes. Remove from the pan and set aside.

In a large bowl, combine the buttermilk and heavy cream, then whisk in the sour cream.

Add the reserved peppers, jicama and cucumber mixture, the shrimp and the basil. Combine thoroughly. Season with additional salt to taste.

Chill thoroughly before serving.

If preparing ahead, STOP. Cover and refrigerate.

A nice garnish would be a paper-thin cucumber slice with the green skin left on.

CHILLED FALLBROOK SOUP

Fallbrook is a small agricultural community between Riverside and San Diego that is known for abundant avocado orchards.

SERVES: 6
PREP TIME: 15 minutes
COOKING TIME: none
MAY BE PREPARED AHEAD: Up to 6 hours

INGREDIENTS:

2 avocados
4 small tomatoes, peeled, finely chopped
1/4 cup finely chopped green onion
Dash tabasco
1/2 cup dairy sour cream
1 can (10-1/2 oz.) condensed beef bouillon
1 tsp. salt
2 tbsp. lemon juice
sour cream for garnish

PREPARATION:

Cut avocados lengthwise into halves; remove seeds and skin.

Process avocados, tomatoes, onions, and tabasco in blender.

Mix well with sour cream. Stir in other ingredients (adding the undiluted bouillon a little at a time) and chill before serving.

Garnish with a design of sour cream or Créme Fraiche and cracked black pepper.

Variance in avocado color may give you a revolting and unappetizing greenish-brown colored soup, so if you must, add a drop or two of green food coloring for aesthestics.

GAZPACHO

The fresh tarragon and wine vinegar
make the difference.

SERVES: 6
PREP TIME: 10 minutes
COOKING TIME: none
MAY BE PREPARED AHEAD: 3 days

INGREDIENTS:

1-1/2 lbs. fresh or canned ripe tomatoes
1 clove garlic, chopped
1 cup tomato juice
2 small lemon cucumbers, or 1 small
    cucumber, peeled, cut into pieces
1/4 tsp. sugar
1 medium green pepper, cut in pieces
1 small onion, cut in pieces
salt to taste
4 tbsp. red wine vinegar
1/4 tsp. tarragon
Diced cucumber, green pepper, tomato,
    green onions for garnish

PREPARATION:

Place all ingredients except the garnish
in the bowl of a processor or blender, in
several steps if necessary. Blend until
no large pieces remain and strain,
pressing with the back of a wooden spoon
to extract as much liquid as possible.

Correct the seasoning, adding more salt
and vinegar if desired.

Chill very well, preferably overnight.

TO SERVE:

Ladle into bowls or goblets and garnish with
chopped cucumber, pepper, or scallions.

GUACAMOLE

Everyone's favorite southwestern appetizer.

SERVES: 4 cups
PREP TIME: 15 minutes
COOKING TIME: none
MAY BE PREPARED AHEAD: 6 hours

INGREDIENTS:

5 avocados, chopped
1 large tomato, diced fine
juice of 1 lemon
1 medium onion, diced fine
3 yellow chiles, minced
salt and pepper to taste

PREPARATION:

Cut avocados into halves.

With spoon, pull out the pulp only
and discard the seed.

Mix with the remaining ingredients
and mash until nearly pureed.

Correct seasonings and taste.

*If preparing ahead, STOP. Replace avocado
pit in guacamole or cover with thin film of
mayonnaise to prevent browning. Cover
with plastic wrap and store in refrigerator.*

TO SERVE:

Place in serving bowl and garnish
with whole chili or chopped tomato.

If guacamole has been stored, remove
pit or stir in light film of mayonnaise
before garishing.

Serve with torilla chips.

To prevent avocado dishes
from browning, store pit in mixture.

HERB DIP with FLOWER PETALS

Serve with fresh vegetables
or small thin crackers.

SERVES: 1-1/2 cups
PREP TIME: 5 minutes
COOKING TIME: None
MAY BE PREPARED AHEAD:

INGREDIENTS:

8 oz. cream cheese
2 tbsp. sour cream
1 tbsp. fresh summer savory
1 tbsp. fresh lemon thyme
1 tbsp. fresh dill
1/4 tsp. freshly ground black pepper
2 tbsp. fresh flower petals (violets,
    johnny jump ups, nasteriums,
    calendulas, marigolds)

PREPARATION:

Beat all ingredients together except
petals until well blended.

Add flower petals, mixing well.

SMALL MELONS with PORT

Be certain melons are VERY ripe.
This simple recipe offers a
wonderful mix of lush flavors.

SERVES: 6
PREP TIME: 15 minutes
COOKING TIME: None
MAY BE PREPARED AHEAD: 4 hours

INGREDIENTS:

3 French melons or small cantelopes,
    about 4" - 5" in diameter
1-1/2 cups Port

PREPARATION:

Using a "V" shaped knife, cut around
circumference of melon to flute edges.
A regular knife works, but it's much harder.

Scoop out seeds and place fluted halves
in stemmed large goblets.

Add 1/4 cup Port to each melon "bowl".
Allow to stand at room temperature
for at least 1 hour. Melons may marinate
up to 4 hours at room temperature.
Cover with plastic wrap.

ANGEL HAIR PASTA with HERBED TOMATO VINAIGRETTE

This is especially good as a COLD appetizer, and is great to prepare ahead for summer dinner parties.

SERVES: 4 appetizer servings or
    2 entree servings
PREP TIME: Mise en place
COOKING TIME: 15 minutes
MAY BE PREPARED AHEAD: 24 hours

INGREDIENTS:

1 large sweet onion, chopped
2/3 cup extra virgin olive oil
1/4 cup white wine vinegar
2 medium tomatoes, (3/4 cup) blanched,
    peeled, seeded, coarsely chopped
1/4 cup mixed fresh herbs (basil, marjoram,
    tarragon, thyme or fennel), minced
8 oz. angel hair pasta, cooked

PREPARATION: Mise en place

TO COOK:

In saute pan over medium heat, saute onion in 3 tbsp. of olive oil until translucent but not brown.

Add white wine vinegar; cook to reduce, about 5 minutes.

Combine remaining olive oil, tomatoes, herbs and sauteed onion mixture.
Stir gently and briefly.

If preparing ahead, STOP. Cover and refrigerate. Reheat before serving if desired.

Serve over hot or cold pasta.

To seed tomatoes, cut in half and squeeze over sink in rolling motion. Seeds will pour out.

TRI-COLOR PEPPERS STUFFED with CHEVRE

This offers a dramatic plate presentation, and so is a favorite for sit down dinner parties.

SERVES: 6
PREP TIME: 20 minutes
COOKING TIME: 3 - 5 minutes
MAY BE PREPARED AHEAD: 24 hours

INGREDIENTS:

1 of each red, yellow, green bell pepper
6 tbsp. butter
1 cup finely chopped onions
1 clove garlic, minced
1/2 cup chopped chives
12 oz. goat cheese
1/2 tsp. cumino
1/4 tsp. cayenne pepper
salt and pepper to taste
1/2 cup pine nuts

PREPARATION:

Slice tops off peppers and remove ribs and seeds.

Melt butter in a medium pan and saute onion and garlic until translucent.

Combine with all remaining ingredients in mix-er or food processor (if using processor, add pine nuts at the end so they aren't finely chopped).

Stuff peppers with mixture and smooth tops; refrigerate for 3 hours.

If preparing ahead, STOP. Refrigerate for up to 24 hours.

TO COOK:

When cheese mixture is hard, cut into 6 slices, discarding bottoms of peppers.

Put slices under broiler for a few minutes until glazed.

TO SERVE:

Serve in tri-color portions.

Garnish with ornamental kale or cilantro.

GOAT CHEESE and TOMATO TART

A very varietal Sauvignon Blanc or dry Gewurtztraminer would be delicious with this.

SERVES: 4-6
PREP TIME: 30 minutes
COOKING TIME: 15 - 20 minutes
MAY BE PREPARED AHEAD: 30 minutes

INGREDIENTS:

1 tsp. shortening
1 lb. frozen bread dough*
1-1/2 tbsp. green onions, washed,
    ends removed, minced
7 oz. mild soft goat cheese, mashed
2 large eggs, beaten lightly
1/2 cup heavy cream
1/4 cup fresh basil leaves, washed,
    dried, minced
salt to taste
pepper to taste
2 tbsp. olive oil
4 tomatoes, washed, cored,
    cut into 1/3-in. thick slices
1 garlic clove, peeled,
    ends removed, minced
basil sprigs, optional

*May substitute with 1 large prebaked crust, puff pastry, or Pate Brisée (see page 117).

PREPARATION:

Preheat oven to 400 degrees. Grease a pizza pan with shortening, shape bread dough into pizza shape, and bake 15 minutes until set but not golden. Remove from oven and set aside.

In a large bowl, whisk together the green onion, goat cheese, eggs, heavy cream, basil, salt and pepper until the mixture is smooth.

In a large skillet, heat the olive oil over moderately high heat until it is hot but not smoking. Working in batches, saute the tomato slices and garlic in oil for 1 to 2 minutes on each side, or until they are browned lightly. Transfer to plate and repeat with remaining tomatoes.

Spread cheese custard mixture evenly over the precooked bread dough and arrange tomatoes decoratively.

TO COOK:

Bake the tart in the middle of oven for 15 to 20 minutes or until the custard is pale golden and set. Remove from oven.

Carefully remove the tart from the baking sheet with 2 spatulas and let cool on a wire rack for 15 minutes. Garnish the tart with basil sprigs if desired, and serve at room temperature.

COUNTRY SAUSAGE PATÉ

A perfect picnic paté or elegant first course for a formal meal.

SERVES: 12 - 16
PREP TIME: 5 minutes
COOKING TIME: 45 minutes
MAY BE PREPARED AHEAD:
    1 week - refrigerated; 3 weeks - frozen

INGREDIENTS:

2 lbs. good bulk country style pork sausage
2 lbs. fresh spinach, chopped, patted dry
1/2 tsp. mace
2 tsp. salt
1/2 tsp. cinnamon
1/2 tsp. thyme
1-1/2 tsp. minced fresh basil

PREPARATION:

Preheat oven to 375 degrees.

Mix all ingredients well in a food processor.

Pack into a 9-inch loaf pan.

TO COOK:

Bake for 45 minutes.

Remove from oven and weigh down immediately with a brick wrapped in foil or with several heavy cans.

Cool, wrap well, and refrigerate.

If preparing ahead, STOP. This keeps well refrigerated for 1 week, or frozen for 3 weeks.

TO SERVE:

Unmold on serving plate and scrape off any excess fat.

Slice and serve with crackers, cornichon pickles, capers or chopped sweet onions.
OR
Serve as a first course on a red lettuce leaf, garnished with cherry tomatoes, french bread and the above relishes.

SPICY RATATIOULLE

This may be served warm as well, but it is so delicious cold, you won't want to bother! Ratatioulle is also a great way to utilize a variety of garden vegetables.

SERVES: 6-8
PREP TIME:30 minutes
COOKING TIME: 1 hour
MAY BE PREPARED AHEAD: 8-15 days

INGREDIENTS:

4 medium-sized tomatoes, peeled, sliced
3 zucchini, unpeeled, sliced
1 medium-sized eggplant, peeled, sliced
2 onions, sliced
2 green peppers, trimmed, sliced
2 jalapeño chilies, seeded, chopped
2 garlic cloves, chopped fine
1/2 tsp. sugar
1/2 cup olive oil
1/4 tsp. dried thyme
salt and pepper to taste
juice of 1 lemon
6-8 leaves purple cabbage or red lettuce

PREPARATION:

Prepare all of the vegetables, the chilies and garlic; place them separately on a large platter. Sprinkle sugar on tomatoes.

TO COOK:

Heat oil in a heavy metal saucepan over high heat; add the onions and brown lightly.

Add the eggplant and cook, stirring, for about 3 minutes, or until lightly softened. Add the tomatoes and crush into the mixture with a wooden spoon, stirring and blending for another 3 minutes.

Add the zucchini, garlic, green peppers and chilies; stir until well mixed.

Cook over high heat for a few minutes, stirring frequently; season with salt and pepper to taste.

Add the thyme, salt and pepper, and then cook, uncovered, over low heat, for about one hour, stirring occasionally (by that time, the mixture should have the texture of a thick tomato sauce).

If preparing ahead, STOP. Cover and refrigerate. Dish is best if allowed to set for flavor mixing for 10-12 hours.

TO SERVE:

Before serving, stir in the lemon juice. Serve at room temperature or cold as appetizer course or as a side dish. Present ratatioulle as a first course in the center of a purple cabbage leaf.

BLUEBERRY BLEU SALAD with RASPBERRY VINAIGRETTE

SERVES: 8
PREP TIME: 15 minutes
COOKING TIME: None
MAY BE PREPARED AHEAD:
    Salad - 2 hours; Dressing - 1 week

INGREDIENTS:

12 oz. blueberries, rinsed and drained
4 heads Bibb lettuce
12 oz. bleu cheese, crumbled
4 oz. pecan halves, sauteed in olive oil
12 oz. raspberry vinaigrette

Raspberry Vinaigrette
1 cup raspberry vinegar
1/2 cup raspberries
1/2 cup honey
1 cup olive oil

PREPARATION:

For each serving: Break 1/2 head of Bibb lettuce into bitesize pieces on individual plates. Add 1-1/2 oz. each of blueberries and crumbled bleu cheese, and 1/2 oz. pecans.

Serve with Raspberry Vinaigrette.

Raspberry Vinaigrette
Place vinegar, raspberries and honey in food processor. Process; slowly add olive oil until all ingredients combine.

If preparing ahead, STOP; refrigerate.
Return to room temperature before serving.

WATERCRESS and JICAMA SALAD

SERVES: 4
PREP TIME: 20 minutes
COOKING TIME: None
MAY BE PREPARED AHEAD: 8 hours

INGREDIENTS:

Salad
1 cup jicama cut in julienne strips
1 Mexican lime
1 tsp. sea salt
1 tsp. crushed red chile
2 cups watercress with stems removed

Dressing
1 large garlic clove, crushed
1 tsp. dijon mustard
1/4 cup walnut oil
1/4 cup raspberry vinegar

PREPARATION:

Spread jicama over the bottom of a shallow glass pan. Sprinkle with lime, salt and chile, and allow to stand for 30 minutes.

Dressing
Whisk together garlic, mustard, oil and vinegar.

If preparing ahead, STOP. Store all ingredients in refrigerator separately.

TO SERVE:

Combine jicama, watercress and dressing. Toss well and serve in red cabbage cups.

Purchase walnut oil in smallest available container. It will remain fresh for 1 - 2 months only.

SUMMER GARDEN SALAD with GOAT CHEESE DRESSING

SERVES: 8
PREP TIME: 10 minutes
COOKING TIME: None
MAY BE PREPARED AHEAD:
    Dressing - 24 hours

INGREDIENTS:

3 tomatoes, sliced
3 cucumbers, peeled, scored, sliced
3 Haas avocados, quartered, peeled,
    sprinkled with lemon juice
3 oranges, peeled, sliced
1 red onion, peeled, sliced
8 sprigs mint

Goat Cheese Dressing
3-1/2 oz. goat cheese
1/3 cup sour cream
1/4 tsp. tarragon
1 tbsp. raspberry or blueberry vinegar
1/4 tsp. basil
1/4 tsp. mint

PREPARATION:

Dressing
Combine all ingredients in food processor and blend for 1 minute.

If preparing ahead, STOP. Cover and refrigerate for up to 24 hours. Mix well before serving.

TO SERVE:

Arrange tomato, cucumber, avocado, oranges and red onion on individual plates.

DATES with MINT and PROSCIUTTO

Serve as an appetizer or as part of
an antipasto.

SERVES: 18 Antipasto or 6 appetizer
    servings of 3 each
PREP TIME: 10 minutes
COOKING TIME: None
MAY BE PREPARED AHEAD: 24 hours

INGREDIENTS:

18 dates, pits removed
18 paper-thin strips of prosciutto
18 fresh mint leaves

PREPARATION:

Tuck a fresh mint leaf into each date.

Roll a strip of prosciutto around each
date and secure with toothpicks.

*If preparing ahead, STOP. Cover and
refrigerate. Return to room temperature
before serving.*

Summer

Entree Salads

SOUTHWESTERN PASTA SALAD with SMOKED CHICKEN and SUN-DRIED TOMATOES

SERVES: 6 to 8
PREP TIME: 15 minutes
COOKING TIME: 15 minutes
MAY BE PREPARED AHEAD: 3 hours

INGREDIENTS:

Dressing
2 tbsp. chopped fresh cilantro
1 tbsp. chopped fresh thyme
2 tbsp. chopped basil
2 garlic cloves, minced
2 shallots, minced
1 tbsp. dry white wine
2 tbsp. white wine vinegar
1 tbsp. balsamic vinegar
3/4 cups olive oil
salt and pepper to taste

Pasta Salad
9 oz. dried pasta, such as fusilli or penne
3 tbsp. olive oil
1/2 cup cooked black beans
1/2 medium red bell pepper,
    cut into 1/4-inch strips
1/2 medium yellow bell pepper,
    cut into 1/4-inch strips
1 small carrot, coarsely chopped
5 tomatillos, husked, rinsed, cored
    and cut into 1/4-inch dice
4 oz. fresh mozzarella, cut into 1/4-inch dice
1 8-oz. boneless smoked chicken breast,*
    cut into 1/4-inch dice
1 cup sun-dried tomatoes in oil

*If smoked chicken is unavailable,
substitute diced grilled or roasted chicken.

PREPARATION:

Dressing
In a small bowl, combine the cilantro, thyme and 1 tbsp. basil, half the minced garlic and the shallots. Whisk in the wine, wine vinegar and balsamic vinegar.

Slowly drizzle in 3/4 cup olive oil, whisking constantly. Season to taste with salt and black pepper; set aside.

Pasta
Cook the pasta in a large pot of boiling salted water until al dente. Drain, place in a large serving bowl, add the remaining 3 tbsp. olive oil and toss well. Set aside to cool.

When the pasta is thoroughly cool, add the black beans, red and yellow bell peppers, carrot, tomatillos, mozzarella, smoked chicken breast, sun-dried tomatoes and the remaining basil and garlic.

Toss with the reserved vinaigrette and season to taste with salt and black pepper.

Cover the salad and refrigerate to chill slightly, about 20 minutes. You may leave in refrigerator for up to 3 hours.

BASIL

AZTEC PORK SALAD

Corn muffins are a great accompaniment. Take fresh corn husks and cut into 2 inch strips, about 8 inches long. Place in cross over bottom of muffin tin before adding batter. To remove muffins, just pull up strips.

SERVES: 4
PREP TIME: 10 minutes
COOKING TIME: 5 - 7 minutes
MAY BE PREPARED AHEAD: Lettuce, orange, avocado and red onion may be prepared 1 hour in advance if necessary.

INGREDIENTS:

4 cups lettuce, shredded
1 medium orange, peeled, sliced, cut into quarters
1 avocado, peeled, diced
1 small red onion, sliced, separated into rings
1 tbsp. oil
1 tsp. chili powder
3/4 tsp. salt
1/2 tsp. dried oregano leaves, crushed
1/4 tsp. ground cumin
1 lb. boneless pork loin, cut into 3x 1/2 x 1/4-in. strips

PREPARATION:

Place lettuce on serving platter.

Arrange orange, avocado and red onion in attractive design over lettuce. I make concentric circles of the orange and avocado with the red onion rings over all.

TO COOK:

Heat oil in large frying pan; add chili powder, salt, oregano and cumin.

Add pork loin strips; stir-fry over medium-high heat for 5-7 minutes or until pork is tender.

Spoon hot pork strips in center of orange avocado circles over lettuce mixture.

Brush avocado with orange juice to keep from oxidizing.

GRILLED CHICKEN SALAD with SPICY PEANUT VINAIGRETTE

SERVES: 4
PREP TIME: 15 minutes
    (with chickenpregrilled)
COOKING TIME: None
MAY BE PREPARED AHEAD: 2 hours

INGREDIENTS:

2 cups spinach leaves, washed,
    dried, rough chopped
2 cups bok choy leaves, washed,
    dried, rough chopped
1 1/3 cup cucumbers, cut into 1/2-in. dice
1 cup carrots, sliced in julienne strips
1 cup red cabbage, thinly sliced
4 5-oz. grilled chicken breasts, sliced
    in julienne strips (hot or cold)
6 tbsp. spicy peanut vinaigrette

PREPARATION:

Rough chop spinach and bok choy in food processor. Do not over process.

Add chopped cucumber, carrots, cabbage, chicken breast, and vinaigrette (below). Toss well.

If preparing ahead, STOP. Cover and refrigerate for up to 2 hours

SPICY PEANUT VINAIGRETTE

INGREDIENTS:

5 tbsp. rice wine vinegar
3 tbsp. sugar
1 tbsp. fresh chilies, diced
2-3 tbsp. soy sauce
1/2 cup peanut oil
1/2 cup toasted peanuts, coarsely chopped

PREPARATION:

Combine vinegar, sugar, chilies, and soy sauce, stirring to mix.

Add peanut oil and toasted peanuts and stir to mix.

PASTA SALAD with TUNA

Rosemary foccacio is a good bread to serve with this.

SERVES: 8
PREP TIME: 5 minutes
COOKING TIME: 15 minutes
MAY BE PREPARED AHEAD: 24 hours

INGREDIENTS:

2 oz. sliced ripe olives
12 oz. mixed color vegetable rotelli
6 oz. water packed light tuna
1/2 cup chopped parsley
10 cherry tomatoes, quartered
1/2 red pepper, minced
1/2 green pepper, minced
1 small red onion
1 zucchini, minced
1 tsp. seasoned salt
3/4 cup balsamic vinegar
1/2 cup virgin olive oil

PREPARATION:

Cook vegetable rotelli in boiling water al dente (approximately 15 minutes).

Add olives, tuna, parsley, tomatoes, red pepper, green pepper, onion and zucchini;mix well.

Add seasoned salt, vinegar and oil; mix well.

If preparing ahead, STOP. Cover and refrigerate.

SHRIMP SALAD CARDINALE

SERVES: 6
PREP TIME: 10 minutes
COOKING TIME: None
MAY BE PREPARED AHEAD:
    Not recommended

INGREDIENTS:

6 cups baby lettuce
1/4 cup shredded carrot
3 cups bay shrimp
Cardinale Dressing (below)
6 sprigs parsley or fresh herb
    of choice for garnish

PREPARATION:

Mix lettuces and carrots together.

Put on service plates.

Top each serving with 1/2 cup bay
shrimp and Cardinale dressing to taste.

Garnish with sprig of parsley or herb.

CARDINALE DRESSING

You may use this dressing with
any green salad.

PREP TIME: 10 minutes
COOKING TIME: None
MAY BE PREPARED AHEAD: 2 weeks

INGREDIENTS:

4 oz. bleu cheese
1 clove minced garlic
2 cups vegetable oil
1/3 tsp. salt
1 tbsp. celery salt
1/3 tbsp. Worcestershire sauce
1/4 cup minced onions
1 1/3 cup red wine vinegar
3 tbsp. sugar
1/2 tsp. paprika
1-1/4 tbsp. horseradish or mustard

PREPARATION:

Place all ingredients in blender
and blend until smooth.

Store in covered jar.

BLACK BEAN CORN SALAD

Top this salad with grilled shrimp
(5 medium per serving) or grilled Chili
Cured Chicken (see page 98) for a
super entree salad.

SERVES: 8
PREP TIME: Overnight soak,
    plus 1 hour for beans;
    15 minutes for salad
COOKING TIME: See above
MAY BE PREPARED AHEAD: 1 day

INGREDIENTS:

1 lb. dried black beans, picked over, soaked
    overnight in cold water, and drained
1-1/2 cups cooked fresh corn kernels
    (from about 3 ears of corn)
1-1/2 cups tomato, chopped, seeded
3/4 cup thinly sliced scallions
1/3 cup minced, fresh cilantro,
    plus sprigs for garnish
1/2 cup olive oil
1/2 cup fresh lemon juice (1 to 2 lemons)
2 tsp. salt

PREPARATION:

In a large saucepan, combine the black
beans and enough cold water to cover
them by 2 inches; bring water to a boil,
and simmer the beans for 45 minutes to
1 hour, or until they are just tender, but
not mushy. Do not overcook beans.

Drain the beans, and in a bowl combine
them with the corn, the tomato, the
scallions, and the minced cilantro.

In a small bowl, whisk together the oil,
the lemon juice, and the salt; pour the
dressing over the vegetables while the
beans are still warm, and let the salad
cool, stirring occasionally, until the beans
are room temperature.

If preparing ahead, STOP. Cover and refrigerate.

Serve the salad, garnished with cilantro
sprigs, at room temperature or chilled slightly.

To quick-soak dried beans, combine
beans, picked over and rinsed,
with triple their volume in cold water.
Bring the water to a boil and cook
the beans, uncovered, over moderate
heat for 2 minutes. Remove
the pan from the heat and let the
beans soak for 1 hour.

GRILLED CHICKEN, RASPBERRY and MUSHROOM SALAD

Our best selling entree salad in the restaurant.

SERVES: 4
PREP TIME: Mise en place
COOKING TIME: 15 minutes
MAY BE PREPARED AHEAD:
    Chicken - 24 hours

INGREDIENTS:

4 5-oz. chicken, boneless, skinless
8 oz. fresh sliced mushrooms
4 oz. soybean oil
2 oz. sliced almonds
2 oz. pinenuts
6 oz. raspberry vinegar
1/2 tsp. salt and pepper
4 cups mixed baby greens, (butter lettuce,
    romaine, and radiccio)
6 oz. fresh spinach
4 oz. whole raspberries

PREPARATION: Mise en place

TO COOK:

Brush chicken lightly with soybean oil.
Grill on an open grill.

If preparing ahead, STOP. Cover and refrigerate.

Slice chicken into bite-size pieces.

Saute mushrooms in 4 ounces soybean oil
for 1 minute. Add almonds and chicken and
saute for another minute.

Add pinenuts, and deglaze pan with raspberry vinegar, salt and pepper. Mix well.

TO SERVE:

Place 1 cup mixed greens on each
salad plate.

Place chicken, vinegar and nut mixture over
lettuce and top with whole raspberries.

CHILI PEPPERONI SALAD

This is a zesty entree salad with lots
of unexpected flavors and textures.

SERVES: 10
PREP TIME: 15 Minutes
COOKING TIME: None
MAY BE PREPARED AHEAD: 2 hours

INGREDIENTS:

1 head iceberg lettuce, chopped
8 oz. dark red kidney beans, drained
4 oz. julienne pepperoni
4 oz. pitted ripe olives
1 avocado, mashed
4 oz. sour cream
1/2 cup Dijon Vinaigrette (see page 58)
1 tbsp. chopped canned green chili peppers
1 onion, minced
1 tsp. chili powder
salt and pepper to taste
4 medium tomatoes, cut into wedges
1/2 cup shredded sharp cheddar cheese
tortilla chips

PREPARATION:

In bowl, combine lettuce, beans, pepperoni,
and olives. Chill.

To make dressing, blend avocado and sour
cream. Stir in Vinaigrette dressing, green
chili peppers, onion, chili powder, salt and
pepper. Mix well. Chill.

If preparing ahead, STOP. Store up to two hours.

TO SERVE:

Spoon avocado dressing in center of
salad, arrange tomato wedges in circle
atop salad, top with shredded cheese,
and trim edge of bowl with tortilla chips.

Summer Grills

Almost any meat or vegetable tastes great grilled.
Fire up the barbecue and relax with a cool drink while
the tantalizing aromas waft over the summer breeze.
Portable mini grills are great for picnics.

Save rosemary cuttings or vine trimmings to
toss over the coals for added flavor.

You'll find an assortment of salsas and relishes
under Summer seasonal gifts. All are fine accompaniments
to summer grills or provide easy snacks
with tortilla chips or crackers before your meal.

Herb butters are another great finish for grilled
fish and meat. They can be fixed in advance to save time
and keep you out of the kitchen in the summer.
Use them to finish meats, fish, pastas and breads. Here
are ten favorites, an herb butter for any occasion.

HERB GARDEN BUTTER

Serve with grilled fish or meats.

SERVES: 30 pats
PREP TIME: 15 minutes
COOKING TIME: None
MAY BE PREPARED AHEAD:
    1 week - refrigerated;
    1 month - frozen

INGREDIENTS:

3-4 cloves garlic
1/4 cup chopped parsley
1/4 cup chopped shallots or chives
1 lb. sweet butter, softened
1/3 cup herbs of your choice
salt and pepper to taste

Optional fresh herbs: basil - tarragon - dill

PREPARATION:

Chop the garlic, parsley and shallots
in food processor.

Blend in the butter, herbs and seasonings.

Divide butter in half. Shape into two
10 x 1-1/2-inch rolls on sheets of wax
paper. Cover with plastic wrap and
refrigerate until firm.

*If preparing ahead, STOP. Butter may be
refrigerated for up to 1 week or frozen for
up to 1 month.*

Cut into pats as needed.

BASIL GARLIC BUTTER

Serve with grilled fish or meats.

SERVES: 1 cup
PREP TIME: 5 minutes
COOKING TIME: None
MAY BE PREPARED AHEAD:
    1 week - refrigerated;
    1 month - frozen

INGREDIENTS:

1 cup sweet butter, softened
4 tbsp. finely snipped fresh basil
4 cloves garlic, pressed

PREPARATION:

Combine all ingredients in food processor.

*If preparing ahead, STOP. Store in small
crocks in refrigerator for up to 1 week.*
OR
Shape into long log and wrap in wax paper.
Store in freezer for up to 1 month.

PARSLEY

HAZELNUT-LAVENDAR BUTTER

Serve with grilled chicken, lamb or fish.

SERVES: 8 servings (1 tbsp. each)
PREP TIME: 5 minutes
COOKING TIME: None
MAY BE PREPARED AHEAD:
    1 week - refrigerated;
    1 month - frozen

INGREDIENTS:

1/4 lb. butter, room temperature
1/3 cup hazelnuts, chopped, toasted
1 tsp. Dijon-style mustard
pinch orange zest
1-1/4 tsp. dried lavendar flowers

PREPARATION:

In a food processor, combine all ingredients together.

Use a sheet of plastic wrap to help form butter into a roll approximately 1-inch in diameter and 8-inches long. Overlap plastic wrap around butter and refrigerate or freeze.

If preparing ahead, STOP. Butter may be refrigerated for up to 1 week or frozen for up to 1 month.

ROASTED RED PEPPER BUTTER

Serve with veal, seafood or poultry.

SERVES: 10-12 servings
PREP TIME: 5 minutes
COOKING TIME: None
MAY BE PREPARED AHEAD:
    1 week - refrigerated;
    1 month - frozen

INGREDIENTS:

1/3 lb. unsalted butter
1 shallot, pared, minced
1/4 tsp. Worcestershire sauce
dash of ground black pepper
2 oz. roasted red bell peppers, drained,
    finely chopped
1 tbsp. whole-grain mustard
1 tsp. lemon juice
2 drops hot pepper sauce
    (pickapepper, tabasco)
1/4 tsp. salt

PREPARATION:

Combine all ingredients together in a food processor.

Divide butter in half. On sheets of wax paper, shape into two 10 x 1-1/2 in. rolls. Cover with plastic wrap; refrigerate until firm.

If preparing ahead, STOP. May be stored in refrigerator for up to 1 week; or in the freezer for up to 1 month.

CHUNKY CILANTRO CITRUS BUTTER

Serve with broiled seafood or poultry.

SERVES: 30 pats
PREP TIME: 15 minutes
COOKING TIME: None
MAY BE PREPARED AHEAD:
    1 week - refrigerated;
    1 month - frozen

INGREDIENTS:

1 cup grapefruit, finely chopped
1/2 cup oranges, finely chopped
1/2 cup lemons, finely chopped
1/2 cup limes, finely chopped
1 lb. unsalted butter, softened
3 tbsp. fresh cilantro, chopped
4 tsp. fresh ginger, grated
2 tsp. salt
1/2 tsp. pepper

PREPARATION:

Place grapefruit, orange, lemon and lime in fine strainer; drain well and discard juice.

Using electric mixer, combine butter, cilantro, ginger, salt and pepper until fluffy.

Stir in fruit pulp; drain off any juice that doesn't incorporate into butter.

On sheets of wax paper, shape butter into two 10 x 1-1/2 in. rolls and cover with plastic wrap. Refrigerate until firm.

If preparing ahead, STOP. Butter may be refrigerated for up to 1 week or frozen for up to 1 month.

SPINACH HERB BUTTER

Serve with roasted poultry, beef tenderloin, and seafood or crusty bread.

SERVES: 30 pats
PREP TIME: 15 minutes
COOKING TIME: None
MAY BE PREPARED AHEAD:
    1 week - refrigerated;
    1 month - frozen

INGREDIENTS:

1 lb. unsalted butter, softened
2 tbsp. fresh parsley, chopped
2 tbsp. lemon juice
1/2 tsp. salt
1/2 cup spinach, cooked and
    very well drained
2 tbsp. shallots, pared and finely chopped
4 tsp. tarragon
1/2 tsp. pepper

PREPARATION:

Combine all ingredients together in a bowl of an electric mixer.

Divide butter in half. Shape into two 10 x 1-1/2 inch rolls on sheets of wax paper. Cover with plastic wrap and refrigerate until firm.

If preparing ahead, STOP. Butter may be refrigerated for up to 1 week or frozen for up to 1 month.

GARLIC CHEESE BUTTER

Perfect for garlic bread or simple
buttered pastas

SERVES: 1-1/2 cups
PREP TIME: 5 minutes
COOKING TIME: None
MAY BE PREPARED AHEAD:
    1 week - refrigerated;
    1 month - frozen

INGREDIENTS:

1 cup sweet butter, softened
4 cloves garlic, crushed
1/2 tsp. dried oregano
1/2 cup parmesan cheese
1/2 tsp. dried marjoram

PREPARATION:

Combine all ingredients in food processor.

*If preparing ahead, STOP. Store in small
crocks in refrigerator for up to 1 week.*
OR
Shape into long log and wrap in wax paper.
Store in freezer for up to 1 month.

HONEY BUTTER

Good with all soft homemade breads
and muffins. Use wild flavor honeys for
a more herbal flavor.

SERVES: 1-1/2 cups
PREP TIME: 5 minutes
COOKING TIME: None
MAY BE PREPARED AHEAD:
    1 week - refrigerated;
    1 month - frozen

INGREDIENTS:

1 cup sweet butter, softened
1/2 cup honey

PREPARATION:

Combine all ingredients in food processor.

*If preparing ahead, STOP. Store in small
crocks in refrigerator for up to 1 week.*
OR
Shape into long log and wrap in wax paper.
Store in freezer for up to 1 month.

CURRIED HONEY BUTTER

Wonderful with fresh breads,
Indian Fry Bread or poultry.

SERVES: 1-1/2 cups
PREP TIME: 5 minutes
COOKING TIME: None
MAY BE PREPARED AHEAD:
    1 week - refrigerated;
    1 month - frozen

INGREDIENTS:

1 cup sweet butter, softened
1 tbsp. curry powder
1/2 cup sage honey

PREPARATION:

Combine all ingredients in food processor.

*If preparing ahead, STOP. Store in small
crocks in refrigerator for up to 1 week.*
OR
Shape into long log and wrap in wax paper.
Store in freezer for up to 1 month.

ORANGE HONEY BUTTER

Great with poultry or seafood.

SERVES: 1-1/2 cups
PREP TIME: 5 minutes
COOKING TIME: None
MAY BE PREPARED AHEAD:
    1 week - refrigerated;
    1 month - frozen

INGREDIENTS:

1 cup sweet butter, softened
6 tbsp. orange juice
1/2 cup orange blossom honey
1 tbsp. grated orange zest

PREPARATION:

Combine all ingredients in food processor.

*If preparing ahead, STOP. Store in small
crocks in refrigerator for up to 1 week.*
OR
Shape into long log and wrap in wax paper.
Store in freezer for up to 1 month.

EASY GRILLED FRESH FISH with HERBED BUTTERS

SERVES: 1
PREP TIME: Mise en place
COOKING TIME: 4 to 6 minutes
MAY BE PREPARED AHEAD:
    Not recommended

INGREDIENTS:

8 oz. fresh fish of your choice
1 tsp. vegetable oil
1 tsp. herb butter of your choice

PREPARATION: Mise en place

TO COOK:

Baste both sides of fish with vegetable oil
and grill 2 to 3 minutes on each side
(depending on what type of fish and how
thick the filet is)

Before serving, spread whipped herb
butter on top.

For years, our top selling entree at the
restaurant was grilled fish with herb butter.
Here are some suggested combinations
to spark your creativity:

- *Grilled Albacore with Basil Walnut Butter*
- *Grilled Halibut Steak with Thyme Butter*
- *Grilled Mahi Mahi with Macadamia Nut Butter*
- *Grilled Monk Fish with Curry Butter*
- *Grilled Opah with Chervil Butter*
- *Grilled Red Fish with Summer Savory Butter*
- *Grilled Salmon with Dill Butter*
- *Grilled Sea Bass with Lemon Garlic Butter*
- *Grilled Shark with Cilantro Garlic Butter*
- *Grilled Red Snapper with Tarragon Butter*
- *Grilled Soupfin Shark with Tarragon Butter*
- *Grilled Swordfish with Cilantro Lime Butter*
- *Grilled Thresher Shark with Thyme Butter*
- *Grilled Trout with Toasted Almond Butter*
- *Grilled Tuna with Basil Walnut Butter*
- *Grilled Wahoo with Scallion Parsley Butter*
- *Grilled Yellowtail with Sage Butter*

GAME HENS with HERBS OF PROVENCE

This marinade works equally well with pork chops, lamb chops, chicken breasts and thin steaks.

SERVES: 6
PREP TIME: 10 minutes
COOKING TIME: 25-40 minutes
MAY BE PREPARED AHEAD:
    May be served cold for picnics

INGREDIENTS:

1/2 cup olive oil
1/4 cup balsamic vinegar
1/4 cup Herbs of Provence (see page 61)
6 game hens

PREPARATION:

Mix olive oil, vinegar and Herbs of Provence together.

Place game hens in marinade, cover, and refrigerate for 2 hours.

TO COOK:

Option 1
Grill over barbeque for 25 minutes, basting with marinade.

Option 2
Stuff with fresh rosemary (1 large sprig per bird) and yellow onions (1/4 large onion cut in chunks).

Place in glass baking dish.

Bake at 425 degrees for 10 minutes. Baste with marinade.

Reduce heat to 325 degrees; continue cooking for 30 minutes, basting with marinade every 10 minutes.

GRILLED CHILI CURED CHICKEN

The cornmeal and chili paste forms a flavorful crust.

SERVES: 6
PREP TIME: 10 minutes + 2 hours
    marinating time
COOKING TIME: 25 minutes
MAY BE PREPARED AHEAD: 24 hours

INGREDIENTS:

1 tbsp. ground California chili-pepper*
1 tbsp. ground New Mexico chili-pepper*
1/2 tsp. ground chili de arbol*
pinch dried safflower* (Mexican-saffron)
1/2 tsp. ground cumin*
1/4 tsp. salt*
1/2 tsp. black pepper*
1 tbsp. mild olive or vegetable oil
1/4 - 1/3 cup water
6 chicken breast halves, boned and skinned
1 cup yellow cornmeal
olive oil or canola mist

*These seven items may be pre-mixed in quantity to make "Three Chili Spice" for gifts.

PREPARATION:

Mix chilis, safflower, cumin, salt, and pepper together.

Add oil and water to make a paste.

Cover chicken breast with chili paste and allow paste to set for 10 minutes.

Pat yellow cornmeal on plate and dust each side of chicken breast.

TO COOK:

Place on oil-misted baking sheet and blast in 425 degree oven for 10 minutes.

Reduce heat to 325 degrees for an additional 10 minutes.

Remove chicken. Allow to sit for 10 minutes.

TO SERVE:

Slice chicken in thin slices, and arrange in fanned pattern.

May be served over:
Black Bean Corn Salad (See page 89)
Bed of Mixed Greens with Dijon Vinaigrette
    (See page 58)
Rosemary and Sundried Tomato Rissoto
    (See page 191)

If preparing ahead for summer salads, STOP. Cover and refrigerate for up to 24 hours.

MARGARITA CHICKEN KABOBS

SERVES: 4
PREP TIME: 35 minutes
COOKING TIME: 10-15 minutes
MAY BE PREPARED AHEAD: 24 hours

INGREDIENTS:

1 cup + 2 tsp. lime juice
4 1/8 tsp. sugar
1/2 tsp. salt
1 tsp. ground coriander
1 garlic clove, pared and minced
1 lb. chicken breast, cut into 1-in. cubes
2 tbsp. butter, softened
1 tbsp. minced parsley
2 ears corn, cut into 8 pieces
1 large green or red pepper,
    cut into 1-in. chunks

PREPARATION:

Combine 1 cup lime juice, 4 tsp. sugar, salt, coriander, and garlic. Place chicken in heavy plastic bag and pour marinade over to cover. Marinate for at least 30 minutes.

If preparing ahead, STOP. May be refrigerated up to 24 hours.

Blend butter, 2 tsp. lime juice, 1/8 tsp. sugar, and parsley together well; reserve.

TO COOK:

Thread chicken onto skewers, alternating with pieces of corn and pepper. Grill over hot coals, basting with butter mixture for 10-15 minutes, turning frequently.

GRILLED SAUSAGES

Make your own charcutierre as time permits. No recipes are included in this book. To save time, develop a reliable source, like a German sausage shop, French charciuterie or sympathetic butcher.

There are many fine speciality sausages available. Try beef/pork combinations with onions and jalapeños or turkey with wild sage.

To cook, slit skin in row of diagonal cuts and grill in a very hot stovetop grill or over the barbecue.

Serve with an assortment of salsas, mustards, or relishes.

SANTA FE TOP SIRLOIN

SERVES: 10
PREP TIME: 10 - 15 minutes
COOKING TIME: 15 minutes
MAY BE PREPARED AHEAD: 8 hours

INGREDIENTS:

2 garlic cloves, minced
1/2 oz. chopped parsley
6 oz. melted butter
1/2 tsp. cumin
6 oz. bread crumbs
1 tsp. dried thyme
salt and black pepper to taste
10 8-oz. top sirloin or 6-oz. tournedo

PREPARATION:

Mix all ingredients together (except meat)

If preparing ahead, STOP. Cover container and allow to remain at cool room temperature for up to 8 hours.

TO COOK:

Grill steak or tournedo to slightly less than desired degree of doneness.

Place bread crumb mixture on top of meat.

Bake in a 350 degree oven for 10 minutes to set topping.

GRILLED LAMB CHOPS with TOMATO MINT COULIS

SERVES: 6
PREP TIME: 15 minutes
COOKING TIME: None
MAY BE PREPARED AHEAD:
    Coulis - 8 hours

INGREDIENTS:

12 small lamb chops
minced garlic to taste
salt and pepper to taste
6 sprigs rosemary for garnish

Tomato Mint Coulis
4 medium tomatoes, skin off
1/2 cup chopped fresh mint
salt and pepper to taste
1/2 cup chopped green onions
4 tsp. raspberry vinegar

PREPARATION:

Tomato Mint Coulis
Put all ingredients in a food processor.

Process for one minute until the mixture is pureed.

If preparing ahead, STOP. Cover and refrigerate for up to 8 hours.

TO COOK:

Lamb
Grill lamb to desired doneness over hot coals, seasoning with minced garlic, salt and pepper to taste.

TO SERVE:

Bring Coulis to room temperature.

Place 1/3 cup Coulis on plate. Top each pool of Coulis with two lamb chops.

Garnish plate with rosemary sprigs.

Serve with Country Style Potatoes (see page 32) and Green Beans with Bacon and Onions (see page 107).

GRILLED CHICKEN STUFFED with CILANTRO PECAN PESTO in SWEET PEPPER COULIS

SERVES: 6
PREP TIME: 10 minutes
COOKING TIME: 20 minutes
MAY BE PREPARED AHEAD: 6 hours

INGREDIENTS

6 large chicken halves
1-1/2 cups Cilantro Pecan Pesto (Recipe follows)
juice of 4 lemons
salt and pepper to taste
1-1/2 cups Sweet Red Pepper Coulis
    (Recipe follows)
6 sprigs cilantro, chopped

PREPARATION:

Insert boning knife into center of chicken, and make a large pocket, taking care not to put hole all the way through meat.

Stuff each chicken with 1/4 cup Cilantro Pecan Pesto, and pin hole opening closed with metal poultry pins.

Place in glass baking dish, season with lemon juice, salt and pepper. Allow to sit for 10 minutes.

If preparing ahead, STOP. Cover and refrigerate for up to 6 hours.

TO COOK:

Option 1
Grill over hot coals, turning carefully so you don't dislodge stuffing, until done.

Option 2
Sear on hot grill to lightly brown, about 2 minutes on each side.

Finish in 350 degree oven for 30 minutes.

TO SERVE:

Place 1/4 cup Sweet Red Pepper Coulis on plate.

Top with chicken breast.

Garnish with chopped cilantro.

CILANTRO PECAN PESTO

This is an unusual Southwestern twist to traditional pesto. Use it with pastas, meats or mixed with a little olive oil as a dip for crusty bread.

SERVES: 2 cups
PREP TIME: 5 minutes
COOKING TIME: None
MAY BE PREPARED AHEAD: 3 weeks

INGREDIENTS:

1 cup parsley
1 cup cilantro
4 large garlic cloves
1 cup pecans
1 cup top quality virgin olive oil
1 cup freshly grated parmesan cheese
salt and pepper to taste

PREPARATION:

In food processor, blend parsley, cilantro, garlic and pecans to a paste.

While processor is still running, add olive oil slowly in a stream.

Add parmesan, salt and pepper to taste.

TO SERVE:

Use as a "no cook" sauce over hot linguini.

Stuff chicken breast.

Top a 5 oz. tournedo with 1 tbsp. pesto before serving.

SWEET RED PEPPER COULIS

SERVES: 1-1/2 cups
PREP TIME: 10 minutes
COOKING TIME: 6-8 minutes
MAY BE PREPARED AHEAD: 24 hours

INGREDIENTS:

2 large red bell peppers, peeled
2 tbsp. olive oil
1/4 tsp. salt
1/8 tsp. freshly ground black pepper

PREPARATION:

Core, seed and roughly chop peppers.

Put in 2-1/2 quart casserole and cover.

TO COOK:

Microwave on high (100% power) until tender, 6 to 8 minutes.

Put peppers, cooking juices, olive oil, salt and pepper in food processor and process until smooth.

If preparing ahead, STOP. Cover and refrigerate for up to 24 hours.

TO SERVE:

Use as a sauce under polenta timbales or as an accompaniment to cooked fish or chicken.

To peel peppers, stab with a fork and hold directly over gas stove flame, turning to scorch pepper on all sides. Put in paper bag, close tightly and let sit for 5 minutes. Hold pepper under running water and use fingers to peel off skin.

Summer Sides

*For "Summer Sides," I have included two "no cook"
pasta sauces to keep the kitchen cool. (Cilantro Pecan
Pesto on page 102 is also "no cook.") The pastas
are a delicious accompaniment to Summer Grills, and
can provide a vegetarian entree as well.*

*Most of these summer sides have
a distinct tartness through lemon or vinegar
to offset the heaviness of grilled meats.*

BASIL GREEN CHILI PESTO

SERVES: 4
PREP TIME: 15 minutes
COOKING TIME: none
MAY BE PREPARED AHEAD: 2 days

INGREDIENTS:

2 cups fresh basil leaves, rinsed,
    torn, packed together
1/2 cup virgin olive oil
3 tbsp. piñons
2 large garlic cloves
1/4 tsp. salt, or to taste
1/2 cup finely chopped
    New Mexican green chilies,
    freshly parched and peeled
1/2 cup freshly grated parmesan cheese
3 tbsp. romano cheese
4 sprigs fresh basil for garnish

PREPARATION:

Process basil, oil, piñon nuts, garlic,
and salt in a food processor until pureed,
being careful not to over-process.

Pour into a 1-quart mixing bowl and add the
green chile and cheeses. Stir until evenly
mixed together.

*If preparing ahead, STOP. Cover and refriger-
ate. Bring to room temperature before serving.*

TO SERVE:

Cook 16 ounces pasta and drain well.
Mix with sauce and garnish with sprig
of fresh basil.

ARTICHOKE, ROASTED RED PEPPER and SUN-DRIED TOMATO SAUCE

SERVES: 4
PREP TIME: 15 minutes
COOKING TIME: none
MAY BE PREPARED AHEAD: 8 hours

INGREDIENTS:

1 jar (6 oz.) marinated artichokes,
    rinsed, drained, and chopped well
1/4 cup chopped Italian flat-leaved parsley
1 tbsp. pitted & slivered brine-cured
    black olives
1 tbsp. red wine vinegar
1/8 tsp. freshly ground black pepper
1 jar (7 oz.) roasted red peppers, rinsed,
    well drained, and chopped well
2 tbsp. minced sun-dried tomatoes
    in oil, drained
1/2 cup olive oil
1 garlic clove, crushed

PREPARATION:

Combine all ingredients in a small bowl;
stir well to blend.

*If preparing ahead, STOP. Cover and store
in refrigerator. Bring to room temperature
before serving.*

TO SERVE:

Cook 16 ounces pasta and drain well.
Mix with sauce and garnish with a
cherry pepper.

BASIL

SOUTHWESTERN CORN SLAW

This spicy, sweet slaw makes a great partner to smoked or grilled meats. If you heat it, it's also an unusual vegetable side dish.

SERVES: 10
PREP TIME: Mise en place
COOKING TIME: 15 minutes
MAY BE PREPARED AHEAD: 3 days

INGREDIENTS:

1 small head green cabbage, sliced into
    thin strips
1 cup chopped green bell pepper
1 chopped chile
1/2 cup diced red pimiento
3 tomatoes, diced
1-1/4 cups salad oil
1 tbsp. celery seed
1/4 tsp. ground cumin
1/2 tsp. ground black pepper
2 lbs. corn
1 cup corn syrup
2/3 cup cider vinegar

PREPARATION: Mise en place

TO COOK:

Saute the fresh vegetables except corn in oil with spices for five minutes; set aside.

Cook the corn in steamer or hot water, then strain and mix with the vegetables. Add corn syrup and cider vinegar, and mix well.

If preparing ahead, STOP. Cover and refrigerate.

TO SERVE:

Serve cool. May be used as a buffet salad or salad course. For salad course, serve in a "cup" from a purple cabbage leaf.

THREE BEAN SALAD

The longer you marinate this salad, the richer and more garlicky the flavor. This salad is a good accent for all barbecue grilled meats.

SERVES: 6
PREP TIME: 5 minutes
COOKING TIME: None
MAY BE PREPARED AHEAD: 1 week

INGREDIENTS:

1 #2 can green beans*
1 #2 can kidney beans
1 medium chopped onion
3 tsp. salt
3/4 cup salad oil
2 whole cloves garlic
1 #2 can wax beans*
1 #2 can garbanzo beans
2/3 cup sugar
1-1/2 tsp. pepper
1 cup vinegar

*Substitute 2 cups fresh cooked beans whenever possible.

PREPARATION:

Mix all ingredients well.

Allow to marinate for one day. If preparing ahead, cover tightly and refrigerate for up to 1 week.

NEW POTATO SALAD VINAIGRETTE

For an unusual zest, add 1/4 tsp. chopped lavender leaves.

SERVES: 6
PREP TIME: 10 minutes
COOKING TIME: None
MAY BE PREPARED AHEAD: 2 days

INGREDIENTS:

18 baby new potatoes with skins on, cooked, cut in 3/4-in. cubes
6 scallions, finely chopped
2 hard boiled eggs, chopped
1/2 cup Tarragon Dijon Vinaigrette
    (see page 58)
1/4 tsp. chopped lavender leaves (optional)

PREPARATION:

Mix all ingredients together.

Allow flavors to marry for 2 hours in refrigerator. If preparing ahead, store covered in refrigerator for up to 2 days.

TARRAGON

VALENCIA SALAD

Potato Salad with the touch of Southern Spain — oranges, onions, pimiento, and cilantro.

SERVES: 4 for light entree;
        6 for appetizer course
PREP TIME: 15 minutes
COOKING TIME: none required
MAY BE PREPARED AHEAD: 24 hours

INGREDIENTS:

3 medium red waxy potatoes, boiled, skinned, cut into 1-in. chunks
1/2 cup slivered Spanish onion
1 orange, peeled, cut into 1/4-in. slices, quartered
1 pimiento, homemade or imported, cut into thin strips
2 tbsp. red wine vinegar
4 tbsp. salad oil
salt to taste
freshly ground pepper to taste
4-8 leaves of butter lettuce
4-6 sprigs of cilantro for garnish

PREPARATION:

In a bowl, combine with a rubber spatula the potatoes, onion, orange pieces, and pimiento.

In a small bowl, beat together the vinegar and oil. Gently fold into the salad. Season with salt and pepper. Refrigerate until well chilled.

If preparing ahead, STOP. Cover with plastic wrap and store in refrigerator.

TO SERVE:

Place leaves of butter lettuce on plates. Top with potato mixture and garnish with cilantro.

GREEN BEANS with BACON AND SWEET ONIONS

SERVES: 6
PREP TIME: Mise en place
COOKING TIME: 20 minutes
MAY BE PREPARED AHEAD: 2 hours

INGREDIENTS:

12 oz. green beans, ends and
    strings removed
4 slices bacon, cut in small pieces
1 medium sweet onion, minced
1/2 tsp. salt
2 tbsp. raspberry vinegar

PREPARATION: Mise en place

TO COOK:

Bring saucepan of water with salt to
boil. Add beans and cook 15 minutes,
until tender. Drain.

Meanwhile, in a large saucepan, saute
bacon and onions together until bacon
is cooked and onions are clear.

Drain off excess bacon drippings, allowing
approximately 2 tbsp. of drippings to remain.
Add salt and vinegar and deglaze pan. Add
beans to saute pan and mix well to coat.

*If preparing ahead, STOP. Cover saute pan
and leave on stovetop for up to 2 hours.
Reheat to serve.*

ROASTED PLUM TOMATOES

The balsamic vinegar and herbs lift
an ordinary tomato to new heights.

SERVES: 4
PREP TIME: 3 minutes
COOKING TIME: 8 minutes
MAY BE PREPARED AHEAD: 4 hours

INGREDIENTS:

4 plum tomatoes, quartered
3 cloves garlic, peeled, thinly sliced
3 bay leaves
8 sprigs parsley
2 sprigs fresh oregano
8 sprigs fresh basil
1/2 tsp. kosher salt
1/2 tsp. fresh cracked pepper
1/4 cup balsamic vinegar
1/4 cup extra-virgin olive oil

PREPARATION:

Preheat oven to 500 degrees.

Place the tomatoes in a single layer in
a shallow baking dish. Sprinkle with
garlic and herbs. Season with salt and
pepper and drizzle evenly with the
vinegar and olive oil.

*If preparing ahead, STOP. Cover and
hold for up to 4 hours.*

TO COOK:

Roast the tomatoes for 8 minutes
until they are lightly caramelized but
still keep their shape. Remove from
the oven and cool.

MARINATED MUSHROOMS

SERVES: 4
PREP TIME: 4 to 6 hour marinade
COOKING TIME: None
MAY BE PREPARED AHEAD: 24 hours

INGREDIENTS:

1/2 cup salad oil
2/3 cup tarragon vinegar
1 medium clove garlic, minced
1 tbsp. sugar
1-1/2 tsp. salt
dash tabasco
2 tbsp. water
1 lb.mushroom buttons, quartered
1 medium onion (1-1/2 cups),
   sliced into thin strips

PREPARATION:

Mix oil, vinegar, water and seasonings.
Toss gently with mushrooms and onions.

*Marinate for 4 to 6 hours. If preparing ahead,
store in refrigerator for up to 24 hours.*

MUSHROOM SCALLION RICE

SERVES: 4
PREP TIME: Mise en place
COOKING TIME: 40 minutes
MAY BE PREPARED AHEAD: 1 hour

INGREDIENTS:

1/2 lb. sliced mushrooms
6 scallions, sliced
4 tbsp. butter
1 cup rice
2 cans beef bouillon
1 cup water
4 tbsp. fresh parsley, chopped

PREPARATION: Mise en place

TO COOK:

Saute mushrooms and scallions in
butter until cooked, about 10 minutes.
Add rice and saute until well coated.

Add beef bouillon and water. Cover and
cook over medium heat for 30 minutes,
or until rice has been thoroughly absorbed.

Add parsley and allow to stand 10 minutes.

*If preparing ahead, STOP. Keep tightly
covered in warm oven for up to 1 hour,
adding additional water and stirring if rice
begins to dry out.*

PARSLEY

COUSCOUS with LEMON and TOMATO

SERVES: 6
PREP TIME: 5 minutes
COOKING TIME: 1 hour
MAY BE PREPARED AHEAD:
    Not recommended

INGREDIENTS:

2 cups couscous
2 tbsp. lemon zest
1/4 cup lemon juice
1/2 cup chopped tomato, seeded
1 tbsp. olive oil
2 cups chicken broth
1 tsp. salt

PREPARATION:

Mix all ingredients well.

TO COOK:

Bake in low 300 degree oven for
1 hour or until broth is absorbed.

BULGAR with PARSLEY and LEMON

SERVES: 6
PREP TIME: Mise en place
COOKING TIME: 30 minutes
MAY BE PREPARED AHEAD:
    Not recommended

INGREDIENTS:

2 cups water
1 cup bulgar
1/2 tsp. salt
2 tbsp. butter
1/4 cup chopped parsley
1 tbsp. fresh lemon juice
2 tbsp. lemon zest

PREPARATION: Mise en place

TO COOK:

Bring water to boil.

Add bulgar, reduce heat, and simmer,
covered, for approximately 30 minutes,
until grain is soft.

Remove from heat and add salt, butter,
parsley and lemon juice, and lemon zest.

ORANGE CINNAMON ICED TEA

SERVES: 3 quarts
PREP TIME: 10 minutes
COOKING TIME: None
MAY BE PREPARED AHEAD: 48 hours

INGREDIENTS:

2 cinnamon sticks
1 tbsp. dried or 3 tbsp. fresh orange peel
    (remove as much white as possible)
1-1/2 quarts boiling water
6 tea bags of choice
1/3 cup orange juice
1-1/2 quarts cold water
orange slice garnish

PREPARATION:

Simmer cinnamon, orange peel and boiling water for 5 minutes.

Remove from heat and add tea bags.

Let stand until cool, and then strain.

Add orange juice and cold water.

If preparing ahead, STOP. Keep well chilled for up to 48 hours.

Garnish with orange slice.

MARGARITA PUNCH

SERVES: 2 gallons
PREP TIME: 10 minutes
COOKING TIME: None
MAY BE PREPARED AHEAD: 4 hours

INGREDIENTS:

2-1/2 quarts white tequila
2 cups triple sec
12 oz. can frozen limeade
4 quarts ice cubes
2 fresh limes, sliced, for garnish

PREPARATION:

Process all ingredients (except garnish) in blender in small batches.

Serve punch in bowl with ice ring. You may freeze lime wheels or flowers into ring.

Garnish with fresh limes.

If preparing ahead, STOP. You may mix all ingredients except ice up to 4 hours ahead.

Use "block" ice for punches.
Create decorative designs or rings
using jello molds. Incorporate
flowers and herbs or colored ice.

STRAWBERRY MARGARITA PUNCH

SERVES: 2 gallons
PREP TIME: 10 minutes
COOKING TIME: None
MAY BE PREPARED AHEAD: 4 hours

INGREDIENTS:

2-1/2 quarts white tequila
2 cups triple sec
12 oz. can frozen limeade
4 quarts ice cubes
1-1/2 quarts fresh or frozen strawberries
10 fresh strawberries for garnish
2 fresh limes, sliced, for garnish

PREPARATION:

Process all ingredients (except garnish)
in blender in small batches.

Serve punch in bowl with decorative
ice ring made with strawberries and lime.

*If preparing ahead, STOP. You may mix
all ingredients except ice up to 4 hours ahead.*

SANGRIA

Originally from Spain, this fruity cooler has
become a Southwestern favorite.

SERVES: 6 - 8
PREP TIME: 5 minutes
COOKING TIME: None
MAY BE PREPARED AHEAD: 24 hours

INGREDIENTS:

24 oz. burgundy
2 tbsp. orange juice
2 tbsp. Grand Marnier
1 tbsp. sugar
1 cup sparkling soda
orange and lemon slices for garnish

PREPARATION:

Mix burgundy, orange juice, Grand Marnier,
and sugar together well.

*Refrigerate for 3 hours. If preparing ahead,
keep in refrigerator for up to 24 hours.*

TO SERVE:

Fill balloon wine glass with 3 parts
wine mixture to 1 part soda. For a
4 ounce serving, this is 3 ounces wine
to 1 ounce soda.

Garnish with orange slice.

BAJA BREEZES

SERVES: 1 drink/ 1 gallon
PREP TIME: 1 minute
COOKING TIME: None
MAY BE PREPARED AHEAD: No

INGREDIENTS:

1 drink
1/2 cup cranberry juice
1/2 cup orange juice
1 oz. white tequila

1 gallon
2 quarts cranberry juice
2 quarts fresh orange juice
16 oz. white tequila

PREPARATION:

Mix all ingredients well.

Serve in a tall glass over ice.

Garnish with an orange slice and cherry.

Summer

Desserts

*Summer meals demand a fresh, light ending.
The Summer desserts you'll find here emphasize
fresh fruits, creams, sorbets and cheeses.*

*The simplest of all finales to a Summer repast is
fresh fruit and cheese. I have included some
delicious taste combinations.*

Cheese and Fruit Chart

Bel Paese	Pineapple, honeydew melon, pears, green grapes, apples.
Blue Gorgonzola	Pears, apples, honeydew melon, plums.
Brick	Pineapple, apples, pears, honeydew melon, green grapes.
Brie	Green grapes, pineapple, apples, honeydew melon, plums, peaches.
Camembert	Green grapes, pineapple, apples, honeydew melon, plums, pears.
Cheddar	Apples, pears, green grapes, honeydew melon, pineapple.
Edam	Apples, pineapple, pears, green grapes, plums.
Gouda	Green grapes, pears, pineapple, honeydew melon, apples.
Monterey Jack	Pineapple, green grapes, pears, apples, honeydew melon.
Muenster	Apples, pears, pineapple, green grapes, cantaloupe.
Port de Salut	Pineapple, plums, pears, honeydew melon, cantaloupe.
Provolone	Pineapple, pears, apples, green grapes, plums.
Swiss	Apples, pineapple, green grapes, pears, plums, honeydew melon.

SIMPLEST STRAWBERRIES

Offer Summer's juiciest
strawberries with a dish of
Créme Fraiche and a
dish of dark brown sugar to dip.

SUMMER PUDDING

SERVES: 6 - 8
PREP TIME: 30 minutes
COOKING TIME: None
MAY BE PREPARED AHEAD: 24 hours

INGREDIENTS:

2 quarts (about 3 lbs.) fresh ripe raspberries,
    blackberries, blueberries, or red currants
1-1/4 cup superfine sugar
10-12 slices homemade white bread
1 cup heavy cream, whipped

PREPARATION:

Wash berries, discarding stems, caps, and bruised or moldy berries; shake dry, and drain on paper towels.

If the berries are not fully ripened and soft, combine the fruit and sugar in a heavy 3- to 4-quart saucepan, and cook over low heat for about 5 minutes, shaking the pan frequently.

Place berries in a large mixing bowl, sprinkle with sugar and toss gently with a large spoon until sugar dissolves completely. Add more sugar to taste if necessary, cover tightly and set berries aside.

With a small, sharp knife, cut 1 slice of bread into a circle or octagon so that it will exactly fit the bottom of a 2-quart English pudding basin, a 2-quart deep bowl, or a charlotte mold, and set in place.

Trim 6 or 7 slices of bread into truncated wedge shapes 3 to 4 inches wide across the top and about 3 inches wide across the bottom. Stand the wedges of bread, narrow end down, around the inner surface of the mold, overlapping them by about 1/4 inch.

Ladle the fruit mixture into the mold, and cover the top completely with the remaining bread.

Cover the top of the mold with a flat plate, and then set a 3- to 4-pound kitchen weight or a heavy pan or casserole on top of the plate.

Refrigerate the pudding for at least 12 hours, until the bread is completely saturated with the fruit syrup. If preparing ahead, keep refrigerated for up to 24 hours.

TO SERVE:

To remove the pudding from the mold, place a chilled serving plate upside down over it and, grasping the plate and mold firmly together, quickly invert them. The pudding should slide out easily.

Serve the whipped cream separately from the pudding.

BLUEBERRY TARTE with ALMOND CINNAMON CREAM

SERVES: 6
PREP TIME: 5 minutes
COOKING TIME: 30 minutes
MAY BE PREPARED AHEAD:
    Cream - 2 hours

INGREDIENTS:

1 sheet prepared puff pastry
2 cups blueberries
4 tbsp. Demara sugar
1 tsp. ground cinnamon

Almond Cinnamon Cream
1 cup whipped cream
1/2 tsp. almond flavoring
1/4 tsp. ground cinnamon
2 tsp. powdered sugar

PREPARATION:

Preheat oven to 350 degrees and
spray tarte or quiche pan with non-stick
spray (like Pam).

Place puff pastry in pan,
trimming and fluting edges as needed.

Prick puff pastry with fork to prevent
uneven bulges.

Sprinkle 2 tbsp. sugar and 1/2 tsp.
cinnamon over pastry.

Spread blueberries over pastry, and sprinkle
with remaining sugar and ground cinnamon.

TO COOK:

Bake for 30 minutes until crust is
puffed and filling is stewing in juices.

Almond Cinnamon Cream
Mix all ingredients together and
whip until fluffy.

*If preparing ahead, STOP. Cover
and refrigerate for up to 2 hours.*

TO SERVE:

Cut in wedges and top with
Almond Cinnamon Cream.

Serve warm or cool.

PLUM TARTE

SERVES: 6
PREP TIME: 10 minutes
COOKING TIME: 40 - 50 minutes
MAY BE PREPARED AHEAD: 4 hours

INGREDIENTS:

9-10 in. pie shell (see Pate Brisée, this page)
1 whole egg
2 egg yolks
1/4 cup sugar
3 tbsp. milk
3 tbsp. Créme Fraiche or heavy cream
1/3 cup ground almonds
2-1/4 lb. ripe mirabelles or prune plums,
    washed, dried, pitted, halved

PREPARATION:

Preheat oven to 350 degrees. Line a pie pan
or tart ring with the pastry dough and prick
lightly all over.

Mix the whole egg and egg yolks. Add sugar,
then stir in the milk and cream little by little.

Sprinkle the ground almonds over the dough.

Arrange the plums over the top in a circular
pattern. Do not pile them on top of each other.

Pour in enough custard mixture to cover.

TO COOK:

Bake for about 40 to 50 minutes. When
cooked, underside of the pastry should have
browned nicely. Turn out and allow to cool.

NOTE: Many fruits (apples, pears, Damson
plums, cherries, etc.) may be baked with
a custard filling as described here.

To grind almonds, use coffee grinder
to finely grind almonds without skins.
Add a minute amount of flour to
reduce oil in ground nuts if needed.

FOOD PROCESSOR PASTRY (PATE BRISÉE)

SERVES: a 9 to 10 inch pastry shell
PREP TIME: 5 minutes
COOKING TIME: none
MAY BE PREPARED AHEAD: 24 hours.
    Dough may be frozen.

INGREDIENTS:

1-1/2 cups all purpose flour
8 tbsp. frozen butter cut into pieces OR
4 tbsp. frozen butter and 1/4 cup shortening
1/4 tsp. salt
1/4 cup ice water

PREPARATION:

Place flour, butter (or butter and shortening)
and salt in a food processor fitted with the
metal blade. Blend using pulse method until
the mixture resembles a fine meal.

Gradually add up to 1/4 cup of ice water
through the feed tube with the processor
running. When the pastry begins to form
a ball, turn off the processor.

Remove the pastry from the processor
and form it into a ball. Flatten the
dough slightly, dust it with flour, and
cover with plastic wrap. Refrigerate
for 30 minutes before rolling.

FRESH FRUIT SAUCES

Serve fruit sauces over ice cream, pound cake, or bread puddings. They make great glazes for custard tartes. Here is a full assortment to utilize summer's freshest fruits. These may also be bottled for gifts.

SERVES: 6-8
MAY BE PREPARED AHEAD:
    3 weeks refrigerated

NOTE: For any fresh fruit sauce, the amount of sugar can vary depending upon the acidity of the fruit, so it is best to add it progressively and judge according to taste.

Apricot Sauce
1 cup water
6-1/2 tbsp. sugar
1 vanilla bean
12 apricots, halved and pitted
3 tbsp. apricot brandy

Make sugar syrup by placing the water, sugar and vanilla in a saucepan and bringing to a boil. Add the apricots, and poach for 20 to 25 minutes stirring from time to time.

Take out the vanilla bean. Work the fruit and syrup through a food mill. Strain the sauce and add the apricot brandy.

Black Currant Sauce
6 tbsp. water
2/3 cup sugar
3 tbsp. black currant puree

Make a sugar syrup by placing the water and sugar in a saucepan and bringing to a boil. Remove from heat and add the black currant puree. Mix to combine and then strain.

NOTE: If making the sauce from fresh black currants, cook them first in a saucepan with a little water, work them through a food mill and sieve before adding to sugar syrup.

Lime Sauce
5-1/2 tbsp. water
6-1/2 tbsp. sugar
3 limes
3 tbsp. apricot jam

Make a sugar syrup by placing the water and sugar in a saucepan and bringing to a boil. Remove from heat and reserve.

Zest 1 lime and cut the zests into thin julienne strips. Drop the zests into boiling water for 2 minutes; drain. Place the zests in a saucepan with 5 tbsp. of the sugar syrup and simmer gently for 10 to 15 minutes. Reserve.

Cut off the peel and whitish inner skin from 2 limes and detach the wedges from between the thin membranes that surround them. Save their juice.

Squeeze the third lime and mix all the lime juice with the apricot jam in a blender. Sieve juice. Add the zests and the remaining syrup to the sauce.

Dice the lime wedges reserved earlier and add to the sauce.

Raspberry or Strawberry Sauce
1-1/4 cups raspberries or strawberries
4-1/2 tbsp. sugar
1 tbsp. lemon juice

Work the fruit through a food mill.
Add sugar and lemon juice, and then sieve.

Mixed Berry Sauce

2 tbsp. sugar (to make 3 tbsp. syrup)
3 tbsp. water
1 3/4 oz. frozen blackberries, chopped
6 tbsp. raspberry puree
2 strawberries, thinly sliced
juice of 1/2 lemon

Make a sugar syrup by placing the water and sugar in a saucepan and bringing to a boil.

Remove from heat and, while still hot, stir in first the chopped frozen blackberries, then the raspberry puree, and finally the sliced strawberries and lemon juice. Allow to cool, and chill until ready to serve.

Passion Fruit Sauce

6 passion fruits
orange juice
3 tbsp. apricot sauce

Cut 5 passion fruits in half and empty into mixing bowl. Add orange juice and place in a blender or food processor with the apricot sauce. Process.

Strain the sauce and then open the sixth passion fruit and add its contents to the sauce.

Orange Sauce

2 oranges
5 tbsp. apricot sauce
Grand Marnier or Cointreau

Peel the oranges and remove the whitish inner skin. Detach the wedges from between the thin membranes that surround them. Save as much of the juice as possible.

Dice the orange wedges and reserve. Place the juice in a food processor or blender with the apricot sauce and process. Strain, add the diced orange and liqueur.

SNOW BLUFF

This is perfect for using up egg whites left when you use yolks alone in mousses and creams.

It's light and flavorful. Use any of the preceding fruit sauce recipes.

SERVES: 4
PREP TIME: 15 minutes
COOKING TIME: None
MAY BE PREPARED AHEAD: 2 hours

INGREDIENTS:

1 egg white
1/2 cup confectioners sugar
3 tbsp. fruit sauce

PREPARATION:

Beat egg white until fluffy.

Add sugar and fruit sauce and mix well.

If preparing ahead, STOP. Cover and refrigerate for up to 2 hours.

Pile in sherbet dishes and serve with small cookies or sponge cake.

HEARTS of CREME

SERVES: 12 individual hearts
PREP TIME: 15 minutes +
    24 hours refrigeration
COOKING TIME: 15 minutes
MAY BE PREPARED AHEAD:
    hearts - 48 hours;
    sauce - 4 hours

INGREDIENTS:

2 cups farmer's cheese
3 cups cream cheese
1/2 cup confectioner's sugar
1 cup whipping cream
1 quart strawberries for garnish
12 sprigs mint for garnish

Chocolate Sauce
1 bar dark baking chocolate (16 oz.)
1/2 cup brown sugar
1-1/2tsp. vanilla
1/4 cup water
1 cup sour cream

PREPARATION:

Process cheeses in food processor until smooth. Add sugar and cream and process until smooth.

Line 12 individual heart molds with perforated bottoms (coeur a la creme molds) with a double layer of dampened cheese cloth.

Fill the molds with the cheese mixture and place on rack in shallow pan.

Refrigerate 24 hours. If preparing ahead, may be refrigerated for an additional 24 hours (48 hour total).

TO COOK:

Chocolate Sauce
Combine chocolate, sugar, vanilla and water in a double boiler. Heat until chocolate is melted.

Remove from heat and stir in sour cream.

If preparing ahead, STOP. Cover and refrigerate for up to 4 hours.

TO SERVE:

Spoon 1-1/2ounces of chocolate sauce on plate.

Unmold each heart onto sauce and garnish with strawberries and mint.

Note: Any individual or large molds with drainage holes will work. I have used molds without holes, but one must pour off excess liquid every couple hours as curds and whey separate.

WATERMELON LIME SORBET and OTHER FRUIT SORBETS

SERVES: 12 (2 quarts)
PREP TIME: 5 minutes
    (+ 4 hours freeze time)
COOKING TIME: None
MAY BE PREPARED AHEAD: 1 month

INGREDIENTS:

8 cups cubed seedless watermelon,
    very ripe*
juice of 1 Mexican lime

*Honeydew, cantalope, or mangoes may
also be used in this recipe. You may want
to add a little lime zest also.

PREPARATION:

Process watermelon and lime in food processor.

Place in a metal bowl and freeze for 4 hours,
stirring every 30 minutes. If preparing ahead,
sorbet will keep in freezer for up to 1 month.

If frozen solid, move to refrigerator 2 hours
before serving.

TO SERVE:

Serve 3 to 4 little balls in a goblet.

Sprinkle confectioner's sugar and fresh
rose petals over the underliner plate in
place of a doily. Encourage guests to
taste the rose petals.

CHAMPAGNE SORBET

SERVES: 6
PREP TIME: Mise en place
    (+ 2 hours freezing time)
COOKING TIME: 35 minutes
MAY BE PREPARED AHEAD: 1 month

INGREDIENTS:

1/2 cup sugar
3/4 cup water
peel of 1 orange
peel of 1 lemon
1-1/4 cup orange juice
    (may substitute any berry juice)
1/4 cup lemon juice
3/4 cup champagne
    (may substitute any muscat wine)

PREPARATION: Mise en place

TO COOK:

Bring sugar, water and fruit peels to boil,
reduce heat and simmer for 30 minutes,
and then add orange juice, lemon juice
and champagne.

Transfer to a freezer tray or ice cream
machine and chill for approximately 2 hours.

*If preparing ahead, STOP. Will keep
in freezer for up to 1 month. Move to
refrigerator 2 hours before serving.*

BALSAMIC VINEGAR and PEPPERED STRAWBERRIES

Spoon strawberries over slices
of toasted pound cake.

SERVES: 6
PREP TIME: 20 minutes
COOKING TIME: None
MAY BE PREPARED AHEAD: 8 hours

INGREDIENTS:

3 tbsp. balsamic vinegar
1 tbsp. sugar
1/2 tsp. freshly ground black pepper
3 cups strawberries, hulled, washed, halved

PREPARATION:

In a small bowl, whisk together vinegar,
sugar and pepper. Pour over strawberries
and marinate for about 15 minutes.

*If preparing ahead, STOP. Cover and
refrigerate for up to 8 hours. Bring to
room temperature to serve.*

ORANGE FLOWER CREME

Use a fresh flower garnish.

SERVES: 8
PREP TIME: 15 minutes
      (+ 3 hours chilling time)
COOKING TIME: 45 minutes
MAY BE PREPARED AHEAD: 24 hours

INGREDIENTS:

1/2 cup sugar
2 cups heavy cream
1/2 tsp. vanilla extract
1 tbsp. orange flower water
6 egg yolks

PREPARATION:

Mix sugar and cream together until sugar
is dissolved. Scald mixture. (Bring to
boiling point, but do not allow to boil.)
Add vanilla and orange flower water.

Beat the egg yolks until thick and very
pale. Gradually pour the cream into
the egg yolks, stirring briskly.

Pour into 8 individual custard cups.

TO COOK:

Put the cups in 1 inch of hot water and
bake in a preheated 350 degree oven
until knife inserted into custard comes
out clean — about 45 minutes.

*Chill for 3 hours. If preparing ahead, may
be refrigerated for up to 24 hours.*

VARIATIONS:

Chocolate Creme
Use only 1/2 cup sugar and 4 egg yolks. Melt 4 square semisweet chocolate with 1 cup water or coffee. Beat into egg yolks. Add 1 tsp. vanilla.

Proceed as above.

Caramel Creme
Carmelize the sugar with 2 tbsp. water.

Proceed as above.

Pistachio Creme

Scald the cream with 1/2 cup finely chopped pistachios. Beat 1 whole egg and 4 yolks.

Proceed as above, adding a little green coloring before pouring into custard cups.

PEACHES (PEARS) in RED WINE

SERVES: 8
PREP TIME: 15
COOKING TIME: 45
MAY BE PREPARED AHEAD: 24 hours

INGREDIENTS:

8 ripe white peaches (or pears)
1-1/2 bottles red wine
1/2 cup sugar
1 tbsp. powdered sugar
1 stick cinnamon
3 to 4 peppercorns
1 piece lemon zest
1/3 cup black currant jam
fresh mint for garnish

PREPARATION:

Parboil the peaches/pears and remove the skin.

In a saucepan, bring the red wine to a boil with the sugar, cinnamon, peppercorns and lemon zest. Simmer gently for about 10 minutes.

Add peaches/pears to red wine mixture, and continue poaching until perfectly tender. Drain the peaches/pears and reduce the wine by half. Add the currant jam, strain, and allow to cool completely.

Pour the cold syrup over the peaches/pears and chill until ready to serve.

If preparing ahead, STOP. Cover peaches/pears for up to 24 hours.

Garnish with fresh mint leaves.

NOTE: If desired, 6 tbsp. black currant liqueur or 3 1/2 oz. crushed black currants may be used.

CHOCOLATE CHERRY CAKE with FRESH MINT CREAM

SERVES: 8 or 16 cupcakes
PREP TIME: 10 minutes
COOKING TIME: 45 minutes
MAY BE PREPARED AHEAD: 2 days

INGREDIENTS:

1-1/4 cup sugar
4 large eggs
1/2 lb. butter, softened
1/2 lb. bittersweet chocolate, melted
3 cups sifted cake flour
1/2 cup walnuts
12-16 marachino cherries, chopped

Mint Cream
1 cup heavy cream, whipped
2 tbsp. powdered sugar
1 tsp. spearmint extract
1/4 cup chopped fresh spearmint

PREPARATION:

Preheat oven to 350 degrees and butter
a bundt cake pan, individual cake mold,
or line muffin tins with paper cups.

Cream sugar and eggs until light and fluffy
and add to butter and melted chocolate.
Add flour and mix well.

Add nuts and cherries. If making cupcakes,
place 1 whole cherry in each cake.

TO COOK:

Bake cake 45 minutes; cupcakes
30-35 minutes or until tester comes clean.
Allow cake to cool in pan before removing.

*If preparing ahead, STOP. Store in cool place
for up to 2 days.*

TO MAKE WHIPPED CREAM

Whip together heavy cream,
sugar and flavoring until fluffy.
Fold in chopped mint.

TO SERVE:

Top cake with a dollop of mint cream.

Always use confectioner's
sugar to sweeten whipped cream.

LEMON ALMOND BUTTER COOKIES

SERVES: 48 cookies
PREP TIME: 15 minutes
COOKING TIME: 10-12 minutes
MAY BE PREPARED AHEAD: 1 month

INGREDIENTS:

1 cup butter
3/4 cup sugar
1 egg
1-1/4 tsp. almond extract
1 tsp. lemon extract
2-1/4 cups sifted flour
1/2 tsp. baking powder
pinch salt

PREPARATION:

Cream together butter, sugar, egg, and lemon and almond extracts.

Sift together dry ingredients and mix into butter mixture.

TO COOK:

Use cookie press for fancy design, or roll into small balls and press a nut or fruit jelly into center of dough. Bake cookies on ungreased cookie sheets at 400 degrees for 10 to 12 minutes.

If preparing ahead, STOP. Cookies may be frozen for up to 1 month.

HONEY LIME FRUIT DIP

Serve with assorted fresh summer fruits cut into slices.

SERVES: 2 cups
PREP TIME: 5 minutes
COOKING TIME: None
MAY BE PREPARED AHEAD: 48 hours

INGREDIENTS:

1 cup sour cream
2 tbsp. lime juice
1/4 cup half and half
3/4 cup honey
2 tbsp. lime peels
green food coloring

PREPARATION:

Mix all ingredients well.

If preparing ahead, STOP. Refrigerate in tightly covered container.

MEXICAN WEDDING COOKIES

SERVES: 4 dozen
PREP TIME: 5 minutes,
     plus 1/2 hour chilling time
COOKING TIME: 12 minutes
     per cookie sheet
MAY BE PREPARED AHEAD:
     1 week; may be frozen for 1 month

INGREDIENTS:

1 cup butter
1/4 tsp. salt
1/2 cup sugar
1 tsp. vanilla
2 cups flour
1 cup chopped pecans
1 cup confectioners sugar

PREPARATION:

Cream butter, salt, sugar, and vanilla.
Add flour and chopped nuts and chill
1/2 hour in refrigerator.

TO COOK:

Place on ungreased cookie sheet and
bake at 375 degrees for 12 minutes; then
roll in confectioners sugar.

LEMON BARS

Really rich and intensely flavored.

SERVES: 60 bars
PREP TIME: 5 minutes
COOKING TIME: 50 minutes
MAY BE PREPARED AHEAD:
     1 week refrigerated or
     1 month frozen

INGREDIENTS:

Crust
2 cups flour
1/2 cup confectioner's sugar
1/2 lb. butter

Filling
4 eggs, lightly beaten
2 cups granulated sugar
6 tbsp. lemon juice
4 tbsp. flour
1/2 tsp. baking powder
1 tsp. lemon zest
1/2 tsp. ground nutmeg
confectioner's sugar for dusting

PREPARATION:

Crust
Place all ingredients in food processor
and process using pastry blade. Mix until
dough follows blade in a ball.

Press dough into a 9 x 13 inch glass
baking pan and bake for 25 minutes
in a 300 degree oven.

Filling
Combine eggs, sugar, lemon juice, flour,
baking powder, lemon zest and nutmeg.

When crust is ready, spread lemon
mixture over crust.

Bake at 300 degrees for 25 minutes.

Cool. Cut in bars and dust with
confectioner's sugar.

*If preparing ahead, STOP. Store in tightly
covered container in refrigerator for up
to 1 week or in freezer for up to 1 month.*

Summer

Seasonal Gifts

CANDIED FLOWERS

Use violets, pansies, marigolds, primroses or rose petals. You may also use this method to candy fruit. Grapes, small plums, or cherries work best.

AMOUNT: 3 dozen small flowers
PREP TIME: 5 minutes
COOKING TIME: None
MAY BE PREPARED AHEAD: 24 hours

INGREDIENTS:

1 egg white
3 dozen flower petals or small flowers
1/2 cup granulated sugar

PREPARATION:

Beat egg white until frothy, but not peaked.

Paint petals with egg white.

Sprinkle with granulated sugar.
Shake off excess.

If preparing ahead, STOP. Store in airtight container for up to 24 hours.

LONGER LASTING CANDIED FLOWERS

INGREDIENTS:

2 tbsp. vodka
1 tsp. gum arabic
3 dozen flower petals or small flowers
1/2 cup granulated sugar

PREPARATION:

Mix vodka with gum arabic.

Coat petals with vodka mixture.

Sprinkle with sugar. Shake off excess.

If preparing ahead, STOP. Store in airtight container for up to 2 weeks.

HONEY POPPY SEED DRESSING

Serve over assorted summer fruits, or with iceberg lettuce, sliced avocado, sweet red onion, and sliced oranges.

SERVES: 1-1/2 cups
PREP TIME: 5 minutes
COOKING TIME: None
MAY BE PREPARED AHEAD: 1 week

INGREDIENTS:

3/4 cup fragrant blossom honey
1 tsp. dry mustard
1-1/2 tbsp. chopped onion
1 cup soy or peanut oil
1 tsp. salt
1/3 cup white wine vinegar
1-1/2 tbsp. poppy seeds

PREPARATION:

Place all ingredients in a blender jar or food processor and process until well blended. Keep at room temperature until ready to use.

If preparing ahead, STOP. Bottle and refrigerate for up to 1 week.

Bottle in a decorative container.
Tie on a card with serving ideas and refrigeration instructions.

SWEET and SOUR MUSTARD

SERVES: 3 cups
PREP TIME: Overnight
COOKING TIME: 10-15 minutes
MAY BE PREPARED AHEAD: 1 month

INGREDIENTS:

1 cup Coleman's dry mustard
1 cup vinegar
2 eggs
1 cup brown sugar
dash of salt

PREPARATION:

Mix dry mustard and vinegar in a saucepan.
Cover and let sit overnight.

Combine eggs, brown sugar, and salt in a
blender. Add vinegar-mustard mixture and
blend for 1 minute.

TO COOK:

Pour back in saucepan and bring to a boil.
Reduce heat and simmer for 5 minutes.

Cool and pour into sterilized jars.
Mustard will keep for up to 1 month.

THREE CHILI MIX

This is great in chili con carne recipes
or to season boiled beans.

PREP TIME: 10 minutes
COOKING TIME: None
MAY BE PREPARED AHEAD: 6 months

INGREDIENTS:

1 tbsp. ground California chili-pepper (mild)
1/2 tsp. ground chili de arbol (hot)
1/2 tsp. ground cumin
1/2 tsp. black pepper
1 tbsp. ground New Mexico chili-pepper (mild)
1/4 tsp. salt
pinch dried safflower (Mexican-saffron)

PREPARATION:

Pound in mortar, sift through fine sieve,
and bottle. Mix will keep for up to 6 months.

Include recipe card for Grilled Chili
Cured Chicken (see page 98) or
Winter Chilis (see pages 257-259).

VARIOUS SALSA COMBINATIONS and IDEAS

- Be inventive with salsas. Serve with tortilla chips or crackers as an appetizer. For gift giving, package in decorative containers with a package of chips and colorful cocktail napkins.
- Papaya, mint, cilantro, lime zest, and grapefruit to serve over grilled fish.
- French lentils, bacon, and blue cheese as a topping for grilled chicken or quail.
- Papaya, mango, and lime zest with a dash of brown sugar and honey, served over ice cream.
- Mango, mango-plum, or papaya salsa to complement grilled fish.
- Cucumber with chilies, tomatoes, and orange, lime, and grapefruit juices for turkey fajitas.

MANGO LIME SALSA

SERVES: 4
PREP TIME: 5 minutes
COOKING TIME: None
MAY BE PREPARED AHEAD: 2 days

INGREDIENTS:

3/4 cup chopped mango (fresh or canned)
1/4 cup red onion, finely chopped
A dash of finely chopped red pepper flakes
1/4 cup cilantro, chopped
1 tbsp. lime juice (approx. 1/2 lime)

PREPARATION:

Mix all ingredients well.

Refrigerate for 8 hours to marry flavors.

If preparing ahead, STOP. Salsa will keep in refrigerator for up to 2 days.

SALSA MEXICANA

SERVES: 5 cups
PREP TIME: 5 minutes
COOKING TIME: None
MAY BE PREPARED AHEAD: 48 hours

INGREDIENTS:

3 cups chopped tomatoes
2 garlic cloves, chopped
1/2 cup fresh cilantro, finely chopped
5 yellow chiles, finely chopped
1 cup chopped onion
2 tsp. dried oregano
1/4 cup red wine vinegar
salt and pepper to taste

PREPARATION:

Place all ingredients in a food processor and pulse gently to chop and mix well.

If preparing ahead, STOP. Refrigerate in tightly covered container for up to 48 hours.

SALSA FRESCA

The simplest of all. I first had this on a cattle branding expedition in the wilds of Nayarit, Mexico. Carne asada was grilled over an open fire, and this simple salsa was made up on the spot. I wondered how the surrounding longhorn cattle felt about our grilled beefsteak feast.

SERVES: 5 cups
PREP TIME: 5 minutes
COOKING TIME: None
MAY BE PREPARED AHEAD: 48 hours

INGREDIENTS:

3 cups chopped tomatoes
1-1/2 cup scallions, chopped
salt to taste
3 small green chilis, finely chopped
1/2 cup cilantro, chopped

PREPARATION:

Mix all ingredients together well.

If preparing ahead, STOP. Cover and refrigerate for up to 48 hours.

TOMATILLO SALSA

SERVES: 2 cups
PREP TIME: Mise en place
COOKING TIME: 15 minutes
MAY BE PREPARED AHEAD:
    24 hours - 3 days

INGREDIENTS:

1 lb. fresh tomatillos,
    husks removed, washed OR
    1 3/4 cup canned tomatillas
2 jalapeño chilies, roasted, peeled, seeded
1 clove garlic, minced
5 sprigs cilantro, minced
1/4 tsp. salt

PREPARATION: Mise en place

TO COOK:

In saucepan, cover tomatillos with water and bring to a boil for 15 minutes, until skin splits. Drain off liquid. (If using canned tomatillos, just drain off liquid.)

Process all ingredients except salt in food processor until finely chopped.

Refrigerate overnight to marry flavors. Salsa will keep in refrigerator for 2 more days.

Add salt before serving.

PIONEER SALSA

From the early days of the Southwest, this salsa is more of a chutney. It dates back to the early 1800s.

SERVES: 6 pints
PREP TIME: Mise en place
COOKING TIME: 1 hour
MAY BE PREPARED AHEAD: 1 year

INGREDIENTS:

12 large tomatoes, chopped fine
12 large apples, chopped fine
3 large onions, chopped fine
2 cups vinegar
1/4 cup salt
2-1/2 cups sugar
1 tsp. dry mustard
1 tsp. black pepper
1/2 tsp. cloves
1 tsp. cinnamon

PREPARATION: Mise en place

TO COOK:

Mix all ingredients and cook until thick, about 1 hour.

Put into sterilized jars. Seal well.

If preparing ahead, STOP. Keep jars in cool, dark place for up to 1 year.

JALAPEÑO and PINEAPPLE SALSA

Delicious with grilled chicken and black beans.

SERVES: 12
PREP TIME: 5 minutes
COOKING TIME: None
MAY BE PREPARED AHEAD: 3 days

INGREDIENTS:

1 small jalapeño, cored, seeded, minced
1 chopped red bell pepper
2 tsp. rice wine vinegar
1 chopped garlic clove
3 cups chopped fresh pineapple
5 sliced tomatillos
1 tbsp. olive oil

PREPARATION:

Place all ingredients in a food processor and pulse about 4 times, until chopped.

Transfer to a bowl and let flavors blend for 60 minutes. If preparing ahead, cover tightly and refrigerate for up to 3 days.

PEACH SALSA

A wonderful relish to serve with game, such as roast pheasant, duck or venison.

SERVES: 30 2-oz. servings
PREP TIME: 10 minutes
COOKING TIME: None
MAY BE PREPARED AHEAD: 1 month

INGREDIENTS:

1 #10 can plum tomatoes, chopped
1/2 cup lemon juice
5 tbsp. jalapeño peppers, minced, seeded
1 cup wine vinegar
2 tbsp. honey
1 #10 can sliced peaches, chopped
30 green onions, chopped
1 cup vegetable oil
1 cup sherry wine

PREPARATION:

Combine all ingredients together well.
Put in tightly covered canning jars

If preparing ahead, STOP.
Keep refrigerated for up to 1 month.

BLACK BEAN TEQUILA SALSA

SERVES: 3 cups
PREP TIME: Beans: 1 hour;
    Salsa: 10 minutes
COOKING TIME: None
MAY BE PREPARED AHEAD: 3 days

INGREDIENTS:

3 cups cooked black beans, drained
1 tsp. orange zest
4 tbsp. sauteed minced bacon with fat
4 tbsp. minced canned jalapeños
1 medium sweet red pepper,
    roasted, peeled, diced
1 medium sweet yellow pepper,
    roasted, peeled, diced
1 tsp Orange Zest
2 tsp. gold tequila
2 tsp. fresh lime juice
2 tbsp. extra virgin olive oil
2 cloves garlic, roasted, peeled, minced
2 tbsp. minced cilantro
1 tbsp. minced marjoram

PREPARATION:

Put beans in a bowl and fold in remaining salsa ingredients, being careful not to crush the beans.

If preparing ahead, STOP. Cover
and refrigerate for up to 3 days.

TO SERVE:

Serve hot or at room temperature.

SUN-DRIED and FRESH TOMATO RELISH

SERVES: 4
PREP TIME: 15 minutes
COOKING TIME: None
MAY BE PREPARED AHEAD: 4 hours

INGREDIENTS:

1/2 pound finely chopped plum tomatoes
1/4 cup finely chopped drained
    oil-packed sun-dried tomatoes
2 tbsp. minced fresh basil and
    2 tbsp. fresh parsley, mixed
1 garlic clove, minced
1-1/2 tbsp. olive oil
1 tsp. balsamic or red wine vinegar
1/4 to 1/2 tsp. hot pepper sauce

PREPARATION:

In medium bowl, combine sun-dried
tomatoes, plum tomatoes, basil/parsley
mixture, garlic, olive oil, balsamic
vinegar and hot sauce.

Cover and let stand at room
temperature at least 15 minutes.

If preparing ahead, STOP.
Cover and refrigerate for up to 4 hours.

OLD FASHIONED CORN RELISH

An old time recipe that comes from
the Indian Territories in the 1860s.

SERVES: 6 pints
PREP TIME: 10 minutes
COOKING TIME: 30 minutes
MAY BE PREPARED AHEAD: 1 year

INGREDIENTS:

18 large ears corn
8 large green peppers, minced
5 large red peppers, minced
5 large onions, minced
2 quarts cider vinegar
3-1/2 cups sugar
1/4 cup salt
2 tbsp. ground mustard

PREPARATION:

Cut corn from cobs and chop fine
with other ingredients.

TO COOK:

Boil 30 minutes and put in jars
boiling hot and seal.

If preparing ahead, STOP. Keep
jars in cool, dark place for up to 1 year.

BASIL

STRAWBERRY HONEY BUTTER

Serve with toast, English muffins, waffles, or French toast. Package in an unusual crock for gift giving and tie on a card with serving suggestions. Try a basket of muffin or pancake mixes, a crock of honey butter, and a jug of specialty syrup.

SERVES: 8
PREP TIME: 10 minutes
COOKING TIME: none
MAY BE PREPARED AHEAD:
    refrigerated - 1 week;
    frozen - 1 month

INGREDIENTS:

1-1/2 cups frozen whole or fresh
    unsweetened strawberries
2 cups butter, softened
2 oz. honey

PREPARATION:

Thaw strawberries completely. Puree in food processor. Allow puree to come to room temperature. Remove to bowl.

Beat together butter and honey in food processor. Beat in strawberry puree until light and fluffy. If butter separates, ingredients are too cold. Allow ingredients to warm, then beat until smooth.

Cover and chill. If preparing ahead, store in small crocks in refrigerator for up to 1 week, or shape into long log and wrap in wax paper. Store in freezer for up to 6 months.

BERRY BUTTERS

My favorites are strawberry, raspberry, and black currant.

SERVES: 1 2/3 cup
PREP TIME: 5 minutes
COOKING TIME: None
MAY BE PREPARED AHEAD:
    refrigerated - 1 week;
    frozen - 1 month

INGREDIENTS:

1 cup sweet butter, softened
1 tbsp. lemon juice
2/3 cup berry jam w/ heavy fruit
1 tsp. confectioners sugar

PREPARATION:

Combine all ingredients in food processor.

If preparing ahead, STOP. Store in small crocks in refrigerator for up to 1 week, or shape into long log and wrap in wax paper. Store in freezer for up to 6 months.

SPICED ZUCCHINI PICKLES

SERVES: 5 pints
PREP TIME: 15 minutes + overnight soak
COOKING TIME: 30 minutes
MAY BE PREPARED AHEAD: 6 months

INGREDIENTS:

4 cups vinegar
4-1/2 cups sugar
2 tsp. celery seed
2 tsp. pickling spice
2 tsp. whole cloves
2 tsp. salt
3-1/2 lbs. zucchini, sliced

PREPARATION:

Bring vinegar and sugar to a boil, adding
the spices. Pour vinegar/sugar mixture
over zucchini in a glass container or crock
and soak overnight in refrigerator.

Bring zucchini mixture to a boil, cooking
until clear, approximately 30 minutes.

Seal in hot, sterilized jars.

ZUCCHINI MARMALADE

SERVES: 6 jars
PREP TIME: 5 minutes
COOKING TIME: 20 minutes
MAY BE PREPARED AHEAD: 1 year

INGREDIENTS:

6 cups zucchini, ground (approx. 8)
3 oranges, ground
2 lemons, ground
1 cup crushed pineapple
1 pkg. SureJel or other powdered pectin
6-1/2 cups sugar

PREPARATION:

Put zucchini and fruit in a food processor,
and process until smooth.

Add SureJel to 4 cups of the zucchini/fruit
mixture and bring to a rolling boil. Boil for
1 minute. Add sugar, and bring back to a
full boil. Boil for 1 minute.

Allow to sit for 7 minutes. Skim and pour
into sterilized jars. Seal with parafin.

BATH SACHETS

YIELD: 10
This gift item is not edible.

PREP TIME: 2 weeks

INGREDIENTS:

2 cups fresh eucalyptus leaves,
    roughly cut with scissors
1 lime peel, cut into strips
    (remove most of the white
    portion by scraping with a spoon)
3 drops rosemary oil
2 cups fresh rosemary
1 orange peel, cut in strips
    (remove most of the white
    portion by scraping with a spoon)
3 drops eucalyptus oil

PREPARATION:

Mix all ingredients well.

Store in covered jar in dark place
for 2 weeks, shaking daily.

Spoon into bath bags.

BATH BAGS

INGREDIENTS:
This gift item is not edible.

1/3 yard lace curtain material (45" wide)
    cut into ten 6" x 9" rectangles
    (select tightly woven pattern)
4 yards satin ribbon 1/4" wide,
    cut into ten 9" pieces

PREPARATION:

Fold rectangles in half to form 4.5" x 6"
rectangle, and stitch 3 sides closed
beginning with 6" side.

Make 1/2" pocket in top, leaving
opening in pocket to insert ribbon.

Turn inside out so seams are on the
inside, and thread ribbon through
pocket; knot both ends.

Fill with sachet, and draw strings tight.
Finish with ribbon bow. Store in tightly
covered container in dark place.

TO USE:

Tie sachet over faucet so that water
flows through herb sachet bag.

When bath is run, re-tie ribbon in bow
and allow to steep in bath while bathing.

To make Bath Bags

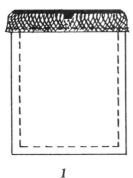

1

2

3

HERBAL SCENT BAGS

Scent bags or sachets were used to scent clothes and linen drawers. These two scent bags are from **Miss Shote's American Housewife**, 1879.

LAVENDAR, THYME and MINT SCENT BAGS

INGREDIENTS:
This gift item is not edible.

1/2 lb. lavender flowers
1/2 oz. dried mint
1/4 oz. carroway
1/2 oz. dried thyme
1/4 oz. ground cloves
1 oz. dried rock salt

PREPARATION:

Mix all ingredients well and put into sachet bags.

GENTLEMEN'S SCENT BAGS

INGREDIENTS:
This gift item is not edible.

1 oz. lavender flowers
1/2 oz. bruised rosemary leaves
5 drops altar of rose
1/4 oz. ground orris root
5 grains musk

PREPARATION:

Mix all ingredients well and put into sachet bags.

TO MAKE SACHET BAGS

1) Sew 4" x 6" rectangles of cloth on 3 sides.

2) Turn inside out and fold top 2" inside bag.

3) Stuff with sachet and tie with ribbon or cord.

For Women
Floral prints with grosgrain ties
Calico with antique lace ties
Moire with French silk ribbons

For Men
Masculine stripes with silk cords
Blue Cambrey with leather thongs

To make Scent Bags

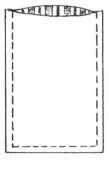

1

2

3

SUMMER HARVEST CALENDAR

SOUTHERN CALIFORNIA[1]

FRUITS AND VEGETABLES

apples, apricots, asparagus, avocados, boysenberries, blackberries, broccoli, cabbage, cantalope, carrots, cauliflower, celery, corn, cucumbers, eggplant, figs, grapefruit, grapes, green onions, honeydew melons, lemons, lettuce and greens, melons, mushrooms, nectarines, naval oranges, onions, peaches, pears, peppers, plums, potatoes, raspberries, squash, spinach, strawberries, sweet corn, sweet onions, sweet potatoes, tomatoes, watermelons, Valencia oranges, zucchini

OTHER PRODUCTS

beans, dried fruits and nuts, eggs, farm fresh scallops, honey

NEW MEXICO[2]

FRUITS AND VEGETABLES

chiles, corn, lettuce, onions, potatoes

ARIZONA[3]

FRUITS AND VEGETABLES

bell peppers, black-eyed peas, cantalope, carrots, cassava melons, chile peppers, cucumbers, golden delicious apples, green beans, honeydew melons, lettuce, melons, onions, okra, peaches, pears, potatoes, red delicious apples, sweet corn, tomatoes, watermelons, white (tamale) corn, yellow squash,

OTHER PRODUCTS

honey

[1]From the Cooperative Extension Service, University of San Diego, the Produce Marketing Association's Produce Availability and Merchandising Guide, and Western Growers Association's 1992 Export Directory.

[2]From the Cooperative Extension Service, New Mexico State University and the Produce Marketing Association's 1992 Produce Availability and Merchandising Guide.

[3]From the Cooperative Extension Service, University of Ariziona, the Produce Marketing Associations's Produce Availability and Merchandising Guide, and Western Growers Association's 1992 Export Directory.

Autumn

"And so the ripe year wanes.
From turfy slopes afar the breeze brings
delicious, pungent, spicy odors..."

Thaxter

Autumn's arrival brings days of abundant harvest, home winemaking, cozy fireplaces, sports outings, and preparations for the holidays ahead. Trees don their fall attire of multihued brilliance. Days shorten and become cool and brisk.

Fall is a perfect season for family outings. Gather pumpkins, pick apples or pinenuts, and attend sporting events. Take leisurely drives to see the autumn colors, purchase the season's firewood supply, and picnic in the mountains to breathe the clean brisk air. Projects that waited while you drifted through those lazy summer days can receive new attention and enthusiasm. During childhood, my father left on week-end hunting expeditions, and the rest of the family threw themselves enthusiastically into preparations for the holidays ahead.

Autumn is always a busy season, so let your meals take on an "Anytime – Easytime" ambiance. Make meals of hearty soups or special sandwiches that can be gobbled between projects or taken on your many impromptu outings. Autumn is also the time when game is fresh from the hunt — venison, duck, pheasant, quail and dove. This season, more than any other, is a time to appreciate and celebrate nature's abundance.

Welcome autumn by gathering dried grain shocks, Indian corn and gourds to decorate your home. Gather brightly covered leaves, each one a work of art, and place them among votives as a sweet smelling, colorful table runner. Pick apples if you can. Baskets of them provide color and fragrance in your home, and there are endless ways to use them: in soups, entrees and desserts, or even studded with cloves as pomander for your closet.

Spend time in front of the fireplace, reading from collections of real ghost stories — British writers seem to do them best. Save herb trimmings from Fall pruning. Dry them and use in your fireplace as a natural woodsy incense.

If you live near local wineries, call to learn their harvest dates. Ask if they allow visitors, and watch the fruit being picked and crushed. Return for the first release of the wine you saw harvested. Stock up on wine for the holidays. Consider making your own.

Make chutneys, relishes and wine jellies for holiday use or gifts. Begin making holiday plans in Autumn, so you can relax and enjoy your guests and the hospitality of the coming season.

Take time to appreciate the result of spring and summer seasons of sowing, growing and reaping.

Autumn Lore
Nuts and Seeds

NUTS

There are many nuts grown in the Southwest, and they strongly influence the cuisine.

Almonds. These nuts were brought into California and New Mexico by the Spanish Padres in the sixteenth century and grow abundantly. Where you find Missions, you find almond groves marking the explorations of the missionary priests.

The nuts are grown commercially chiefly in the interior valleys of central California. After gathering, they must be hulled, cured or dried, then bleached.

To prepare blanched almonds, which most recipes call for, simply pour boiling water over the shelled almonds, and let stand just until the brown skins can be easily slipped off — 2 to 5 minutes should be sufficient. Drain, slip off skins, and dry the nuts before using.

Walnuts. The English or Persian walnut is one of the leading food products of the Coast, particularly southern California. The nuts range in size from the enormous giant down to very small. Medium-sized nuts are, of course, most common and therefore the most economical to buy.

The walnuts, after being gathered, hulled, and dried or cured for a short time, are bleached by quick immersion in a chloride of lime solution, then carefully dried again.

Pecans. Pecans are grown in various localities throughout the West. The shell varies from very thin to thick and hard and the meat is oily and sweet.

Pine Nuts or Piñons. Numerous species of pines, yielding edible nuts, are found on the Pacific slope and in California, New Mexico, and Arizona. With the increased use of all nuts, pine nuts, often called Indian nuts, piñons, or by the Mexicans, "piñones," are coming on the market in increasing quantities.

Pistachios. The pistachio, or green almond, grows well in the warm interior valleys of California and Arizona. The nuts, strange to say, must be processed before being eaten. This is done by soaking them in a strong salt brine; then they are roasted, which causes the shells to open slightly. Pistachio nuts supply a most interesting flavor and green color to candies, ice creams, and various other desserts. It also adds subtle variety and texture to vegetable and rice dishes.

The pistachio tree is very hardy and not particular as to soil requirements. It should be popular for home gardens. The trees, when loaded down with their large, grape-like clusters of nuts, are strikingly beautiful.

Chestnuts. Chestnuts are grown to a rather limited extent in the West, the Italian variety being predominant. The fruit, in its characteristic burr coating, ripens in October.

Chestnuts are relished as a dessert nut when freshly roasted; are steamed or roasted for use in sauces, dressings, puddings, etc.; and are ground into meal, for thickening soups or for bread-making.

Macadamias. Macadamia nuts are hard-shelled, somewhat resembling a filbert, and produced by an Australian evergreen tree of the protea family that is cultivated extensively in Hawaii and California. It may be used in recipes calling for pecans.

As children, we gathered walnuts on my grandmother's ranch, removed the fragrant green and black skins, and stored bagfuls of the nuts to crack for holiday treats.

Gather or buy your winter's supply of nuts. Set aside a morning for a nut cracking party. Serve hot chocolate, and cinnamon toast. Use a hammer to crack the nuts; it's faster than a nut cracker. Then have everyone pick the nutmeats from the shells. The very youngest family members as well as the very oldest can enjoy this activity. Store the nuts in tightly covered jars. Recycled mayonnaise jars work well. Put the nutshells in paper grocery bags and tie tightly to save for starting your autumn fires.

This activity works for any of the local nuts, almonds, pecans, pistachios. Nuts may be frozen to preserve freshness. I recommend using within four months for optimum flavor.

Another favorite fall activity was gathering nuts from the piñon pine. I asked my 87 year old father to refresh my memory on these outings. He was taught by the Piute Indians. Here are his instructions verbatim:

"Picking or Gathering Pine Nuts"

"The cones are picked by hand or using pole hooks (a long pole with a metal hook screwed into the end) from the larger pinon trees. Disposable cotton or other cloth gloves are a must, because the cones are covered with pitch that doesn't wash off. If you do get it on your hands, use kerosene. It's about the only way to get the pitch off. Cones are bagged in burlap sacks for transporting home. They are then left in the open air, spread out to dry. When dried out, the cones open up and most of the nuts can be removed by tapping with a piece of broom stick or whatever is handy. The nuts are then placed in a pail of water. Those that float to the top are bad — hollow, due to worms or bugs.

Eight or ten percent are usually bad. Then dry them out, roast, and they are yummy!

P.S. There is also an enjoyable side benefit that can't be overlooked. The anticipation, and preparation, usually by two or three couples, for a mini vacation of hard work, and solitude in the pine nut hills is fun. The air is clean and the warm late September sun is most enjoyable. Plenty of good food and cold beer make one forget it is really hard work."

Now you can appreciate the high price tag on pine nuts in the stores. Commercial growers gather the nuts later in the year waiting for the cones to dry and open up on the trees. Canvas ground covers are placed under the trees, and mechanical shakers are used to shake the nuts from the cones.

Use pine nuts in salads, with pastas, and to make pesto. They have a particular affinity for goat cheese and sun-dried tomatoes.

SEEDS

Harvest seeds and experience a connection to early mankind who gathered rather than cultivated his food supply.

If you grow sunflowers, roast the seeds to use in salads, or leave them for the birds' treat.

Pumpkin or squash seeds can be roasted in the oven (350 degrees for thirty minutes). Spray lightly with olive oil and lightly salt, if desired. Add minced garlic and a dash of chile colorado for an unusual variation. Enjoy them as snacks. Make an exotic pumpkin seed sauce for chicken or vegetarian burritos (see page 190).

Autumn Menus

∼ Anytime Easytime ∼

Chili Corn Chowder
"The Beefeater" Sandwich
Baked Apple

Curried Zucchini Soup
"Pollo Pita" Sandwich
Fruit Cobbler

Black Bean Soup
"The Big Bird" Sandwich
Hazelnut Cakes

Cream of Artichoke and Pecan Soup
Crab Meat Gruyere Sandwich
Apple Cream

Garden Vegetable-Sausage Soup
Chic-Che-Apple Sandwich
Banana Pumpkin Flan

∼ Dinner ∼

Smoked Chicken Bisque in Bolillo
Mom's Pheasant
Nutted Rice
Broccoli Timbales
with Sweet Red Pepper Puree
Pumpkin Bombe

Butternut Soup with Jalapeño Salsa
Quail Stuffed with
Sausage and Shitake Mushrooms
Country Style Herbed Lentils
Autumn Carrots
Pippin Tansy

Black Bean Terrine
with Goat Cheese and Salsas
Duck Breast Stuffed
with Wild Mushrooms
Angel Hair Flans
Squash with Piñons and Lemon Thyme
Kahlua Pecan Brulé

Apple-Pumpkin Soup
Chicken Cutlets
with Hazelnut Sauce
Tortellini with
Forest Mushroom Sauce
Tomatoes Stuffed with Peas Potage
Chocolate Silk Pudding

Autumn

"Anytime Easytime"
Soups and Sandwiches

*Hearty soups can be a meal in themselves. Prepare
them ahead, allow flavors to mingle and serve them piping hot
with garlic bread, rosemary tomato focaccio, or muffins.*

*Pair soup with unusual hot or cold sandwiches
for a quick, satisfying repast that requires little time out
from your many autumn activities.*

*Something should be said here about what
I call "Sunday Soup." It is a spin-off on the concept of a
"Pot on the Fire" of bygone days, when ingredients were
added day by day to a continuously bubbling pot. It is called
Sunday Soup because we clear all leftovers from the
refrigerator on Sunday and discard or recycle. The "recipe"
for this soup is at the end of the soup section.*

CHILI CORN CHOWDER
with TOMATILLO SALSA

This is a showy first course for guests with its floating island of zesty tomatillo salsa.

SERVES: 6
PREP TIME: Mise en place
COOKING TIME: 1 hour
MAY BE PREPARED AHEAD: 48 hours

INGREDIENTS:

4 slices bacon
1 jalapeño chile (fresh or canned),
    finely minced
1/2 cup chopped onion
1 green pepper, finely chopped
2 stalks celery, finely chopped
2 medium potatoes, diced
2-1/2 cups chicken broth
1 bay leaf
1-1/2 tbsp. flour
2-1/2 cups milk
16 oz. corn kernels, fresh or frozen
1 corn tortilla
3 tsp. tomatillo salsa (see page 131)

PREPARATION: Mise en place

TO COOK:

Saute bacon until crisp; drain and crumble.

Saute jalapeño until soft; remove with slotted spoon; drain and reserve.

Saute onion, green peppers, and celery in bacon drippings until tender. Drain excess fat.

Add potatoes, sauteed vegetable mixture, bacon, chicken broth, bay leaf and flour.

Bring to a boil, cover and simmer until potatoes are tender. Remove from heat.

Puree mixture in food processor. (Remove bay leaf before pureeing.)

Add milk, corn, and jalapeño. Bring back to a boil. (Return bay leaf.) Cover and simmer until corn is tender. Remove bay leaf and adjust seasoning.

If preparing ahead, STOP. Cover and refrigerate for up to 48 hours.

Using hors doeuvre cutter, cut six 1-1/2 inch "flower" from corn tortilla.

Spray baking sheet with Pam and place tortilla flowers on sheet. Bake 5 minutes at 400 degrees.

TO SERVE:

Ladle soup into serving bowls. Float tortilla flower with 1/2 tsp. of tomatillo salsa in center.

SMOKED CHICKEN BISQUE in BOLILLO

This hearty bisque is served in an edible bowl.

SERVES: 4-6
PREP TIME: Mise en Place
COOKING TIME: 1 hour
MAY BE PREPARED AHEAD: 24 hours

INGREDIENTS:

6 tbsp. sweet butter
2 cups finely chopped yellow onion
2 carrots, peeled and chopped
5 cups chicken stock
6 parsley sprigs
1 lb. shredded smoked chicken
Salt and freshly ground black pepper to taste
1 cup half-and-half
6 bolillos or crusty Mexican rolls
6 sprigs cilantro for garnish

PREPARATION: Mise en place

TO COOK:

Melt the butter in a pot. Add onions and carrots, and cook over low heat, covered, until tender, about 25 minutes, stirring occasionally.

Add the stock and parsley; bring soup to a boil, reduce heat, and cover. Simmer for 10 minutes.

Strain the soup and transfer the solids to the bowl of a food processor fitted with a steel blade, or puree the vegetables in the pot using a hand held mixer/emulsifer. If using food processor, add 1 cup of the cooking liquid to the vegetables and process until smooth. Reserve the rest of the stock.

Return pureed vegetable and broth to pot and add half-and-half. Stir in additional cooking stock, about 4 cups, until soup reaches desired consistency.

Add shredded smoked chicken and simmer for 15 minutes. Season to taste with salt and pepper, and serve immediately.

If preparing ahead, STOP. Cover and refrigerate. Reheat before serving.

TO PREPARE BOWLS:

Slice 1/4 top off large rolls. Hollow out bolillos, brush lightly with olive oil and toast/dry in slow oven at 250 degrees for 15 minutes. Grill mark tops.

TO SERVE:

Ladle soup into rolls.

Garnish with cilantro.

Serve roll top on the side.

BLACK BEAN SOUP

One of our most requested recipes from the restaurant, this velvety soup draws "oohs and ahhs," especially with the web design Créme Fraiche garnish (see page 29).

SERVES: 6
PREP TIME: Overnight plus 2.5 hours
COOKING TIME: 1 hour
MAY BE PREPARED AHEAD: Up to 5 days

INGREDIENTS:

1 cup dry black beans
6 cups water
4 slices bacon
1/2 cup chopped onion
1 clove garlic, minced
1 large tomato, chopped
2 tsp. salt
1/2 tsp. dried oregano, crushed
1/4 tsp. crushed red pepper
Dash of pepper
1/3 cup dry sherry
6 lime slices for garnish
2 tbsp. sour cream or Créme Fraiche

PREPARATION:

In 3-quart saucepan, combine beans and water; soak overnight. Cook for 2-1/2 hours or until beans are tender.

TO COOK:

In small skillet, cook bacon until crisp; drain, reserving 2 tablespoons drippings. Crumble bacon and set aside.

Cook onions and garlic in reserved drippings until tender.

Add to beans, along with tomato, salt, oregano, crushed red pepper, and pepper; simmer about 30 minutes.

Press bean mixture through sieve or process in blender, half at a time, until smooth.

If preparing ahead, STOP. Cover and refrigerate for up to 5 days.

TO SERVE:

Return to saucepan; stir in sherry. Heat through, 5-10 minutes.

Garnish with crumbled bacon, lime slice, and 1 tsp. sour cream or Créme Fraiche.

APPLE PUMPKIN SOUP

Serve with cranberry muffins
and honey butter.

SERVES: 8
PREP TIME: Mise en place
COOKING TIME: 20 minutes
MAY BE PREPARED AHEAD: 24 hours

INGREDIENTS:

2 cups cooked pumpkin, mashed
2 cups apples, diced
3-1/2 cups milk
1/2 tsp. cinnamon
3 tbsp. brown sugar
2 tbsp. butter
2 tbsp. grated lemon peel
1/2 tsp. salt
1/2 tsp. nutmeg

PREPARATION: Mise en place

TO COOK:

Combine ingredients and heat thoroughly
(over medium heat), but do not boil
(20 minutes).

*If preparing ahead, STOP. Cover and
refrigerate for up to 24 hours. Reheat,
but do not boil, before serving.*

CREAM of ARTICHOKE and PECAN SOUP

These unusual flavors and textures will surprise you with their delicious compatibility.

SERVES: 6
PREP TIME: 5 minutes
COOKING TIME: 15 minutes
MAY BE PREPARED AHEAD: 24 hours

INGREDIENTS:

1/2 cup roasted pecans
1 cup chopped canned artichoke hearts
1 cup chicken broth
1 cup half and half
2 tbsp. lemon juice*
1/2 tsp. ground black pepper
2 tbsp. chopped chives or
    18 chive flowers for garnish

*You may wish to add an additional
tbsp. of lemon juice to taste.

PREPARATION:

Chop pecans and place in a sauce pan
with the artichoke hearts, chicken broth,
half and half, lemon juice and black pepper.

TO COOK:

Cook over medium heat, stirring frequently,
until soup begins to boil.

Place soup into a blender and puree.
Return to saucepan.

If preparing ahead, STOP. Cover and refrigerate.

Reheat just until boiling.

TO SERVE:

Garnish with chopped chives or purple
chive flowers (3 per serving).

Use a hand held blender to
puree soups right in the saucepan.
It saves time and mess!

CURRIED ZUCCHINI SOUP

SERVES: 8-10
PREP TIME: Mise en place
COOKING TIME: 45 minutes
MAY BE PREPARED AHEAD: 24 hours

INGREDIENTS:

5 tbsp. unsalted butter
2 coarsely chopped onions
5 tsp. curry powder
6 cups chicken stock, or canned stock
2 potatoes, peeled and cubed
1 tsp. salt
1 tsp. freshly ground black pepper
6 zucchini cut julienne style
1-1/2 cups heavy cream
chives for garnish

PREPARATION: Mise en place

TO COOK:

Melt 4 tbsp. of the butter in soup pot;
add the onions and curry powder, and
cook until the onions are wilted.

Add the stock and potatoes and simmer
for 15 minutes; season with salt and pepper.

Slice 5 of the zucchini and add them to
the soup pot; simmer for ten minutes.

Puree the soup, in batches, in a food
processor or blender. While the machine
is running, add the cream through the
food tube in a slow, steady stream.

Pass the mixture through a food mil or
a fine-mesh sieve, and then return it
to the pot. Keep it hot.

Julienne the reserved zucchini; heat the
remaining 1 tbsp. butter in a small skillet,
add the zucchini, and saute over medium
heat until just wilted; add this to the soup.

*If preparing ahead, STOP. Cover and
refrigerate. Reheat before serving.*

TO SERVE:

Garnish with chives, and serve.

GARDEN VEGETABLE SAUSAGE SOUP

A great rainy day soup.

SERVES: 6
PREP TIME: Mise en place
COOKING TIME: 30 minutes
MAY BE PREPARED AHEAD: 24 hours

INGREDIENTS:

1 lb. hot or sweet Italian sausage,
    casings removed
1 large onion, chopped
2 carrots, sliced
1 cup mushrooms, sliced
1/3 cup fresh parsley, chopped
2 garlic cloves, minced
3 cups beef broth
15-1/2 oz. chickpeas
    (garbanzo beans) drained
2 cups water
1 cup beer
1 tsp. dried basil, crumbled
1/2 tsp. ground sage
salt and pepper to taste
additional chopped fresh parsley for garnish

PREPARATION: Mise en place

TO COOK:

Cook sausage in medium Dutch oven over
medium-high heat until brown, breaking
up with fork, about 7 minutes.

Add onion, carrots, mushrooms, parsley
and garlic. Cook until onion is translucent,
stirring frequently, about 5 minutes.

Mix in broth, chickpeas, water, beer,
basil, and sage, and simmer for 15 minutes.
Season with salt and pepper to taste.

*If preparing ahead, STOP. Cover and
refrigerate. Reheat before serving.*

TO SERVE:

Ladle soup into bowls. Sprinkle with
additional parsley for garnish.

CREAM of BROCCOLI SOUP

SERVES: 10
PREP TIME: 5 minutes
COOKING TIME: 30 minutes
MAY BE PREPARED AHEAD: 24 hours

INGREDIENTS:

2 lbs. fresh broccoli florets
1 large onion
1 oz. fresh garlic
2 oz. cream cheese
1 quart milk
1 pt. half & half
1/4 tsp. nutmeg
1 tsp. salt
1/4 tsp. white pepper
Tabasco sauce (a few drops to taste)
Worchestershire sauce (a few drops to taste)
1 cup chicken stock
1/2 cup cornstarch (if desired)
1 cup cold water
chopped parsley for garnish

PREPARATION:

Chop broccoli, onions, garlic, and cream cheese in food processor (or very fine by hand).

TO COOK:

Place milk and half & half in saucepan and bring to boil.

Once the milk mixture is boiling, add the chopped ingredients, spices, tabasco and Worchestershire sauce and chicken stock. Cook for 20 minutes.

Mix cornstarch with cold water until dissolved and add to soup to thicken it.

NOTE: If soup seems sufficiently thick, you may wish to omit the cornstarch and water, and substitute an additional cup of chicken stock. To make soup thicker without the cornstarch, try using a hand held mixer to puree ingredients in the soup pot itself

Continue to cook for an additional 5 - 10 minutes, stirring constantly. Correct seasonings.

If preparing ahead, STOP. Cover and refrigerate. Reheat to serve.

TO SERVE:

Garnish with chopped parsley.

Rinse metal pan with water
before adding milk or cream
to prevent sticking.

EMERALD SOUP

Emerald soup plain is a fine, flavorful
vegetable potage. Adding the cream changes
and expands the flavor considerably. This
is a good novelty soup for dinner parties,
when flavor differences make a good topic
of conversation. Guests can taste the flavorful vegetable soup, then stir in cream to
change the flavor. Diet conscious friends
can opt to omit the cream.

SERVES: 10
PREP TIME: 15 minutes
COOKING TIME: 35 minutes
MAY BE PREPARED AHEAD: 24 hours

INGREDIENTS:

1 quart chicken broth
1 large potato, peeled and chopped
8 oz. green beans, chopped
8 oz. mushrooms, sliced
8 oz. spinach, chopped
4 oz. scallions, chopped
parsley and basil to taste
1 cup heavy cream (optional)
salt and pepper to taste

PREPARATION:

Combine all ingredients except cream
in large kettle.

TO COOK:

Bring to a rolling boil, lower heat and
cook until potatoes are done.

Put soup in food processor in small
quantities, and puree until smooth or
use hand held processor.

*If preparing ahead, STOP. Cover and
refrigerate. Reheat to serve.*

TO SERVE:

Offer guests the heavy cream in a pitcher
to add at the table if desired.

CREAM of WILD MUSHROOM SOUP

The rich and earthy flavors of wild mushrooms
go well with game. Any wild mushrooms
may be substituted for the shitaki or porcini.

SERVES: 8
PREP TIME: Mise en place
COOKING TIME: 45 minutes
MAY BE PREPARED AHEAD: 24 hours

INGREDIENTS:

1/2 cup Shitaki mushrooms
1/2 cup porcini mushrooms
1 lb. fresh mushrooms, cut into quarters
10 pieces green onions, 1 in. long
2 tbsp. minced garlic
6 cups beef stock
6 tbsp. softened butter
4 tbsp. flour
1 tsp. salt
1/2 tsp. Granada Seasoning (see page 287)
2 cups heavy cream

PREPARATION: Mise en place

TO COOK:

Lightly saute mushrooms, green onions,
and garlic in 4 tbsp. butter.

Add to beef stock and simmer for 30 minutes.

Make a roux by stirring slowly 2 tbsp.
butter and 4 tbsp. flour over low heat.
Slowly stir the roux into the beef stock.

Add salt and Granada Seasoning,
and cook over medium heat for about
15 minutes, stirring occasionally.

Add the cream and heat through.

*If preparing ahead, STOP. Cover
and refrigerate for up to 24 hours.
Reheat to serve.*

BUTTERNUT SQUASH SOUP with JALAPEÑO CILANTRO SALSA

Consider making "corn squash" bowls for this soup by removing tops and seeds of fresh, uncooked squash.

SERVES: 8
PREP TIME: 35 minutes
COOKING TIME: 15 minutes
MAY BE PREPARED AHEAD: 1 day

INGREDIENTS:

2 cups chopped onion
2 tbsp. unsalted butter
2 tbsp. vegetable oil
3-3-1/2lb. butternut squash, peeled, halved, seeds and strings discarded, flesh cut into 1/2-inch pieces (see tip below)
1/2 cup water
6 cups chicken broth
2 - 4 inch strips orange zest
1-1/2 cups freshly squeezed orange juice
8 cilantro sprigs for garnish
jalapeño cilantro salsa (recipe follows)

PREPARATION:

In a kettle, cook the onion in the butter and oil over moderately low heat, stirring until it is softened.

Add the squash and water, and cook the mixture, covered, over moderately low heat for 20-30 minutes, or until the squash is tender.

Add the broth, zest, and the orange juice, and simmer the mixture, uncovered, for 15 minutes.

In a blender or food processor, puree the mixture in batches and strain it through a sieve into a large bowl. You may use hand held blender for this task.

If preparing ahead, STOP. Cover and refrigerate for up to 1 day.

Ladle the soup into 8 bowls and add to each serving about a tablespoon of the salsa, to be stirred into the soup. Garnish with cilantro sprig.

Cutting a fresh hard-shelled squash or pumpkin can be very difficult. To make cutting easier, cook in microwave for 5 minutes on medium to soften. It will be much easier to cut, seed, and chop.

JALAPEÑO CILANTRO SALSA

SERVES: approximately 1/2 cup
PREP TIME: 2 minutes
COOKING TIME: None
MAY BE PREPARED AHEAD: 24 hours

INGREDIENTS:

1/4 cup sliced almonds
1/4 cup coconut
2 jalapeño chilies, seeded,
    chopped coarse (use gloves)
1/4 tsp. salt
1/3 cup water
2 cups packed cilantro leaves

PREPARATION:

In a blender or food processor, blend the
almonds, coconut, jalapenos, salt and
water until the mixture is ground fine.

Add the cilantro and blend the mixture
until it is ground fine.

*If preparing ahead, STOP. Cover
and refrigerate for up to 24 hours.*

TORTILLA SOUP

This is the Cafe's most popular soup and
one of the most frequently requested recipes.
It is a meal in itself.

SERVES: 4
PREP TIME: 5 minutes
COOKING TIME: 20 minutes
MAY BE PREPARED AHEAD: 24 hours

INGREDIENTS:

4 medium-sized peeled tomatoes
8 oz. tomato sauce
4 tbsp. chopped onion
2 garlic cloves, chopped
4 tbsp. chopped fresh oregano
4 tbsp. chopped fresh cilantro
4 cups chicken broth
1 tsp. salt (if necessary)
8 oz. tortillas
8 oz. vegetable shortening/oil (for frying)
5 oz. grated monterey jack cheese
1 avocado slices for garnish

PREPARATION:

In blender, combine tomatoes, tomato
sauce, onions, garlic, oregano, and cilantro;
blend until nearly smooth.

Put tomato mixture in saucepan; stir in
chicken broth. (Adjust with salt if needed.)

TO COOK:

Bring to a boil, and then simmer for 20 minutes.

*If preparing ahead, STOP. Cover and
refrigerate. Reheat before serving.*

Cut tortillas in strips 1/2 inch wide and
2 inches long, and fry them in hot oil until
crisp and lightly browned; drain off excess
oil. May not be prepared ahead.

TO SERVE:

Put strips in soup bowl with cheese and
ladle soup over. Garnish with avocado slices.

SUNDAY SOUP

Sunday Soup begins with 1 quart of chicken or beef stock, and contains compatible leftovers: meats, vegetables, pastas, rice. Mix ingredients and allow to simmer for an hour. Correct seasonings, and add milk if you want a cream soup or some chopped fresh ingredients like scallions, tomatoes or parsley to perk up flavors.

Experiment with your own Sunday Soup. It's another way to avoid waste. Some Sunday Soups turn out to be so delicious that we regret they're one of a kind, and we haven't a recipe to allow duplication.

Tips for Sunday Soups

Choose leftovers with compatible flavors.

Avoid including two strongly flavored dishes that would compete with each other.

Simmer together for one hour to mix flavors before adding milk, seasonings, or fresh ingredients.

Develop herbal flavors present in the leftover dishes, or add a single stronger flavor note like tarragon or curry.

Do this slowly. Stir, taste, and see what you can create.

Examples of Compatible Combinations

#1
Leftovers
Sauerbraten (cut in pieces)
Sweet and Sour Red Cabbage
German Style Potato Salad with Bacon
Dilled Carrots

Fresh Additions
Beef Broth
Tomatoes
Parsley
Seasonings

#2
Leftovers
Spaghetti with Marinara Sauce
Sausage Meatballs (cut in pieces)
Corn on the Cob (cut off cob)
Peas and Mushrooms

Fresh Additions
Chicken Broth
Milk
Scallions
Curry

#3
Leftovers
Wild Rice Pilaf
Turkey
Bread Stuffing with Celery,
    Onions and Herbs
Relish Plate: Carrots, Broccoli, Zucchini,
Celery, Scallions (chopped)

Fresh Additions
Chicken Broth
Sage
Parsley

THE BEEFEATER

SERVES: 4
PREP TIME: 10 minutes
COOKING TIME: 3 minutes
MAY BE PREPARED AHEAD: No

INGREDIENTS:

8 oz. mushrooms
8 oz. yellow onion
4 tbsp. garlic butter
1 tsp. Worchestershire sauce
16 oz. roast beef, thinly sliced
4 french rolls
8 oz. jack cheese, shredded

PREPARATION:

Saute mushrooms and onions until tender in 2 tbsp. garlic butter. Season with Worcestershire sauce.

Butter each roll with 1/2 tbsp. garlic butter, pile roast beef onto bottom of roll, cover with mushroom/onion mixture, and top with shredded jack cheese.

Broil until cheese is melted, replace top of roll, and serve.

THE BIG BIRD

SERVES: 4
PREP TIME: 10 minutes
COOKING TIME: 5 minutes
MAY BE PREPARED AHEAD: No

INGREDIENTS:

1 onion, sliced
8 slices rye bread
4 tbsp. garlic butter
16 oz. fresh chicken breast, thinly sliced
8 oz. shredded cheddar cheese

PREPARATION:

Saute onion until clear.

Spread rye bread with garlic butter. Place slices of chicken on bread and top with sauteed onions and grated cheddar cheese.

Grill on both sides for approximately 5 minutes until golden brown.

LA TORTA

A great late night supper for after the game or concert. Serve with a crisp green salad.

SERVES: 4
PREP TIME: 5 minutes plus
    Carne Asada Marinade = 2 hours
COOKING TIME: 5 minutes
MAY BE PREPARED AHEAD:
    Not recommended

INGREDIENTS:

4 7-in. torta bread, cut lengthwise
4 tbsp. butter
16 oz. refried beans
8 oz. cheese, jack or cheddar
32 oz. carne asada (recipe follows)
1 avocado, sliced
8 tomato slices
4 pieces of lettuce
8 thin slices of red onion
4 oz. sliced jalapeño peppers

PREPARATION:

Spread butter on each half of the torta bread.

Place bread, butter face down, on flat hot grill. Remove from grill.

Spread 1 oz. beans and 1 oz. cheese on each half of the bread.

Put carne asada on bottom half; top with avocado, tomato, lettuce and onion.

Cover with other half of bread and press down.

Serve with jalapenos on the side.

CARNE ASADA

Juice from 2 lemons
2 tbsp. salad oil (soy bean)
1 tsp. black pepper, coarse
1 tsp. crushed dried oregano
1 tsp. salt
2 garlic clove, finely chopped
32 oz. top sirloin strips

PREPARATION:

In a small bowl, combine all ingredients except sirloin strips. Mix well.

Pour mixture over sirloin strips, and toss. Marinate for 2 hours.

Cook on hot grill for about 2 minutes on each side.

BORDER GRILL

Lots of different flavors here:
smoky, sweet, piquant, sharp

SERVES: 4
PREP TIME: 5 minutes
COOKING TIME: 5 minutes
MAY BE PREPARED AHEAD:
  Not recommended

INGREDIENTS:

4 tbsp. unsalted butter
12 tbsp. jalapeño jelly (see page 285)
8 oz. sharp cheddar cheese, thinly sliced
1 lb. sliced smoked turkey
8 thick slices sourdough or
  country-style white bread, sliced
  1/2 in. thick, from an oval loaf
  about 7 in. across.

PREPARATION:

In a small saucepan, melt the butter
over low heat. Set aside.

Spread one side of each bread slice
with 1-1/2 tbsp. jalapeño jelly.

Lay sliced cheese over the jelly, dividing
evenly between the two slices of bread
(1 oz. on each side).

Fold each slice of turkey in half and
arrange the slices, overlapping slightly,
over the cheese on one slice of bread.

Invert the remaining cheese-covered
bread slice on top of the turkey.

TO COOK:

Heat a medium griddle over cast iron
skillet over moderate heat until just warm.

Generously brush half the melted butter
over the top surface of the sandwich, and
invert the sandwich, butter side down,
onto the heated griddle.

Brush the remaining butter over the
top of the sandwich.

Cover skillet and cook until the bread
is crisp and golden brown on the bottom
and the cheese is beginning to melt,
about 5 minutes. With a wide spatula,
turn and brown the other side.

Transfer the sandwich to a cutting board
and cut in half with a serrated knife.
Serve at once.

POLLO PITA

A savory filling of chicken and fresh vegetables.

SERVES: 4
PREP TIME: 15 minutes
COOKING TIME: None
MAY BE PREPARED AHEAD: 24 hours

INGREDIENTS:

1/2 tsp. dried basil
1/4 tsp. dried thyme
1/4 tsp. savory
1/2 tsp. crushed dried oregano
1/2 tsp. black pepper
1/2 tsp. salt
2 cloves garlic, finely chopped
1-1/2 cups salad oil
1/2 cup red wine vinegar
1/2 cup diced celery
1/2 cup diced carrots
1/2 cup diced red onion
1/2 cup small broccoli buds
16 oz. chicken, cooked and diced
4 pita bread

PREPARATION:

Mix herbs, salt, pepper and garlic with oil and vinegar to make dressing.

In another bowl, combine vegetables and chicken. Pour 1 cup of the dressing over chicken and mix well. Add more dressing to taste or serve on side if desired.

Marinate for 2 hours in refrigerator.

If preparing ahead, STOP. May be stored in refrigerator for 24 hours.

TO SERVE:

Cut pita bread in half and stuff with chicken.

CRAB MEAT GRUYERE SANDWICH

SERVES: 4
PREP TIME: 5 minutes
COOKING TIME: 5 minutes
MAY BE PREPARED AHEAD: 24 hours

INGREDIENTS:

1 cup fresh crab meat
1/2 tsp. salt
1 tbsp. sauterne
2 tbsp. mayonnaise
1/4 cup shredded Gruyere cheese
1/2 tsp. dijon mustard
4 English muffins, halved
4 parsley sprigs for garnish

PREPARATION:

Mix all ingredients together.

If preparing ahead, STOP. Cover and refrigerate.

Pile high on rounds of English muffins.

TO COOK:

Place in a 450 degree oven until hot and cheese is melted. (Approximately 5 minutes)

Garnish with parsley sprigs.

KING NEPTUNE'S CROISSANT

SERVES: 4
PREP TIME: 10 minutes
COOKING TIME: none
MAY BE PREPARED AHEAD: 24 hours

INGREDIENTS:

16 oz. bay shrimp
4 scallions, finely chopped
3 tbsp. mayonnaise
1 tsp. lemon juice
1 tbsp. fresh tarragon, chopped
1 cucumber, thinly sliced
1 avocado, sliced in 16 pieces
4 croissant
Garlic Ranch Dressing

PREPARATION:

Mix bay shrimp, scallions, mayonnaise,
lemon juice and fresh tarragon.

If preparing ahead, STOP. Cover and refrigerate.

TO SERVE:

Split croissant lengthwise. Place 5 cucumber
slices on bread, spread with 4 oz. bay shrimp
salad, and top with 4 avocado slices. Place
other half of croissant on top.

Serve with side of Garlic Ranch
(see page 58).

CURRIED TUNA MELT

SERVES: 4
PREP TIME: 10 minutes
COOKING TIME: 2-3 minutes
MAY BE PREPARED AHEAD: 24 hours

INGREDIENTS:

1 7-oz. can tuna, drained
1/4 cup chopped celery
2 tbsp. raisins
2 tbsp. sliced scallions
1/4 cup mayonnaise
2 tsp. lemon juice
1/3 tsp. curry powder
2 tsp. salt
4 English muffins, split & lightly buttered
4 oz. shredded cheddar cheese
celery leaves to garnish

PREPARATION:

Combine tuna, celery, raisins and
scallions in small bowl.

In a measuring cup, stir together
mayonnaise, lemon juice, curry powder
and salt. Fold into tuna mixture.

If preparing ahead, STOP.
Cover and refrigerate.

TO COOK:

Toast English muffins. Immediately
spoon tuna mixture onto muffins, and
top with shredded cheese.

Broil for 2 to 3 minutes or until
cheese melts.

TO SERVE:

Serve hot, open-faced.
Garnish with celery leaves.

HOT ITALIAN HERO

SERVES: 4
PREP TIME: 15 minutes
COOKING TIME: 5 minutes
MAY BE PREPARED AHEAD: 24 hours

INGREDIENTS:

1/4 cup butter, room temperature
1 tbsp. minced fresh parsley
1 tbsp. Dijon mustard
1 garlic clove, crushed
6 oz. Italian salami, thinly sliced
3 sweet peppers, seeded and diced
2 medium tomatoes, thinly sliced
1 medium onion, thinly sliced
6 oz. mozzarella cheese, thinly sliced
1/2 tsp. red pepper flakes, crushed
4 French rolls

PREPARATION:

Mix butter, mustard, parsley, garlic
and red pepper together.

If preparing ahead, STOP.
Cover and refrigerate.

Slice rolls 3/4 through.
Spread with butter mixture.

Arrange tomatoes, onions, cheese,
meats and peppers in side of rolls.

TO COOK:

Heat under broiler until cheese is melted.

CHIC-CHE-APPLE SANDWICH

SERVES: 6
PREP TIME: 15 minutes
COOKING TIME: None
MAY BE PREPARED AHEAD: 24 hours

INGREDIENTS:

1 cup Camembert cheese
   (room temperature)
1 cup diced peeled apples
1/4 cup chopped walnuts
1 cup diced cooked chicken
3 tbsp. mayonnaise
3 tbsp. sour cream
12 slices rye or sourdough bread
6 lettuce leaves
salt and pepper to taste

PREPARATION:

Combine cheese, apples, nuts and
chicken in bowl.

Blend mayonnaise and sour cream
in small bowl. Add to chicken and apple
mixture, tossing to coat.

If preparing ahead, STOP. Cover tightly
and refrigerate.

Place lettuce leaf on bread with chicken
mixture. Top with remaining bread.

BERMUDA TRIANGLE

SERVES: 4
PREP TIME: 10 minutes
COOKING TIME: None
MAY BE PREPARED AHEAD:
    Not recommended

INGREDIENTS:

4 tsp. lemon juice
2 tbsp. mayonnaise
8 slices sourdough bread
4 slice swiss cheese
16 slices bacon, cooked
1 bermuda onion, thinly sliced
1 avocado, sliced into 16 pieces
4 cherry tomatoes and 4 parsley sprigs

PREPARATION:

Mix lemon juice with mayonnaise and
spread bread with mayonnaise mixture.
Top with swiss cheese, bacon, bermuda
onion rings, and avocado — in that order.

Cut into triangles and garnish with
cherry tomato and parsley.

REUBEN SALAD SANDWICH

SERVES: 4
PREP TIME: 10 minutes +
    1 hour marinade time
COOKING TIME: 3 minutes
MAY BE PREPARED AHEAD: 24 hours

INGREDIENTS:

1/2 lb. corned beef, thinly sliced
2/3 cup sauerkraut, drained
1/2 cup Italian dressing
8 slices rye bread, toasted with mustard
2 tbsp. rough grain mustard
1 medium tomato, diced
1/3 red onion slices, separated into rings
1 cup shredded lettuce
1/2 cup shredded Swiss cheese

PREPARATION:

Combine corned beef, tomato,
sauerkraut, onion and dressing
into bowl. Refrigerate 1 hour.

*If preparing ahead, STOP. Mixture may be
covered and refrigerated for up to 24 hours.*

Drain corned beef mixture,
add lettuce, and toss to combine.

Spread 4 slices of toast with mustard.
Top each with corned beef mixture
and sprinkle with shredded cheese.

TO COOK:

Broil until cheese melts.
Top with remaining toast, and serve.

WHAT TO SERVE WITH SANDWICHES
(Besides Soup)

- Crudites - Fresh Vegetable Nibbles

- Fresh Fruit Slices

- Homemade Potato and Sweet Potato Chips

- Southwestern Slaw (see page 105)

- Three Bean Salad (see page 105)

- New Potato Salad with Dijon Vinaigrette (See page 106)

Autumn

Appetizers

ANGEL HAIR FLANS

Serve as an appetizer or as
a side dish with game.

SERVES: 8
PREP TIME: 15 minutes
COOKING TIME: 20 minutes
MAY BE PREPARED AHEAD: 8 hours

INGREDIENTS:

1 cup whipping cream
3 large eggs
1 tsp. minced fresh thyme
1/2 tsp. ground nutmeg
1 cup freshly grated parmesan cheese
3 oz. angel hair pasta, freshly cooked
salt and pepper to taste

PREPARATION:

Preheat oven to 350 degrees. Butter
eight 1/2 cup souffle dishes or ramekins.

Whisk cream, eggs, thyme and nutmeg
in medium bowl to blend. Season
generously with salt and pepper. Stir
in 2/3 cup parmesan cheese.

Divide freshly cooked pasta evenly
among prepared souffle dishes. Pour egg
mixture over angel hair pasta. Sprinkle flans
with remaining 1/3 cup parmesan cheese.

If preparing ahead, STOP. Cover and
refrigerate for up to 8 hours.

TO COOK:

Bake until flans are set and golden
brown, about 20 minutes. Run small
sharp knife around sides of souffle
dishes to loosen. Unmold and serve.

TO SERVE:

As an appetizer, serve on top of a leaf
of red lettuce with a cherry tomato rose
(see page 28).

TORTELLINI with FOREST MUSHROOM SAUCE

The earthiness of porcini works
well with game.

SERVES: 6
PREP TIME: 1 hour
COOKING TIME: 35 minutes
MAY BE PREPARED AHEAD:
    Not recommended

INGREDIENTS:

1/4 cup dried or 3/4 cup fresh porcini
    or cepes
1 cup fresh mushrooms, sauteed in oil
3 cups cream
1/2 cup brandy
salt and pepper to taste
16 oz. tortellini, cooked
1 cup parmesan cheese
1/2 cup parsley

PREPARATION:

If using dried porcini, Rehydrate
in hot water for 1 hour. Drain.

Saute fresh mushrooms in 2 tbsp. olive
oil. Add rehydrated porcini. Reserve.

TO COOK:

Cook cream 10 minutes.

Add brandy and simmer for 5 minutes.

Add sauteed mushrooms, season to
taste with salt and pepper. Simmer until
thick and richly perfumed with porcini
and mushrooms (about 20 minutes).

Toss mushroom cream sauce with pasta
immediately. Add parsley and parmesan.

COUNTRY STYLE HERBED LENTILS

Serve as an appetizer or as a side dish
with grilled meat or fish.

SERVES: 10
PREP TIME: Mise en place
COOKING TIME: 20 minutes
MAY BE PREPARED AHEAD: 4 - 24 hours

INGREDIENTS:

2 cups lentils, rinsed
6 cups cold water
1/2 tbsp. oregano
1/2 tsp. thyme
1/2 cup olive oil
1/2 lb. slab bacon, finely diced
1 cup red onion, peeled, minced
1/4 cup chopped parsley
2 tbsp. fresh basil, finely chopped
1/2 tsp. oregano
1/2 tsp. cracked black pepper

PREPARATION: Mise en place

TO COOK:

Place rinsed lentils in large pot and
pour water over beans. Heat to simmer.

Add oregano and thyme and simmer
for 10 minutes or until lentils are tender
(Do not overcook)

Strain off liquid and transfer lentils
to large metal bowl.

In large skillet, heat olive oil. Add bacon
and saute until golden brown. Add red
onion and saute until tender.

Transfer bacon and onions to large pot or
roasting pan and add lentils. Heat until warm.

*If preparing ahead, STOP. Lentils may be
held in warm 200 degree oven for 4 hours or
refrigerated overnight in covered container.
Reheat to serve.*

Add parsley, basil and black pepper.
Stir gently, but well.

TO SERVE:

As an appetizer, serve on a red cabbage
cup and garnish with a sprig of fresh basil.

As a side, serve with grilled seafood
(shrimp is recommended), mixed fried-fish
assortment (whitefish is recommended)
or grilled chops.

SAGE

BLACK BEAN TERRINE with GOAT CHEESE and SALSAS

This is an easy appetizer for large dinner parties because it can be done well in advance and is easy to serve.

SERVES: 12
PREP TIME: 1 hour + overnight soak
for beans; 30 minutes for terrine
COOKING TIME: 5 minutes
MAY BE PREPARED AHEAD: 1 week

INGREDIENTS:

1 lb. dried black beans
3 garlic cloves
1/4 cup epazote
1/2 lb. bacon
1/2 lb. chorizo
3 tbsp. butter (cut into small pieces)
1/2 tsp. tabasco
1 tsp. salt
1 log (9 oz.) goat cheese
or three 3-1/2-oz. logs
12 sprigs cilantro

PREPARATION:

Soak beans overnight in 1 quart water.

Add another quart water, and cook the beans over medium heat with garlic and epazote in approximately 2 quarts of water for 1 hour until tender. Allow the beans to cool in the liquid — this keeps them very black and flavorful.

Puree 3/4 of the beans in a food processor until very smooth; combine the puree with the whole beans.

Finely grind the bacon in a meat grinder; saute bacon over medium heat until the fat is rendered (about 10 minutes) and the meat is slightly caramelized; pour off the fat.

Saute the chorizo until done (about 10 minutes). Do not drain fat.

Add the black bean mixture and bacon; work the puree into the chorizo.

Cook the puree over medium heat to evaporate the excess water until it is very thick and pulls away from the sides of the pan (this is a crucial step in the recipe, for if the mixture isn't thick enough, i.e., contains excess water, the mixture will not firmly set in the terrines. It is better to overcook the mixture than undercook it).

Work the butter into the bean puree until fully incorporated; add the tabasco and salt. Remove from the heat.

Fill three quarters of the terrines with the warm black bean mixture. Press a log of goat cheese into the center of each terrine and cover with more of the black bean mixture.

Cover with plastic wrap and allow to chill overnight; when completely chilled, the terrine should be very firm.

If preparing ahead, STOP. May be stored in the refrigerator for one week.

TO COOK:

Remove from refrigerator and slice one inch thick.

Warm on grill for 2-3 minutes on each side. If preparing in large volume, place rolls on baking sheet and warm in oven at 350 degrees for 10 minutes.

TO SERVE:

Place on plate and garnish with sprig of cilantro.

Serve with fresh tomato/serrano chili salsa and corn/red pepper salsa. Actually, any of the salsas work well.

For a circular shape, plastic two-quart soft drink bottles may also be used as molds. Just cut off the top of the bottle, place goat cheese log in center, and surround with black bean mixture.

LIMESTONE LETTUCE and ENDIVE with GRILLED QUAIL and GOAT CHEESE VINAIGRETTE

This warm salad works well as an appetizer or light supper with a soup or warmed apple or pear compote.

SERVES: 4
PREP TIME: 8 hours
COOKING TIME: 15 minutes
MAY BE PREPARED AHEAD: 4 hours

INGREDIENTS:

2 quail breasts
3/4 cup virgin olive oil
4 sprigs fresh thyme
3 tbsp. red wine vinegar
salt and pepper to taste
12 stalks endive, washed
4 2-1/2-in. diameter rounds of fresh
    goat cheese, each 1/2-in. thick
4 handfuls limestone lettuce,
    broken in bite-size pieces & sliced
4 cherry tomatoes

PREPARATION:

Marinate the breasts in 1/4 cup of the olive oil and sprigs of fresh thyme for eight hours.

To prepare vinaigrette dressing, whisk remainder of olive oil with vinegar; add salt and pepper to taste.

TO COOK:

Grill quail on barred grill for 4 minutes.

Cut each quail breast into six pieces lengthwise.

Spread each endive with 1/3 round goat cheese and 1 piece of grilled quail.

If preparing ahead, STOP. Lettuce and prepared endive/quail/cheese may be covered and stored in refrigerator for 4 hours.

TO SERVE:

Toss the lettuce with enough vinagrette to lightly coat, and arrange them on round salad plates.

Place endive/cheese/quail on top of dressed greens in spoke design with cherry tomato rose in center.

Autumn

Wild Game and Poultry

Game tastes best paired with strong herbal, berry or earthy mushroom flavors. Stuffings infuse the meat with flavors and provide tasty side dishes.

Included are five favorite stuffings: an herbal cornbread stuffing, a chestnut stuffing, a sausage stuffing, a mushroom stuffing and a liver based stuffing. In addition to stuffing poultry, try them with a loin of pork or with veal birds.

Flavorful sauces finish wild game dishes. You'll find a reduced madiera sauce recipe with a short cut version following. The hunter sauce recipe can be used with all game. The sun-dried tomato sauce is a more unusual choice. The game bird stock is an excellent soup base, and can be further reduced to a flavorful sauce.

GARLIC THYME CORNBREAD STUFFING

SERVES: 4-6 depending on size of bird
PREP TIME: Mise en place
COOKING TIME: 15 minutes
MAY BE PREPARED AHEAD: 4 hours

INGREDIENTS:

1/2 lb. fresh mushrooms, sliced
7 tbsp. unsalted butter
2 cloves minced garlic
1/2 red onion, diced
1 stalk celery, diced
2 cups crumbled corn bread
2 tbsp. minced parsley
1 tsp. fresh minced thyme
salt and pepper to taste
2 tbsp. heavy cream

PREPARATION: Mise en place

TO COOK:

Cook mushrooms and 1 clove minced
garlic in 4 tbsp. butter for 5-7 minutes.

Saute red onion and celery with 1 clove
minced garlic in 3 tbsp. butter until
soft, about 3 minutes.

Mix mushrooms, juice, onions, celery,
and garlic with corn bread in bowl.

Add parsley, thyme, and season
with salt and pepper to taste.

Stir in heavy cream to bind stuffing.

If preparing ahead, STOP.
Cover and store in refrigerator.

CHESTNUT STUFFING

STUFFS: 1 Turkey; 8-12 Quail; 4 Pheasant
PREP TIME: Mise en place
COOKING TIME: 25 minutes
MAY BE PREPARED AHEAD: 24 hours

INGREDIENTS:

2 tsp. butter
1/2 onion, diced
1 stalk celery, diced
1 cup game bird stock
2 tsp. fresh sage, chopped
4 cups cubed bread, toasted
1-1/2 cup whole chestnuts, finely chopped

PREPARATION: Mise en place

TO COOK:

Melt butter in a saucepan large enough
to hold all the bread.

Add the onion and celery cover and sweat
until soft, do not brown.

Add the stock and sage, reduce slightly.

Stir in bread and chestnuts, adjust seasoning
with salt and pepper.

Remove from heat and cover, let stand
for 10 minutes. The mixture should be moist
but not sticky, add more stock if needed.

If preparing ahead, STOP. Cover and refrigerate.

THYME

PORCINI MUSHROOM STUFFING

SERVES: 4 Duck or Chicken Breasts;
    8 Veal Roulades
PREP TIME: Mise en place
COOKING TIME: 45 minutes
MAY BE PREPARED AHEAD: 8 hours

INGREDIENTS:

1-1/2 cup veal stock
2 oz. dried porcini mushrooms
1/3 cup butter
2 tbsp. shallots, chopped
1-1/2lb. mushrooms, chopped
1/3 cup cognac
3 tbsp. tomato paste
1 tsp. flour
1/2 cup cream
salt & pepper to taste

PREPARATION: Mise en place

TO COOK:

In a small saucepan bring veal stock
to a boil, add porcini and remove
from heat. Cover and let sit until soft
approximately 30 minutes.

Melt butter in a large saucepan. Add
shallots saute one minute. Do not brown.
Add mushrooms and cook over medium
heat until mushrooms have rendered their
liquid. Strain stock from porcini through
cheesecloth into mushrooms.

Rinse and dice porcini add to mushroom
mixture. Reduce until liquid is almost
gone, add cognac, tomato paste and flour
stir to blend.

Add cream, reduce adjust seasoning
with salt and pepper. Cool.

If preparing ahead, STOP. Cover and refrigerate.

SAUSAGE DRESSING

A filling side dish, excellent with gravy.
Garnish with fresh sage or parsley.

SERVES: enough to stuff a 14-16 lb. big bird
    or 8 partridge or 16 quail
PREP TIME: 20 minutes
COOKING TIME: Same as bird
MAY BE PREPARED AHEAD: 24 hours

INGREDIENTS:

1 onion, finely chopped
1 cup celery, finely chopped
2 tbsp. butter
1/2 lb. lean bulk pork sausage
2-1/2 lbs. ground beef
1 egg
1 tsp. poultry seasoning (see page 208)
1 tsp. beau monde or celery salt
1/4 tsp. pepper
1 tsp. salt
7 - 8 slices bread, cut into small squares
water as needed
2 tbsp. chopped fresh parsley or sage

PREPARATION:

Saute onions and celery in 2 tbsp.
butter until transparent. Place in large
bowl with meats.

Add egg and seasonings. Mix well.

Add bread cubes and mix well.
Dressing will be texture of uncooked
meatloaf. Add small amount of water
to bind mixture if too dry.

*If preparing ahead, STOP. Cover and
refrigerate for up to 24 hours.*

TO USE:

Stuff turkey, goose or quail.

Roast bird as required according
to weight.

Remove dressing to serving plate.
Garnish with fresh sage or parsley.

FOIS GRAS/WILD MUSHROOM STUFFING

This is a wonderful stuffing to use with duck breasts, boned quail, chicken and veal "birds". Use sparingly because it is a very rich filling and a small amount suffices. This is not recommended for stuffing large birds.

SERVES: 6
PREP TIME: 10 minutes
COOKING TIME: None
MAY BE PREPARED AHEAD: 8 hours

INGREDIENTS:

7 oz. cepe/porcini mushrooms
2 tbsp. butter
3-1/2 oz. cured ham
5 oz. goose foie gras (ok to used canned)
3 egg yolks
salt and pepper to taste

PREPARATION:

Saute porcini mushrooms in 2 tbsp. butter

Chop cured ham, mushrooms and sauteed duck liver into small squares.

Add egg yolks and mushrooms to meat. Yolks will hold stuffing together. Salt and pepper to taste.

MADEIRA SAUCE

SERVES: 6
PREP TIME: Mise en place
COOKING TIME: 3 hours (1 hour cooking and 2 hour reduction)
MAY BE PREPARED AHEAD: 48 hours

INGREDIENTS:

1/4 cup carrots, diced
1/4 cup onion, diced
2 tbsp. leeks, white part only, minced
1/4 oz. bacon, diced
3 cups game bird stock
4 cups chicken stock
2 sprigs thyme
3 tbsp. madeira
1 tbsp. cognac

PREPARATION: Mise en place

TO COOK:

Saute carrots, onion, leeks, and bacon in a small amount of butter until lightly browned.

Add stocks and thyme; reduce slowly one hour. Strain into a clean saucepan and add madeira and cognac.

If preparing ahead, STOP. Cover and refrigerate.

Bring to a boil, and reduce to desired consistency, about 2 hours. Adjust seasoning with salt, pepper, and lemon juice.

SHORT CUT MADEIRA SAUCE

SERVES: 1-1/2 cups
PREP TIME: Mise en place
COOKING TIME: 15 minutes
MAY BE PREPARED AHEAD: 48 hours

INGREDIENTS:

3 tbsp. butter
1-1/2 tbsp. flour
3/4 cup beef stock
1 tsp. Kitchen Bouquet or Bovril
1/4 cup Madeira wine

PREPARATION: Mise en place

TO COOK:

Melt butter in a saucepan, stir in flour
and cook for 5 minutes. Add beef stock,
kitchen bouquet, and Madeira.
Cook until thickened.

*If preparing ahead, STOP. Cover and
refrigerate for up to 48 hours.*

SUN-DRIED TOMATO SAUCE

An excellent sauce for roast pheasant,
duck breast, or chicken.

SERVES: 4
PREP TIME: Mise en place
COOKING TIME: 30 minutes
MAY BE PREPARED AHEAD: 24 hours

INGREDIENTS:

1/4 cup shallots, chopped
1 tbsp. olive oil
1/4 cup sherry
1 bay leaf
2 sprigs thyme
1 oz. sun dried tomatoes in oil, minced
2 peppercorns
2 juniper berries
3 cups game bird stock or chicken stock
1 cup cream
salt & pepper to taste

PREPARATION: Mise en place

TO COOK:

In a medium saucepan saute shallots
in olive oil. Do not brown.

Deglaze with sherry, add bay leaf, thyme,
sun dried tomatoes, peppercorns and
juniper berries.

Cook one minute; add game bird
stock and reduce liquid by 2/3.

Add cream, reduce to desired
consistency, adjust seasoning with salt
and pepper. Strain.

*If preparing ahead, STOP. Cover and
refrigerate for up to 24 hours. Before serving,
reheat, stirring constantly. If needed, add
a bit of stock to thin.*

GAME BIRD STOCK/SAUCE

SERVES: 1 quart stock
PREP TIME: Mise en place
COOKING TIME: 4 hours
MAY BE PREPARED AHEAD: 3 days

INGREDIENTS:

2 lb. game bird carcasses
1/4 cup vegetable oil
1/2 onion
1 small carrot
2 small tomatoes
1/8 cup mushrooms
1 small rib celery
2/3 cup white wine
1 clove garlic
1 sprig parsley
1 sprig thyme
1 bay leaf
4 peppercorns
2 qt. chicken stock

PREPARATION: Mise en place

TO COOK:

Brown carcasses in oil, add vegetables
and cook until slightly softened.

Add white wine, herbs, peppercorns and stock.

Cook 4 hours. Strain, using Chinois to
extract all possible juices.

If preparing ahead, STOP. Cover and refrigerate.

NOTE: To use as a sauce, reduce for another
2 hours until slightly thickened.

QUAIL STUFFED with SAUSAGE and SHITAKE MUSHROOM

SERVES: 6 - 2 birds per serving
PREP TIME: 30 minutes
COOKING TIME: 20 minutes
MAY BE PREPARED AHEAD: 24 hours

INGREDIENTS:

1/2 lb. shiitake mushrooms, sliced
2 tbsp. olive oil
2 shallots, minced
2 garlic cloves, minced
12 boneless quail
5 oz. heavy cream
salt to taste
ground black pepper to taste
8 oz. smoked sausage links, cooked
    and cut into small chunks
1 bunch chives
4 oz. boneless, skinless chicken breast
12 bacon strips for wrapping quail

PREPARATION:

Saute mushrooms in olive oil; stirring
constantly, until cooked. Add shallots
and garlic, saute until softened; cool.

Puree chicken in food processor until
smooth. Add cream, salt and pepper; pulse
until smooth. Refrigerate until chilled.

Mix sausage, chives, and chicken
"mousse" into the mushroom mixture.

*If preparing ahead, STOP. Cover
and refrigerate for up to 24 hours.*

Stuff each quail with this mixture,
then wrap with bacon slices.

TO COOK:

Roast in a 450 degree oven until fat is
golden brown, about 10 minutes. Let
quail rest for 10 minutes longer. Remove
fat or bacon and serve immediately.

QUAIL with ROSEMARY BEURRE BLANC

SERVES: 4
PREP TIME: 10 minutes
COOKING TIME: 15 minutes
MAY BE PREPARED AHEAD: 8 hours

INGREDIENTS:

8 boneless quail
4 cloves garlic
4 2-in. piece rosemary
1/2 cup chardonnay
4 tbsp. cream
8 tbsp. butter
salt & pepper to taste
juice of 1 lemon to taste
4 sprigs rosemary for garnish

PREPARATION:

Stuff quail* and tie if needed.

*If preparing ahead, STOP.
Refrigerate in airtight container.*

TO COOK:

Brown quail in a small amount of olive oil.
Add the garlic, rosemary and chardonnay.

Cover and cook over medium heat
approximately 6 minutes. Remove quail
and keep warm.

Add cream and reduce. Whisk in butter,
and adjust seasoning with salt, pepper and
lemon juice.

Strain sauce over quail.

TO SERVE:

Place on plate, top with sauce,
and garnish with rosemary.

*Stuffing Options
Garlic Thyme Cornbread Stuffing
Chestnut Stuffing

STUFFED DUCK BREAST with MADEIRA SAUCE

Select a large breasted duck like
Muscovy or Peking.

SERVES: 4
PREP TIME: 5 minutes
COOKING TIME: 30 minutes
MAY BE PREPARED AHEAD: No

INGREDIENTS:

4 duck breasts
1 cup Porcini Mushroom Stuffing
   (see page 171)
1/4 cup flour, for dredging
1 egg, beaten
1 cup bread crumbs
4 sprigs fresh rosemary or thyme for garnish
1 cup Madiera Sauce (see page 172)

PREPARATION:

Trim duck breast and remove skin. At the fat
end cut a pocket in the breast using a thin
knife, try not to make too large an opening.

Place a few heaping tsp. of stuffing in
each breast, dredge in flour dip in beaten
egg and roll in bread crumbs.

TO COOK:

Heat a little clarified butter in a non-stick
pan, brown the duck on all sides.

Finish cooking in a 375 degree oven. Remove
and let rest five minutes before slicing.

TO SERVE:

Place 1/4 cup sauce on each plate. Slice into
1/2-inch portions and arrange in a fanned style.

Garnish with fresh rosemary or thyme.

Stuffing Options
Porcini Mushroom Stuffing
Fois Gras Wild Mushroom Stuffing

Sauce Options
Madiera Sauce
Sun Dried Tomato Sauce

WILD DUCK or CHUKAR PARTRIDGE with HUNTER'S SAUCE

Use this sauce to baste chukar, wild ducks or game hens while roasting or serve with meat as a side dish.

SERVES: 2 cups (about 8 game hens
    or 4 ducks or chukar)
PREP TIME: Mise en place
COOKING TIME: 20 minutes
MAY BE PREPARED AHEAD: 24 hours

INGREDIENTS:

1 cup red or black currant jelly or preserves
1 tsp. dry mustard
1/2 tsp. Worcestershire sauce
juice of 2 lemons
1 tbsp. horseradish sauce
1 cup dry red wine

PREPARATION: Mise en place

TO COOK:

Combine all ingredients in a small heavy saucepan, and bring to a boil.

Simmer slowly until slightly thickened.

If preparing ahead, STOP. Cover and refrigerate for up to 24 hours.

To Prepare Birds

Stuff with filling of choice. I often pick the simplest: pieces of onion, celery, and fruit.

See cooking instructions in the following recipe. Cook 30 minutes per pound or until juice is clear when fork is inserted in breast meat.

DOVES or CHUKAR PARTRIDGE with WILD SALAL and SHERRY

You may substitute game hens for the wild birds.

SERVES: 6
PREP TIME: 15 minutes
COOKING TIME: 30-40 minutes
MAY BE PREPARED AHEAD:

INGREDIENTS:

6 game hens, doves or 3 chukar
1/4 cup dry sherry
1 tsp. Worchestershire sauce
1/2 cup wild salal jam (huckleberry or
    black currant jam may also be used)
1 tsp. dijon mustard

PREPARATION:

Heat all ingredients except game hens over low heat, stirring constantly until jam is melted.

Prepare and stuff hens.

Rub hens with bacon drippings or olive oil.

TO COOK:

Sear 10 minutes in 425 degree oven.

Baste with Wild Salal/Sherry Sauce

Reduce heat to 325 degrees.

Continue cooking for 30 minutes, basting frequently.

Serve additional sauce at table as condiment.

STUFFING SUGGESTIONS:

Vegetable Stuffing
2 stalks of celery cut in 6 pieces each
    (12 total)
2 apples cut in 6 pieces each (12 total)
2 onions cut in 6 pieces each (12 total)

Stuff each hen with 2 pieces celery, 2 pieces apple, and 2 pieces onion.

Rissoto with Sun Dried Tomatoes and Wild Mushrooms (see page 191)

Garlic Sage Spoon Bread (see page 270)

GOOSE ROASTED with APPLES

SERVES: 6-8
PREP TIME: 25 minutes
COOKING TIME: 1-1/2-2 hours
MAY BE PREPARED AHEAD:
    1-1/2 - 2 hours oven finish

INGREDIENTS:

2 sour apples, sliced
7 tbsp. butter
2 chicken livers, chopped
2 oz. cooked ham, chopped finely
1 onion, minced
2 shallots, minced
1 bunch parsley, chopped
2 small sprigs sage
1 cup breadcrumbs
1 egg
salt and pepper to taste
1 young goose, 6-7 lbs.

PREPARATION:

Put the sliced apples in a pot and
simmer gently with 1 tbsp. butter.

Mix the chopped chicken livers, ham,
finely chopped onions, shallots and herbs.
Cook this mixture in 3 tbsp. butter until
onions and shallots are transparent.

Stir together the apples, stuffing mixture, and
breadcrumbs which have been moistened
with just enough milk to hold them together.
Bind together with the lightly beaten egg.

Remove the neck and wing tips from
the goose and sew up the neck opening.

Season the stuffing and insert into the goose.

Mash 3 tbsp. butter with salt and pepper
and smear over the goose.

TO COOK:

Place the bird on a rack and put
into a preheated 425 degree oven.

Turn after 10 minutes to brown the other
side. After a further 10 minutes turn
again, and 10 minutes later reduce the
heat to 325 degrees.

Roast for 1-1/2 to 2 hours more,
depending on weight.

At the end of the cooking time, cover
the goose with aluminum foil and leave
without further cooking for 15 minutes.

TO SERVE:

Carve and serve with gravy (see page 179)
and baked apples stuffed with prunes
and nuts (see page 272).

SAGE

PHEASANT JOSEPHINE

This is an easy do-ahead dish for entertaining. The pheasant can be roasting during cocktail hour. It is also a good buffet dish.

SERVES: 6
PREP TIME: 20 minutes
COOKING TIME: 1-1/4 hour
MAY BE PREPARED AHEAD: 8 hours

INGREDIENTS:

2 pheasants, cut in serving pieces
1/2 cup flour, salt, pepper for dredging
2 tbsp. vegetable oil
2 tbsp. butter
1 clove garlic, minced
1 medium onion, minced
1 carrot, grated
1 cup mushrooms, sliced
1 cup chicken stock
1/2 cup dry white wine
1 tbsp. fresh parsley
1 tsp. fresh rosemary
1 tsp. fresh basil

PREPARATION:

Dredge pheasant in seasoned flour.

Brown pheasant in oil and butter with garlic and onion in saute pan. Place in covered baking dish.

Add grated carrot, mushrooms, stock, wine and herbs.

If preparing ahead, STOP.
Cover and refrigerate for up to 8 hours.

TO COOK:

Cook in preheated 350 degree oven for 1 hour, 15 minutes. (Add 15 minutes if dish is chilled.)

Serve in pan sauces with wild rice pilaf (see page 195).

MOM'S PHEASANT

SERVES: 6
PREP TIME: 10 minutes
COOKING TIME: 1 hour and 20 minutes
MAY BE PREPARED AHEAD:
    Not recommended:
    This has a one hour oven finish.

INGREDIENTS:

1 pheasant
1/2 cup all purpose flour
1/2 tsp. salt
1/4 tsp. black pepper
3 tbsp. + 1/4 cup sherry
6 tbsp. butter
2 tbsp. olive oil
12 pearl onions (fresh or frozen)
1/4 cup chicken or game broth

PREPARATION:

Cut pheasant into 6 pieces. (2 thighs, 4 breast pieces, leaving upper wing attached) Discard lower leg and lower wing. The tendons are voluminous because of the pheasant's heavy running habits. Use any leftover leg meat to make a great game broth.

Dredge pieces in flour, salt and pepper.

Mix together 3 tbsp. sherry with 3 tbsp. melted butter; reserve for basting.

TO COOK:

In a large covered frying pan. saute pheasant pieces in 3 tbsp. butter and 2 tbsp. olive oil until brown, about 20 minutes.

Sprinkle with 1/4 cup sherry, and add pearl onions and broth.

Cover and cook over medium heat for 1 hour or until tender, basting every 15 minutes with sherry/butter marinade.

Placing flour, seasoning and meat in a paper bag and shaking vigorously, allows a thorough coating. Hold top securely closed.

ROAST PHEASANT

To roast a pheasant whole, rub inside with salt, and stuff with

1 medium onion, quartered
1 apple, seeded and quartered
1 stalk celery, cut in 4 pieces

OR

Dressing of your choice.

Do not salt outside of bird.

Place in roasting pan and cook in preheated 450 degree oven for 15 minutes.

Reduce heat to 300-350 degrees, place two strips bacon over pheasant and continue cooking for 45-60 minutes until fork inserted runs with clear juice.

Remove from oven, keep covered, and allow to sit for 15 minutes before serving.

PAN GRAVY for ROAST POULTRY

For any roast bird: turkey, duck, pheasant, or goose.

Remove bird from roasting pan and drain off excess grease.

Place roasting pan on top of stove, add 1/2 cup water and 1/4 cup sherry, and deglaze pan. If bits of dressing, meat, or bacon are left in pan, incorporate into gravy.

Remove onions from cavity and place in pan.

Use hand held processor to puree gravy and get smooth consistency.

Add 2 tsp. Kitchen Bouquet add depth of flavor and 1 tbsp. Wondra fine milled flour to thicken.

Correct seasoning with salt and pepper.

Serve separately in gravy boat.

BREAST of TURKEY with LEMON and CAPERS

SERVES: 4
PREP TIME: Mise en place
COOKING TIME: 10 minutes
MAY BE PREPARED AHEAD:
    Not recommended

INGREDIENTS:

20 oz. turkey breast, boneless, skinless
3 oz. flour, seasoned with salt and pepper
4 eggs, beaten
8 slices of zucchini

Sauce
3/4 cup melted butter
2 tsp. chopped capers
2 tsp. chopped parsley
1 tbsp. fresh lemon juice

PREPARATION: Mise en place

TO COOK:

Slice the turkey breast into 2-1/2 oz. slices. Coat both sides of each slice with seasoned flour and dip in egg batter.

Saute slices in a skillet with 1/4 cup cooking oil for 2 minutes on each side.

Use the same procedure with the zucchini slices.

Sauce
Heat the butter in a saucepan. When butter is very hot, add capers, parsley and lemon juice. Set aside.

Alternate the cooked turkey breast and zucchini slices on each plate - 2 slices of each per serving. Pour 1 tbsp. of sauce over the turkey.

MEDALLIONS of VENISON with APPLES and SWEET ONIONS

This calls for about 5 oz. of meat per serving. You may wish to increase this amount. The dish is filling and the medallions become larger with pounding. This recipe may also be used with pork.

SERVES: 6
PREP TIME: Mise en place
COOKING TIME: 30 minutes
MAY BE PREPARED AHEAD:
    Not recommended

INGREDIENTS:

2 lbs. tenderloin of venison
3 tbsp. olive oil
3 tbsp. butter
3 sweet onions, sliced
3 apples peeled, cored, sliced
salt and pepper to taste
1/2 cup applejack brandy
1-1/2 cup half and half

PREPARATION: Mise en place

Slice tenderloin of venison 1" thick;
Pound into medallion.

TO COOK:

Melt oil and butter in saute pan.
Saute onions and apples until soft, approximately 15 minutes.
Remove onions and apples – reserve.

Saute medallions 4 - 5 minutes, seasoning with salt and pepper.
Add applejack brandy and deglaze pan.

Return apples and onions to pan.
Add half and half stirring constantly until sauce begins to thicken.
Serve immediately.

VENISON SCALLOPINI

This recipe will work for veal or chicken medallions also.

SERVES: 6
PREP TIME: 20 minutes
COOKING TIME: 1 hour
MAY BE PREPARED AHEAD: 2 hours

INGREDIENTS:

1-1/2 lbs. venison tenderloin,
    cut 1/2 inch thick
flour, salt, pepper for dredging
2 tbsp. vegetable oil
1 clove garlic, crushed
1 lb. sliced mushrooms
1/2 cup water
1/2 cup white wine
2 tbsp. lemon juice
1 4 oz. can tomato sauce
1 bay leaf
1/4 tsp. thyme
1/4 cup Marsala wine

PREPARATION:

Pound medallions between two pieces of wax paper and dredge in flour, salt and pepper.

Heat oil in covered frying pan with garlic and mushrooms.

Saute medallions until brown.
Add water, wine, lemon juice, tomato sauce and herbs. Cover and simmer for 1 hour, adding water as needed.

If preparing ahead, STOP. Cover and hold on stovetop for up to 2 hours.

Remove medallions to service plate.

Deglaze pan with Marsala wine and reduce sauce slightly. Pour sauce over medallions.

LOIN of VENISON with HUCKLEBERRIES

SERVES: 8-10
PREP TIME: 10 minutes +
    2 hours marinating
COOKING TIME: 1-1/2 hours
MAY BE PREPARED AHEAD:
    Oven finish of 1-1/2 hours

INGREDIENTS:

6 tbsp. vegetable oil
1 bouquet garni
salt and pepper to taste
1 loin of venison, 4 lbs.
1 onion, minced
1 cup beef stock (beef bouillion will do)
1/2 cup heavy cream
2 tbsp. wild huckleberry, salal or
    black currant jam

PREPARATION:

In a bowl, mix together oil, bouquet garni, salt and pepper. After letting this stand for several minutes, brush it carefully all over the meat. Leave for 2 hours to marinate.

Put the meat in a deep dish with the finely chopped onion, bouquet garni and stock.

TO COOK:

Place in a preheated 350 degree oven, and cook for 1-1/2 hours, basting frequently with the juices in the pan.

Place on a hot serving dish and keep warm.

Take out the onion and bouquet garni, and thicken the sauce with the cream.

At the last moment, add 2 tbsp. of huckleberry jam and stir well

Serve the gravy in a sauceboat.

VENISON in HUNTER'S SAUCE

This recipe may also be used
with beef shortribs.

SERVES: 6
PREP TIME: 20 minutes
COOKING TIME: 1 hour
MAY BE PREPARED AHEAD: 2 hours

INGREDIENTS:

2 lbs. short ribs of venison
3 tbsp. vegetable oil
1 onion, minced
1/2 cup chopped celery
1/4 cup cider vinegar
1 tbsp. brown sugar
1/2 cup hot water
2 tbsp. tomato puree
1 tbsp. Worcestershire sauce
2 tsp. dijon mustard
1 tsp. salt

PREPARATION:

Brown ribs in a frying pan. Add onion and celery, cooking until transparent.

Mix together vinegar, sugar, water, tomato puree, mustard, Worcestershire sauce, and salt, and pour over ribs, celery and onions. Add 1 cup hot water.

If preparing ahead, STOP. Cover and hold on stovetop for up to 2 hours.

Cover and simmer until tender.
Serve with pan sauce.

CHICKEN BREAST with CHILI CREAM SAUCE

SERVES: 6
PREP TIME: 20 minutes
COOKING TIME: 15 minutes
MAY BE PREPARED AHEAD: 1 day

INGREDIENTS:

2 fresh Anaheim chilies
1 -1/2 cups Créme Fraiche
1 small red onion, thinly sliced
1/4 cup chopped fresh cilantro
1 garlic clove, minced
6 boneless chicken breast halves
salt and pepper to taste
1 large tomato, peeled, seeded, chopped

PREPARATION:

Char chilies over gas flame or in broiler
until blackened on all sides.

Wrap in paper bag and let stand 10 minutes
to steam. Peel*, seed, and chop chilies.

Combine chilies, cream, onion, cilantro and
garlic in heavy large saucepan over medium-
high heat. Boil until reduced to thick sauce,
stirring occasionally, about 5 minutes.

If preparing ahead, STOP. Cover and refrigerate.

TO COOK:

Prepare barbecue (high heat) or
preheat broiler.

Season chicken with salt and pepper.
Grill or broil until springy to touch,
about 5 minutes per side. Cut chicken
diagonally into thin slices.

Add tomato to chili sauce and bring to simmer.
Season sauce to taste with salt and pepper.

TO SERVE:

Spoon sauce onto plates. Fan chicken
atop sauce and serve.

*It is advisable to use plastic gloves
when handling chilies.

CHICKEN CUTLETS with HAZELNUT SAUCE

SERVES: 6
PREP TIME: 15 minutes
COOKING TIME: 25 minutes
MAY BE PREPARED AHEAD: 4 hours

INGREDIENTS:

6 half breasts of chicken
Olive oil
1/2 cup roasted hazelnuts, finely chopped
6 sheets of phyllo

PREPARATION:

Remove finger-size muscle on back
of chicken half and reserve for other use.
Flatten breast half by pressing gently
with palm of hand.

Dip one side of chicken in olive oil, and then
chopped hazelnuts. Salt and pepper to taste.

Spray one sheet of phyllo with olive oil
mist and place filet on one corner; roll filet
and phyllo toward the opposite corner,
tucking in sides as you go.

*If preparing ahead, STOP. Cover phyllo
wrapped chicken with damp cloth to prevent
drying and refrigerate for up to 4 hours.*

Bake at 375 degrees on a baking sheet
for 20-25 minutes until golden.
Do not crowd pan.

Serve with hazelnut sauce.

HAZELNUT SAUCE

INGREDIENTS:

3/4 lb. unsalted butter
1-2 shallots
3 tbsp. flour
1 cup chicken broth
Tarragon, salt, pepper to taste
1/3 cup cognac or brandy
1 yolk
1/3 cup half-and-half
1/2 cup roasted hazelnuts,
    finely chopped coarse, reserve some
    whole nuts for garnish
chopped chives or parsley for garnish

PREPARATION:

Melt 3 tbsp. butter, then add 3 tbsp. minced shallots; saute until tender, but not brown. Add 3 tbsp. flour and cook until thick.

Slowly add 1 cup chicken broth, tarragon, salt, and pepper, stirring until smooth.

Bring sauce to a boil and add cognac or brandy; remove from heat and add the yolk, which has been beaten with 1/3 cup half-and-half.

Heat over low heat to thicken; do not boil.

Fold in chopped hazelnuts

TO SERVE:

Garnish with whole or chopped hazelnuts and chopped chives or parsley.

Serve sauce on side.

To remove nut skins from roasted hazlenuts, place in clean terrycloth towel and rub together. Skins should fall off easily.

CHICKEN DAMIANA

Damiana is a liqueur made from sage and herbs available in Mexico. It has an unproven reputation as an aphrodesiac. A dinner guest called to thank me for a dinner party a few days later and asked, "When will I begin to feel the effect of the chicken?"

SERVES: 4
PREP TIME: Mise en place
COOKING TIME: 20 minutes
MAY BE PREPARED AHEAD: 2 hours

INGREDIENTS:

1/4 cup chopped scallions
2 flattened breasts, halved
1 tbsp. olive oil
1 tbsp. butter
1/2 tsp. Granada Seasoning (see page 287)
1 tbsp. fresh rosemary; 4 sprigs for garnish
salt and pepper to taste
1/4 cup Damiana*
2 tbsp. chicken broth
1/4 cup cream

*You may use Strega or Jaegermeister liqueur as a substitute.

PREPARATION:

Saute scallions and chicken in oil/butter; season with Granada seasoning, rosemary, salt, and pepper.

Add Damiana, deglaze and reduce; remove chicken to shallow baking dish.

Add chicken broth to scallion and Damiana and reduce; add cream and reduce.

Cover chicken with sauce.

If preparing ahead, STOP. Cover dish with foil; may be held 2 hours in a 250 degree oven.

TO SERVE:

Garnish with sprigs of fresh rosemary.

CHICKEN with APPLES and BRANDY

SERVES: 8
PREP TIME: Mise en place
COOKING TIME: 30 minutes
MAY BE PREPARED AHEAD: 1 hour

INGREDIENTS:

4 chicken breasts, halved & boned
2 tbsp. butter and 2 tbsp. vegetable oil,
mixed for sauteing
salt and pepper to taste
4 medium green apples, cored, peeled, sliced
1 cup Calvados or Apple Jack
1/2 cup heavy cream

PREPARATION: Mise en place

TO COOK:

Flatten the halves of the chicken breasts
to 1/2 inch thickness.

Saute chicken in oil and butter. Add salt
and pepper. Lightly brown on each side,
about 10 minutes.

Add the apple slices and brown them lightly.
Add Calvados, deglaze pan and stir.

If preparing ahead, STOP. Place in foil covered
baking dish and store in a 200 degree oven.

Add cream to cover. Bring to a boil.
Reduce heat and allow cream to thicken.

Mixing butter and oil for
sauteing gives you the benefits of
both: the stability of oil for cooking
and the flavor of butter with less
chance the butter will burn.

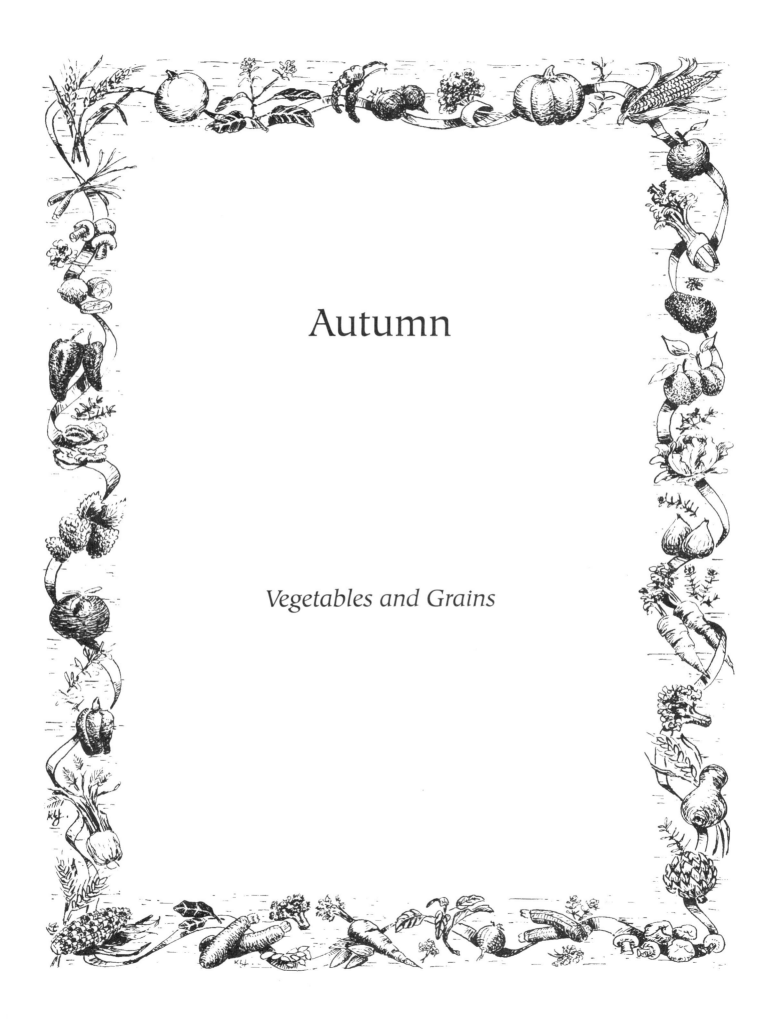

Autumn

Vegetables and Grains

BROCCOLI TIMBALE with SWEET RED PEPPER COULIS

SERVES: 8
PREP TIME: Mise en place
COOKING TIME: 25 minutes
MAY BE PREPARED AHEAD: 4 hours

INGREDIENTS:

3 cups broccoli florets
2 cup peeled, chopped broccoli stems
2 tbsp. lemon juice
1/2 tsp. salt
1/4 tsp. pepper
8 large eggs, beaten
1-1/2 cup half-and-half
1/4 tsp. ground nutmeg
Sweet Red Pepper Coulis (see page 102)

PREPARATION: Mise en place

TO COOK:

Chop broccoli florets fine and put in a
1 quart casserole. Cover and microwave
on high until tender, about 3-4 minutes.
Drain and set aside.

Put broccoli stems, lemon juice, salt
and pepper in a 1-quart casserole.
Cover and microwave on high until
tender, about 5 -7 minutes.

Put in food processor and process
until smooth. Pour into large bowl.

Stir beaten eggs, half-and-half,
nutmeg and chopped broccoli florets
into puree and blend well.

Fill eight 6-oz. custard cups about 2/3 full.
Cover tightly with plastic wrap and arrange
on a large plate in a circle without touching.
(The cups can be placed right on the
microwave oven floor, but they are easier
to rotate if on a plate.)

*If preparing ahead, STOP. Refrigerate for
up to 4 hours.*

Microwave on medium until knife
inserted into the middle comes out clean,
6-8 minutes. Rotate the cups, if necessary,
to help them cook evenly.

Let stand to finish cooking and pull
away from the sides, about 5 minutes.
Remove plastic wrap.

TO SERVE:

Invert a plate on top of the custard cup and
turn the cup upside down to release timbale.

Use a spatula to transfer the timbale
onto a plate lined with lettuce leaves.

Spoon over about 1/2 cup Sweet Pepper
Coulis (see page 102).

ZUCCHINI with TOMATO and BACON

This gets better and better the longer it is kept. The chilling and reheating bring the flavors to new richness.

SERVES: 8
PREP TIME: Mise en place
COOKING TIME: 1 hour
MAY BE PREPARED AHEAD: 1 week

INGREDIENTS:

1 medium onion, minced
1/4 lb. bacon, minced
1 lb. zucchini, sliced
3 cans tomato sauce
1 tbsp. fresh basiL
1 bay leaf
1/4 cup fresh grated parmesan cheese

PREPARATION: Mise en place

TO COOK:

Saute onions and bacon together for 15 minutes. Drain excess bacon fat.

Add zucchini, tomato sauce, and herbs. Simmer for 45 minutes, stirring occasionally.

If preparing ahead, STOP. Cover and refrigerate. Re-heat to serve.

TO SERVE:

Serve this vegetable in small ramikins topped with fresh parmesan cheese.

SQUASH and PIÑONS with LEMON THYME

SERVES: 8
PREP TIME: Mise en place
COOKING TIME: 10 minutes
MAY BE PREPARED AHEAD: 2 hours

INGREDIENTS:

2 cups yellow crookneck squash, sliced
2 cups zucchini, sliced
2 tbsp. butter
1 tbsp. fresh lemon thyme, chopped
1/4 cup piñons

PREPARATION: Mise en place

TO COOK:

Cook squash and zucchini in boiling, salted water until al dente, about 7 to 10 minutes. Drain and add butter, thyme and pinenuts, mixing well.

If preparing ahead, STOP. Cover serving container and keep warm in steam bath or low oven.

SQUASH with WALNUTS

SERVES: 6
PREP TIME: Mise en place
COOKING TIME: 15 minutes
MAY BE PREPARED AHEAD: 1 hour

INGREDIENTS:

1/2 cup olive oil
2 lbs. yellow squash,
    cut in 1/4-in. thick slices
2 tsp. salt
1 cup walnuts, chopped very coarse
    and toasted in the oven

PREPARATION: Mise en place

TO COOK:

Heat oil and saute squash until soft,
but not brown. Drain.

Sprinkle toasted walnuts over squash.

*If preparing ahead, STOP. Place in covered
serving dish and keep warm for up to one hour.*

CARROT PECAN CASSEROLE

SERVES: 6-8
PREP TIME: 10 minutes
COOKING TIME: 20 Minutes
MAY BE PREPARED AHEAD: 24 hours

INGREDIENTS:

2-3 pounds of carrots, cooked, mashed
    (six cups yield)
3/4 cup firmly packed brown sugar
2 eggs, beaten
8 tbsp. butter
3/4 tsp. baking powder
1 tsp. salt
1 tsp. cinnamon
3/4 - 1 cup fresh orange juice
1 cup pecan halves

PREPARATION:

Preheat oven to 375 degrees.
Butter a 2 quart casserole dish.

Combine carrots, eggs, 1/4 cup brown
sugar, 4 tablespoons butter, baking powder,
salt, cinnamon and enough orange juice
to get moist, fluffy consistency.

If preparing ahead, STOP. Cover and refrigerate.

Arrange pecan halves and sprinkle with
remaining brown sugar and melted butter.

TO COOK:

Bake uncovered for 20 minutes.

AUTUMN CARROTS

SERVES: 6
PREP TIME: Mise en place
COOKING TIME: 20 minutes
MAY BE PREPARED AHEAD: 4 hours

INGREDIENTS:

2 lbs. carrots, peeled, cut into julienne strips
1/2 lb. mushrooms, coarsely diced
4 tbsp. sweet butter
salt and pepper to taste
1-1/2tsp. sugar
2 tbsp. parsley, chopped
2 tbsp. tarragon, chopped

PREPARATION: Mise en place

TO COOK:

Boil carrots in salted water for 15 minutes.
Drain well.

Saute mushrooms and carrots in butter.
Season with salt, pepper and sugar. When
lightly browned, place in vegetable casserole.

*If preparing ahead, STOP. Cover and
refrigerate for up to 4 hours. Reheat for
3 minutes in microwave on medium.*

Top with chopped herbs and serve.

"VEGETABLES of the SOUTHWEST" BURRITO

This is an entree item, but it's here to
showcase the use of pumpkin seeds. It is a
popular dish for fat and calorie conscious
guests. You may also use this recipe without
the tortillas and create a "Vegetables of the
Southwest" saute with pumpkin seed sauce.

SERVES: 6
PREP TIME: Mise en place
COOKING TIME: 15 minutes
MAY BE PREPARED AHEAD:
    Not recommended

INGREDIENTS:

1 cup chopped broccoli
1/2 cup onion, finely chopped
2 cloves garlic, finely chopped
2 tbsp. vegetable oil
1/4 tsp. salt
1/2 cup finely chopped red bell pepper
1 tbsp. lemon juice
1 cup julienne strips zucchini
1/4 cup shelled, toasted pumpkin seeds
1 tsp. ground red chiles
1/4 tsp. ground cumin
1 cup julienne strips yellow squash
6 flour tortillas (10 inches in diameter), warmed

PREPARATION: Mise en place

TO COOK:

Cook broccoli, onion and garlic in oil in
10-inch skillet, stirring frequently, until tender.

Stir in remaining ingredients except tortillas.
Cook, stirring occasionally, until squash is
crisp-tender, about 2 minutes. Keep warm.

Spoon about 1/2 cup of the vegetable
mixture onto center of each tortilla. Fold one
end of tortilla up about 1 inch over mixture;
fold right and left sides over folded end,
overlapping. Fold remaining end down.

Serve in a pool of Pepian (Pumpkin Seed
Sauce) with additional sauce drizzled in
a zig-zag pattern for garnish. Calorie
conscious folks should limit the sauce.

PEPIAN (PUMPKIN SEED SAUCE)

Try this on skinless chicken breasts
or medallions of chicken.

SERVES: 3 cups
PREP TIME: Mise en place
COOKING TIME: 20 minutes
MAY BE PREPARED AHEAD: 48 hours

INGREDIENTS:

1 cup shelled pumpkin seeds
1 small onion, chopped (about 1/4 cup)
1 slice white bread, torn into pieces
1 clove garlic, crushed
2 tbsp. vegetable oil
2 tbsp. canned chopped green chiles
1 can (14 oz.) chicken broth
1/2 cup whipping cream
dash of salt

PREPARATION: Mise en place.

TO COOK:

Cook pumpkin seeds, onion, bread and
garlic in oil, stirring frequently, until bread
is golden brown. Stir in chiles.

Place mixture in food processor workbowl
fitted with steel blade; cover and process
until smooth.

Stir in broth, whipping cream and salt.

*If preparing ahead, STOP. Cover and
refrigerate. Reheat in double boiler. Do
not boil or sauce will separate.*

FENNEL with BACON

SERVES: 6
PREP TIME: 15 minutes
COOKING TIME: 1 hour
MAY BE PREPARED AHEAD:
    1 hour stove top finish

INGREDIENTS:

4 large bulbs fennel
2 onions, finely chopped
4 tbsp. butter
6 oz. thick strips of bacon,
    sliced into 1/4-in. pieces
1 bouquet garni
salt and pepper to taste
2 cups chicken bouillon

PREPARATION:

Remove the very hard outer shell of the
fennel; cut the bulbs in quarters and
blanch in boiling salted water for 5 minutes.
Drain well.

Using a heavy saucepan, saute the onions in
butter until transparent. Add the bacon
pieces to the onion and brown on all sides.

Meanwhile, chop the fennel into bite-sized
pieces and add to the browned bacon
and onion mixture. When they are beginning
to turn gold, add the bouquet garni,
seasoning and bouillon.

TO COOK:

Simmer gently for 50-60 minutes.

Remove the bouquet garni, correct
seasoning, and serve as an accompaniment
to grilled or roasted meat.

RISSOTO with SUN DRIED TOMATOES, WILD MUSHROOMS and ROSEMARY

The rich, earthy flavors of the mushroom and sun-dried tomatoes recall the loamy scent of fallen leaves.

SERVES: 6
PREP TIME: Mise en place
COOKING TIME: 45 minutes
MAY BE PREPARED AHEAD: 1 day

INGREDIENTS:

1 cup rissoto
2 cups chicken broth
1 tsp. rosemary
1/2 tsp. salt
1/4 cup sliced shitaki mushrooms
1 cup Blush Chablis
1/4 cup minced sun dried tomatoes

PREPARATION: Mise en place

TO COOK:

Put all ingredients in saucepan, cover and cook over medium heat, stirring as needed, until rissoto has absorbed all liquid and is tender. Add water if needed to cook rissoto until tender.

If preparing ahead, STOP. Cover and refrigerate. Reheat in microwave in covered dish.

SAFFRON RICE

Brought to the New World as one of the most precious spices from Southern Spain. Saffron adds a distinctive flavor and is very expensive. It is the dried stigma of the autumn flowering white crocus. You might try collecting and drying your own. There is an herb called Azafran or "Mexican saffron" that is less expensive and may be used here.

SERVES: 6
PREP TIME: 10 minutes
COOKING TIME: 20 minutes
MAY BE PREPARED AHEAD: 24 hours

INGREDIENTS:

1 medium onion, chopped
6 tbsp. butter
2 cups white long grain rice
4 cups boiling chicken stock
1/4 tsp. saffron
1 cup chopped mushrooms
1/2 cup grated romano cheese

PREPARATION: Mise en place

TO COOK:

Saute onion in 2 tbsp. butter until browned. Add uncooked rice and brown about 1 minute. Add chicken stock, mushrooms and saffron; stir and bring to a boil. Cover, reduce heat and simmer about 20 minutes.

If preparing ahead, STOP. Cover and refrigerate. Add 2-3 tbsp. chicken broth and reheat, stirring constantly, before serving.

When cooked, add remaining 4 tbsp. butter and romano cheese; stir and serve.

MEXICAN RICE

Spicy and flavorful, this rice stands up well to meats and poultry with full flavored sauces.

SERVES: 6
PREP TIME: Mise en place
COOKING TIME: 1 hour
MAY BE PREPARED AHEAD: 30 minute stove top finish

INGREDIENTS:

1/4 lb. chorizo
1 medium onion, chopped
1 cup celery, chopped
1 clove garlic
1 large green pepper, chopped
1 tsp. chili powder
1/4 tsp. cumin
1/4 tsp. black pepper
1 tsp. salt
3 cups fresh tomatoes, chopped
2 cups chicken broth
1 cup red wine
2 cups long grain rice

PREPARATION: Mise en place

TO COOK:

Brown chorizo, add onion, celery, garlic and green pepper. Cook until tender. Add chili powder, cumin, black pepper, salt and tomatoes, and simmer, covered, for 10 minutes to mix flavors.

Add rice, chicken broth, and wine and cook for an additional 10 minutes. Cover and cook for 30 minutes until liquid is absorbed.

HARVEST RICE

SERVES: 6
PREP TIME: Mise en place
COOKING TIME: 30 minutes
MAY BE PREPARED AHEAD: 24 hours

INGREDIENTS:

1/4 cup butter
1 cup long grain rice
2 tbsp. chopped onion
1/4 cup slivered almonds
1/4 tsp. allspice
1/4 tsp. black pepper
1/4 tsp. salt
1/2 cup raisins
1-1/2 cup chicken stock

TO COOK:

Melt butter in a medium saucepan. Add rice, onion and almonds and saute until rice is slightly brown. Stir in allspice, black pepper, salt, and raisins.

Add chicken stock, cover and simmer for 25 minutes.

If preparing ahead, STOP. Cover and refrigerate. Add 1/4 cup additional stock and reheat.

NUTTED RICE

SERVES: 6
PREP TIME: Mise en place
COOKING TIME: 30 minutes
MAY BE PREPARED AHEAD: 24 hours

INGREDIENTS:

2 tbsp. butter
1 cup long grain rice
1/4 cup bulgar
1/4 cup pinenuts
2 cups beef or game stock
1 cup water
1/4 tsp. salt (or to taste)

TO COOK:

Melt butter in saucepan. Add grains and pinenuts and saute until rice and bulgar are light brown and coated.

Add liquids and salt. Cover and simmer for 30 minutes until done.

If preparing ahead, STOP. Cover and refrigerate. Add 1/4 cup stock, stir and reheat.

ORANGE MUSHROOM PILAF

SERVES: 6
PREP TIME: Mise en place
COOKING TIME: 30 minutes
MAY BE PREPARED AHEAD: 24 hours

INGREDIENTS:

1/4 cup butter
1/2 cup finely broken vermicelli
1 cup rice
2 cups boiling hot beef broth
1 tbsp. dried powdered mushrooms
1 tbsp. dried powdered orange zest
salt and pepper to taste

PREPARATION: Mise en place

TO COOK:

In 1-1/2 to 2 quart saucepan over medium heat, melt butter. Add vermicelli and cook until brown, stirring frequently.

Add the rice and cook 2 to 3 minutes, stirring well. Add the beef broth, mushrooms, orange zest, salt and pepper. Reduce heat to low, cover and cook for 20 minutes, until all the liquid is absorbed.

If preparing ahead, STOP. Cover and refrigerate. Add 2-3 tbsp. additional broth and reheat, stirring constantly.

BARLEY with MUSHROOMS and CILANTRO

Energy Saver. This can be cooking along with roast game to save energy.

SERVES: 8
PREP TIME: 10 minutes
COOKING TIME: 1-1/2-2 hours
MAY BE PREPARED AHEAD:
    1-1/2 to 2 hour oven finish

INGREDIENTS:

1 cup uncooked barley
3 tbsp. butter
1 large onion, finely chopped
1/2 lb. fresh mushrooms, sliced
2 cups chicken broth
1 tbsp. pickapepper sauce
1/2 tsp. salt
1/4 tsp. pepper
1 tbsp. minced fresh cilantro for garnish

PREPARATION:

In a saucepan over medium heat, brown barley in butter. Add onions and saute until tender. Add remaining ingredients.

Pour into a greased 2-quart casserole, uncovered, at 300 degrees for 1-1/2 to 2 hours, stirring occasionally. Sprinkle with cilantro before serving.

ORZO with HERBS and PINENUTS

SERVES: 6
PREP TIME: Mise en place
COOKING TIME: 20 minutes
MAY BE PREPARED AHEAD:
    Not recommended

INGREDIENTS:

2 cups orzo
3 tbsp. unsalted butter, cut in small pieces
1/3 cup pinenuts, toasted
1 tbsp. fresh lemon juice
3 tbsp. fresh cilantro, minced
1 tbsp. fresh lemon thyme, minced

PREPARATION: Mise en place

TO COOK:

In a kettle of boiling salted water, boil the orzo until it is al dente; drain well.

Stir in butter, pinenuts, lemon juice and salt and pepper to taste. Add the cilantro and lemon thyme, and toss well.

THYME

WILD RICE with PINE NUTS

SERVES: 6
PREP TIME: 10 minutes
COOKING TIME: 45 minutes
MAY BE PREPARED AHEAD: 2 hours

INGREDIENTS:

1 tsp. olive oil
1 large onion, chopped
1 large clove garlic, chopped
1 cup fresh mushrooms, sliced
1 cup wild rice (uncooked)
2-1/2 cups chicken broth
1/4 cup sherry
1/2 tsp. salt
pepper to taste
1/2 tsp. oregano
1 tsp. basil
1/3 cup chopped parsley
1/2 cup pine nuts

PREPARATION:

In a large non-stick frying pan, heat oil over medium heat, add onion, garlic and mushrooms. Saute until tender (approximately 10 minutes).

TO COOK:

Add rice and cook until lightly browned.

If preparing ahead, STOP. Cover pan and hold on stovetop for up to 2 hours.

Add broth, sherry, salt, pepper, oregano and basil. Bring to a boil, and simmer, covered, for 45 minutes. Remove from heat and let stand for 10 minutes.

Toss with nuts, parsley and serve.

BLANCO BEANS

While these are the texture of refried beans, they are white and made without refrying. This dish offers a nice change from the refried pinto or black beans. Serve them to complement spicy dishes. They go especially well with autumn meats and sauces.

SERVES: 6
PREP TIME: 10 minutes
COOKING TIME: 1-1/4 hour
MAY BE PREPARED AHEAD: 24 hours

INGREDIENTS:

1 lb. white navy beans
1 carrot
1 onion, stuck with 3 cloves
bouquet garni of 8 parsley stems
    and 1 bay leaf
salt and white pepper to taste
scant 1/2 cup light cream
1/4 cup butter
parsley leaves for garnish

PREPARATION:

Put the beans into cold water with the carrot, onion, bouquet garni and salt and pepper. Bring to a boil and cook for 1 to 1-1/4 hour (depending on the size and quality of the beans).

Remove the bouquet garni, and cut carrot and the onion. Put the beans through a sieve or food mill twice or puree with hand held food processor to obtain a smooth puree.

Add the cream and butter, and beat well. If necessary, to make the puree more creamy, add a little of the water in which the beans have been cooked.

If preparing ahead, STOP. Cover and refrigerate for up to 24 hours.

Reheat slowly, stirring to avoid burning. Garnish with fresh parsley and serve with garlic crisps (see page 13).

Autumn

Desserts

PUMPKIN BOMBE

Use miniature jello molds or tartlet molds for this; the more elaborate the better since the frozen consistency holds details of an intricate design well! A large single mold may be used, and a pint of softened vanilla ice cream may be put in the mold prior to adding the pumpkin mixture for a two-tone effect. I prefer the individual decorative molds for ease of service. Garnish and sauce remain the same for either presentation.

SERVES: 6-8
PREP TIME: 5 minutes
COOKING TIME: None
MAY BE PREPARED AHEAD: 2 weeks

INGREDIENTS:

1 cup cooked pumpkin
1/2 cup sugar
1/2 tsp. salt
1/2 tsp. ginger
1/2 tsp. nutmeg
1 cup evaporated milk, whipped
slivered almonds garnish
cinnamon cream anglaise (see page 201)

PREPARATION:

Mix pumpkin, sugar, and spices; fold in whipped milk.

Spray molds with Pam or other non-oil mist, and fill. Cover with a square of wax paper to prevent transfer of flavor in freezer.

If preparing ahead, STOP. Bombe may be stored frozen for 2 weeks.

TO SERVE:

Unmold onto serving plates. Garnish with slivered almonds and serve in a pool of rum cream anglaise or cinnamon cream anglaise. To make rum cream anglaise, substitute 1 teaspoon rum extract for the cinnamon in the cream anglaise.

BANANA PUMPKIN FLAN

SERVES: 8
PREP TIME: 10 minutes
COOKING TIME: 1 hour 10 minutes
MAY BE PREPARED AHEAD:
   up to one week

INGREDIENTS:

1-1/4 + 2/3 cup sugar
2 ripe, medium bananas, peeled
6 eggs, beaten
1 can (16 oz.) pumpkin
2 cups half-and-half
1 tsp. cinnamon
1/2 tsp. ground ginger
1/4 tsp. ground cloves
1/2 tsp. ground nutmeg
1/2 tsp. salt
1 tsp. vanilla extract

PREPARATION:

Melt 1-1/4 cup sugar in a skillet; stir until completely melted and amber in color. Pour into 2-qt. shallow casserole dish, rotating to fix sugar to sides of dish. Ramekins may also be used.

Puree bananas and combine with eggs, pumpkin, half-and-half, 2/3 cup sugar, spices, salt, and vanilla. Mix thoroughly. Pour into casserole; set casserole or ramekins in pan of hot water (Bain Marie).

TO COOK:

Bake in 350 degree oven for 1 hour and 10 minutes. Do not overcook or flan becomes dry. Cool completely before unmolding.

If preparing ahead, STOP. Cover and store in refrigerator.

TO SERVE:

Unmold by running a knife blade around the edge of casserole or ramekin, placing serving dish over casserole or ramekin. Quickly invert and lift off casserole or ramekin.

PIPPIN TANSY

This is a modern version of a 15th century recipe. It is always the one chosen first at a dessert buffet. The original recipe calls for tansy, but modern research tells us that tansy is no longer recommended for consumption. Allspice is an excellent substitution.

SERVES: 12
PREP TIME: 20 minutes
COOKING TIME: 30 - 40 minutes
MAY BE PREPARED AHEAD: 3 days; May be frozen for 1 month

INGREDIENTS:

12-14 apples (green pippin)
1 tbsp. fresh lemon juice
2 tsp. cinnamon
3/4 cup white sugar
1 cup flour
1-1/2 cups oats
3/4 cup brown sugar
1 cup butter
pinch of salt
1/4 tsp. tansy or allspice
1 tbsp. orange zest

PREPARATION:

Peel and slice apples into thin slices; sprinkle with lemon juice and 1/2 tsp. cinnamon, and 1/4 cup white sugar. Fill 12 buttered ramekins 3/4 full of apple-spice mixture.

Mix flour, oats, brown sugar, remainder of white sugar, butter, rest of cinnamon, salt, tansy or allspice, and orange zest. Cover apples with mixture.

TO COOK:

Place ramekins on baking sheet. Bake 30-40 minutes.

TO SERVE:

Serve with a pitcher of fresh double cream (optional).

APPLE CREAM

Here's a modern version of a recipe that dates back to 1658. The herbal flavors give it an unusual twist.

SERVES: 6 - 8
PREP TIME: 30 minutes
COOKING TIME: None
MAY BE PREPARED AHEAD: 24 hours

INGREDIENTS:

6 apples, peeled and quartered
1-1/2 cups sugar
2 cups Rosé wine
rind of 1 lemon
pinch of dried rosemary
pinch of dried thyme
1 envelope unflavored gelatin
1/2 cup sweet sherry
1 cup heavy cream, whipped

PREPARATION:

Place apples in a pan with the sugar, rose wine, lemon rind, rosemary, and thyme. Simmer until apples are very soft. Strain and reserve wine.

Puree apples through a fine strainer into a bowl, add reserve wine.

Soak gelatin in sherry for 5 minutes. Melt in a double broiler and add to apples. Stir well and cool. When apple mixture begins to stiffen, fold in the cream.

Pour into a mold that has been rinsed in cold water and chill in the refrigerator until firm.

If preparing ahead, STOP. Hold in refrigerator for up to 24 hours.

Unmold and serve plain or with Cinnamon Cream Anglaise (see page 201).

BAKED APPLES

This is really "comfort" food and somehow reminds everyone of home or grandma.

SERVES: 6
PREP TIME: 10 minutes
COOKING TIME: 30 minutes
MAY BE PREPARED AHEAD: 24 hours

INGREDIENTS:

6 tbsp. butter, softened
6 tbsp. brown sugar
1 tsp. ground cinnamon
1 cup raisins
1/4 cup walnuts
6 apples, cored

PREPARATION:

Cream together butter, sugar, and cinnamon. Add nuts and raisins, mixing well so that ingredients stick together.

Stuff nut/raisin mixture in center of each apple and place on foil lined baking pan.

If preparing ahead, STOP. Cover and refrigerate for up to 24 hours.

TO COOK:

Bake for 30 minutes at 350 degrees.

TO SERVE:

Spoon any drippings from foil over apples and serve warm or cold with whipped cream or double cream.

APPLESAUCE CAKE

An old fashioned spice cake, this is especially good as a brunch dessert because it's not too sweet.

SERVES: 8
PREP TIME: 15
COOKING TIME: 45 minutes
MAY BE PREPARED AHEAD: 24 hours

INGREDIENTS:

1/2 cup shortening
1 cup sugar
1 egg
1 cup applesauce
2 cups flour
1 tsp. soda
1 tsp. cinnamon
1/4 tsp. cloves
1/2 tsp. allspice
3/4 tsp. salt
1 cup raisins
confectioner's sugar garnish

PREPARATION:

Cream together shortening, sugar, egg, and applesauce.

Sift together dry ingredients. Add dry ingredients to creamed ingredients, mixing well.

TO BAKE:

Grease and flour 9" x 12" pan. Bake 45 minutes at 350 degrees. Dust with confectioner's sugar.

If preparing ahead, STOP. Cover and refrigerate for up to 24 hours.

KAHLUA PECAN BRULÉ

This is very rich, so use your smallest ramekins.

SERVES: 8
PREP TIME: 15 minutes
COOKING TIME: 45 minutes
MAY BE PREPARED AHEAD: 1 week;
    may be frozen for 1 month

INGREDIENTS:

4 oz. German chocolate
1/4 cup butter
1-2/3 cup sugar
3 tbsp. corn starch
2 eggs
1-2/3 cup milk
1 tsp. vanilla
1/4 cup Kahlua liqueur
1/8 tsp. salt
1/2 cup pecans
1-1/3 cup coconut

PREPARATION:

Melt chocolate and butter; remove from heat.

Mix sugar, cornstarch, eggs, milk, vanilla, Kahlua, and salt; stir in chocolate mixture. Fill 8 ramekins or baking cups, and sprinkle pecans and coconut on top.

TO COOK:

Place on cooking sheet. Bake in oven at 375 degrees for 45-50 minutes.

PEARS POACHED in ZINFANDEL with CINNAMON CREAM ANGLAISE

Skip the cream anglaise for your calorie conscious friends.

SERVES: 4
PREP TIME: Mise en place
COOKING TIME: 30 minutes
MAY BE PREPARED AHEAD: 24 hours

INGREDIENTS:

1 cup zinfandel
2 tbsp. lemon juice
2 cinnamon sticks
2 cups water
4 pears, peeled
1/4 cup Cinnamon Cream Anglaise
4 fresh mint sprigs for garnish

PREPARATION: Mise en place

TO COOK:

Bring zinfandel, lemon, cinnamon and water to a boil, add pears; reduce heat, and simmer for 30 minutes.

Remove from heat, cover and allow pears to remain in poaching liquid overnight to absorb color and flavor.

TO SERVE:

Place 1/4 cup Cinnamon Cream Anglaise in large goblet; stand pear upright in goblet and garnish with mint sprig at stem end.

CINNAMON CREAM ANGLAISE

INGREDIENTS:

2 cups milk
4 egg yolks
1/2 cup sugar
1/2 tsp. vanilla
1 tsp. ground cinnamon

PREPARATION:

Heat milk to boiling, then remove
from heat.

Mix together egg yolks, sugar, vanilla
and cinnamon, and add to cooled milk,
mixing well.

Stir constantly over low heat until
mixture thickens.

*If preparing ahead, STOP. Cover and
refrigerate for up to 24 hours.*

HAZELNUT CAKES

SERVES: 12
PREP TIME: 5 minutes
COOKING TIME: 35 minutes
MAY BE PREPARED AHEAD: 1 week

INGREDIENTS:

3 cups all purpose flour
1/2 cup brown sugar
1 tsp. ginger
1 tsp. nutmeg
1/2 cup finely chopped hazelnuts
1 tsp. salt
3 sticks (12 oz.) softened butter
confectioners sugar for dusting

PREPARATION:

Heat oven to 350 degrees. Spray cake
molds with oil coating (like Pam).

Mix flour, brown sugar, spices, nuts and
salt in a large bowl. Cut butter into small
pieces and cut into dry ingredients using
hands. When well mixed, divide dough
into 12 pieces and pat into muffin cups
or decorative cake molds.

TO COOK:

Bake 30 to 35 minutes. Let cool 10 minutes
and unmold to wire rack.

*If preparing ahead, STOP. May be stored in
airtight container for up to 1 week.*

Sprinkle with powdered sugar before serving.

FRUIT COBBLERS

Use any fruit in season. Pears and apples are great in winter; peaches, plums and berries in summer.

SERVES: 8
PREP TIME: 15 minutes
COOKING TIME: 30 minutes
MAY BE PREPARED AHEAD: 24 hours

INGREDIENTS:

Fruit Filling
6 pears, apples, or peaches, peeled,
    cored and cut into 1/4-in. slices
1/2 tsp. minced fresh ginger
3 plums or apricots, pitted and cut into
    1/4-in. slices
1 pint blackberries, blueberries or raspber-
    ries (fresh is best, but frozen will work)
2 tbsp. amaretto liquor
1/4 cup fresh lemon juice
3 tbsp. light brown sugar
1 tbsp. cornstarch
1/2 tsp. cinnamon
1/4 tsp. nutmeg
2 tbsp. chopped pecans or walnuts

Topping
1-1/2 cup all purpose flour
1/2 cup granulated sugar
1/2 tsp. salt
1 tsp. baking powder
1/2 tsp. baking soda
4 tbsp. unsalted butter, cut into pieces
1/3 cup plain yogurt
1/4 cup lowfat milk
1/2 tsp. vanilla extract

PREPARATION:

Fruit Filling
Coat pears, apples or peaches with lemon juice in bowl. Add plums or apricots, berries, amaretto, and ginger.

In another bowl, mix together well sugar, cornstarch, spices and nuts. Add to fruit and toss well. Spoon into saucepan and cook over medium heat, stirring well, until simmer point is reached.

Topping
Preheat oven to 425 degrees.

Sift together flour, 1/3 cup sugar, salt, powder and soda. Cut butter into dry ingredients until crumbly.

In another bowl, mix together yogurt, lowfat milk and vanilla.

Make a well in center of crumb mixture and add yogurt mixture, stirring until dough forms. Dough will be sticky.

Flatten dough between sheets of wax paper by patting into 3/4-inch thick rectangle. Cut into 12 "cobbles" using a 2-1/2-inch round fluted cookie cutter.

Put hot fruit mixture in rectangular baking pan; top with "cobbles" and brush "cobbles" with milk. Sprinkle remaining granulated sugar over all.

TO COOK:

Bake 30 minutes or until cobbles are golden and fruit is bubbling.

If preparing ahead, STOP. Store in cool place for up to 24 hours. Reheat before serving.

TO SERVE:

Best served warm. May serve with double cream, whipped cream or ice cream.

CHOCOLATE SILK MOUSSE

A super quick mousse, that will bring raves.

SERVES: 8
PREP TIME: Mise en place
COOKING TIME: 5 minutes
MAY BE PREPARED AHEAD: 2 days

INGREDIENTS:

12 oz. bittersweet chocolate,
    roughly chopped
1 cup milk
1/4 cup dark rum
4 eggs, separated
1/4 cup sugar
1 cup heavy cream, whipped

PREPARATION: Mise en place

TO COOK:

Combine chocolate and milk in saucepan. Warm over heat until chocolate is melted and well mixed, stir constantly (approximately 3 minutes). Remove from heat and whisk in rum and egg yolks.

Whip egg whites with sugar until stiff. Do not over beat. Whisk chocolate mixture into whipped egg whites, blending well and fold in whipped cream.

Spoon into stemmed glasses and chill for at least 2 hours.

If preparing ahead, STOP. May store in refrigerator for up to 2 days.

Garnish with candied violets or any edible fresh flowers.

You may substitute **pure** chocolate chips for roughly chopped bittersweet chocolate. Be certain no fillers have been added to the chips.

Autumn

Seasonal Gifts

SHERRY ROSEMARY JELLY

Serve with roast pork, lamb or beef.

SERVES: 4 - 6 jars (approx. 3/4 - 1 cup each)
PREP TIME: 5 minutes +
    1 hour steeping time
COOKING TIME: 30 minutes
MAY BE PREPARED AHEAD: 6 months

INGREDIENTS:

2-1/2 cups Sherry
1 cup rosemary
4 cups sugar
1/4 cup cider vinegar
3 oz. liquid pectin
4-6 fresh rosemary sprigs for garnish
parafin to seal

PREPARATION:

Bring wine to a boil.

Pour over fresh rosemary, cover, and allow
to steep until cool (approximately 1 hour).

Press through chinois or fine strainer,
extracting as much flavor as possible.

TO COOK:

In a non-metal pan, combine 2 cups herb
infusion with sugar, and bring to a boil.

When sugar is dissolved, add pectin
and vinegar.

Bring jelly to a boil again,
and boil for 1 minute.

Remove from heat and skim foam.

Pour into jars and allow to cool
approximately 15 minutes.

Add optional sprig of rosemary
and seal with thin layer of parafin.

Top with a colorful square of fabric
and ribbon, raffia, or lace.

LAVENDAR THYME JELLY

SERVES: 4 - 6 jars (approx. 3/4 - 1 cup each)
PREP TIME: 5 minutes +
    1 hour steeping time
COOKING TIME: 30 minutes
MAY BE PREPARED AHEAD: 6 months

INGREDIENTS:

2-1/2 cups Rosé wine
1/2 cup lemon thyme
1/2 cup lavendar
4 cups sugar
1/4 cup lemon juice
3 oz. liquid pectin
parafin to seal

Optional
1-2 drops red food coloring
4-6 sprigs fresh thyme

PREPARATION:

Bring wine to a boil.

Pour over fresh herbs, cover, and allow
to steep until cool (approximately 1 hour).

Press through chinois or fine strainer,
extracting as much flavor as possible.

In a non-metal pan, combine 2 cups herb
infusion with sugar, and bring to a boil.

When sugar is dissolved, add pectin and
lemon juice. If adding color, do so now.

Bring jelly to a boil again, and boil for
1 minute. Remove from heat and skim foam.

Pour into jars and allow to cool
approximately 15 minutes.

Add optional sprig of herb and seal
with thin layer of parafin.

Top with a colorful square of fabric
and ribbon, raffia, or lace.

Use cut crystal goblet "orphans" recycled from antique stores or garage sales
for clear jellies. Be certain to sterilize
them in a hot water both before using.

BANANA JAM

A lovely pinky peach color makes this
a holiday gift favorite

SERVES: 10 medium jars
PREP TIME: 5 minutes
COOKING TIME: 20 minutes
MAY BE PREPARED AHEAD: 12 months

INGREDIENTS:

6 ripe bananas
4 oz. cherries, chopped
20 oz. crushed pineapple
7-1/2 cups sugar
1 bottle liquid pectin

PREPARATION:

Crush bananas in pot with masher or
whip. Add cherries, pineapple and sugar,
and mix well.

TO COOK:

Bring mixture to a full boil (hard) for
1 minute. Remove from heat. Stir in pectin,
and stir and skim for 3 to 5 minutes.

Fill sterilized jars and seal with parafin.

APPLE BUTTER

Serve with muffins, crumpets, scones,
and waffles.

SERVES: 1-1/4 cup
PREP TIME: Mise en place
COOKING TIME: 5 minutes
MAY BE PREPARED AHEAD: 1 month

INGREDIENTS:

2 cups unsweetened applesauce
1 tsp. cinnamon
1/8 tsp. ginger
1/3 cup brown sugar
1/4 tsp. allspice
1/8 tsp. cloves

PREPARATION: Mise en place

TO COOK:

Combine all ingredients in saucepan.
Bring to boil; reduce heat; cook 1/2 hour,
stirring constantly. (Flavor improves
"with age.)

Pour into sterilized gift jars, cover tightly,
and store in refrigerator.

*If preparing ahead, STOP. May be stored
in refrigerator for up to 1 month.*

GARLIC and ONION JAM

Serve with tournedos, roast pork, or roast beef.

SERVES: 8
PREP TIME: Mise en place
COOKING TIME: 1 hour
MAY BE PREPARED AHEAD: 1 week

INGREDIENTS:

2 large Spanish onions, coarsley chopped
6 large garlic cloves, coarsely chopped
1/4 cup extra-virgin oil
1 tsp. fresh lemon juice
1 tsp. salt or to taste
1/2 tsp. freshly ground pepper

PREPARATION: Mise en place

TO COOK:

In a heavy medium saucepan, combine the onions, garlic and olive oil. Cover and cook over very low heat, stirring occasionally, until the onions are very soft, golden brown and slightly carmelized, about 1 hour.

Transfer the onion mixture to a food processor or blender and puree. Stir in the lemon juice, salt and pepper. Scrape the jam into a small glass container and let cool completely.

If preparing ahead, STOP. Cover and refrigerate for up to 1 week.

CRANBERRY ORANGE RELISH

SERVES: 4 cups
PREP TIME: 5 minutes
COOKING TIME: 30 minutes
MAY BE PREPARED AHEAD: 1 week

INGREDIENTS:

1 lb. fresh cranberries
2 cups brown sugar
1 cup walnut pieces, chopped
1 cup orange marmalade

PREPARATION:

Preheat oven to 300 degrees. Mix cranberries and sugar in a tightly covered baking pan.

TO COOK:

Bake 30 minutes, stirring every 10 minutes to dissolve sugar. Allow to cool, and then add nuts and marmalade. Mix well.

If preparing ahead, STOP. Store in tightly covered container and refrigerate.

PEAR and RED PEPPER CHUTNEY

Serve with rosemary pork medallions, grilled ahi, or roast pork.

SERVES: 6
PREP TIME: 5 minutes
COOKING TIME: 5-6 minutes
MAY BE PREPARED AHEAD: 48 hours

INGREDIENTS:

1 medium red pepper, chopped
1 medium onion, chopped
2 medium pears, peeled,
    cored, and chopped
1/2 cup sugar
1 tbsp. fresh ginger, grated
2 tbsp. raspberry vinegar
1/8 tsp. ground cloves

PREPARATION:

Combine the red pepper, onion, pears, sugar, ginger, raspberry vinegar, and cloves in a microwave safe bowl.

TO COOK:

Cover loosely with plastic wrap and microwave on high for 5 to 6 minutes. Remove from the microwave, stir and cool slightly. Served warm or chilled.

POULTRY SEASONING

SERVES: 3/4 cup - three spice jars
PREP TIME: 5 minutes
COOKING TIME: None
MAY BE PREPARED AHEAD: 6 months

INGREDIENTS:

1 tbsp. paprika
1 tbsp. dried sage
1 tbsp. thyme
3 tbsp. dried marjoram
3 tbsp. dried rosemary
3 tbsp. dried basil
4 tbsp. dried tarragon

PREPARATION:

Use an electric coffee grinder to finely grind herbs.

Place in airtight jars, decorate with raffia bow, and attach a recipe card for roast game hen or turkey.

SUN-DRIED TOMATOES in OIL

The intense flavor of sun dried tomatoes perks many dishes. Make your own with the last of the season's crop. While you can dry fruit in the sun, you will have more product control and avoid mildew and spoilage if you use a home dehydrator or dry in the oven on a foil lined baking sheet at 200 degrees for approximately 5 - 7 hours.

Leave door ajar for moisture to escape. Halve tomatoes and lightly salt cut side. Tomatoes are done when they are dry and shriveled but not crisp.

SERVES: 4 pints
PREP TIME: 5-7 hours
COOKING TIME: None
MAY BE PREPARED AHEAD: 3 months

INGREDIENTS:

8 lbs. plum or romano tomatoes, halved
salt to taste
4 sprigs fresh basil
olive oil to cover

Optional Additions
4 cloves garlic
4 pico de pájaro peppers

PREPARATION:

After cooling, pack tomatoes in sterilized jars. Add salt and 1 sprig basil to each jar.

If desired, add 1 clove garlic or 1 hot pepper to each jar. Cover with oil, seal, and store in refrigerator.

SHERRIED WALNUTS

SERVES: 4 cups
PREP TIME: 30 minutes
COOKING TIME: None
MAY BE PREPARED AHEAD: 1 month

INGREDIENTS

1-1/2 cups sugar
1/2 cup cream sherry
1 tsp. light corn syrup
pinch of salt
1-1/2 tsp. grated lemon rind
2-1/2 cups walnuts

PREPARATION:

Combine the sugar, sherry, corn syrup, salt and lemon rind in a small saucepan. Bring to 238 degrees on a candy thermometer.

Remove from heat and add the nuts, stirring until the mixture turns creamy. Turn out onto an oiled cookie sheet, and break up with a fork.

NOTE: If you want to make more, repeat the process. Do not double the recipe.

These nuts should be made
a month before they're given.
They will keep for another
month after that.

ROSEMARY WALNUTS

SERVES: 4 cups
PREP TIME: 5 minutes
COOKING TIME: 15 minutes
MAY BE PREPARED AHEAD: 3 days

INGREDIENTS:

6 tbsp. butter
1 tbsp. salt
1/2 tsp. cayenne pepper
1 tbsp. dried rosemary, crumbled*
4 cups walnut halves

*Use mortar and pestle

PREPARATION:

Melt butter in large skillet. Mix in salt, cayenne and rosemary. Remove from heat.

Toss walnuts in butter mixture.

TO COOK:

Put in one layer on cookie sheet, and bake at 350 degrees for 10-15 minutes, shaking pan every 5 minutes.

If preparing ahead, STOP. Store in an airtight container for up to 3 days. Rewarm before serving.

HERBED HAZELNUTS

Serve over a salad or with grilled chicken.

SERVES: 3/4 cup
PREP TIME: Mise en place
COOKING TIME: 5 minutes
MAY BE PREPARED AHEAD: 1 week

INGREDIENTS:

2 tbsp. butter
1 tsp. fresh oregano, minced
1/4 tsp. ground cumin
salt and freshly ground pepper to taste
3/4 cup hazelnuts, coarsely chopped
1/4 tsp. fresh thyme, minced
1/8 tsp. cayenne pepper

PREPARATION: Mise en place

TO COOK:

Melt butter in heavy medium skillet over medium heat. Add remaining ingredients and stir until hazelnuts are lightly toasted, about 5 minutes.

If preparing ahead, STOP. Store in a tightly covered jar for up to 1 week.

SPICED PECANS

SERVES: 4 cups
PREP TIME: Mise en place
COOKING TIME: 25 minutes
MAY BE PREPARED AHEAD: 1 week

INGREDIENTS:

1/2 cup butter
4 cups pecan halves
1-1/2 cup confectioners sugar
1 tbsp. ground cloves
1 tbsp. cinnamon
1 tbsp. nutmeg

PREPARATION: Mise en place

TO COOK:

Melt butter in a large skillet. Saute pecan halves over low heat for 20 minutes, stirring constantly. Drain on towel.

Mix sugar and spices in paper bag. Add warm nuts. Shake thoroughly to coat well and allow to dry on paper towel. Store in airtight container.

If preparing ahead, STOP. Pecans will keep for one week in airtight container.

POMANDER BUG REPELLENT

MAKES: 6 pomanders
This gift item is not edible.
PREP TIME: 2 weeks drying time +
    20 minutes per apple or lime
COOKING TIME: None
MAY BE PREPARED AHEAD: 1 year

INGREDIENTS:

6 lady apples or Mexican limes
1 cup whole cloves
2 lengths ribbon, 12 - 15 inches each

PREPARATION:

Cover apples or limes with cloves. Allow to dry for 2 weeks. I often add these pomanders to holiday potpourri while they are curing.

When dry, tie a 12 - 15 inch ribbon around apple or lime, and form large loop for hanger. Tie a 12 - 15 inch ribbon crossways, ending in a bow on top.

Place over hangers or on hooks in closet.

MOTH REPELLENT SACHET

MAKES: 10 bags
This gift item is not edible.
PREP TIME: 5 minutes
COOKING TIME: None
MAY BE PREPARED AHEAD: 1 year

INGREDIENTS:

1 cup dried rosemary
1 cup dried vetiver
1 cup dried pennyroyal
5 whole bruised bay leaves
1/4 cup whole cloves

PREPARATION:

Mix together all ingredients.

Place in small sachet bags and tie with a pretty ribbon. (See page 138 for instructions on making sachet bags.)

Experiment with your own scents!
Other natural repellants include: camphor, wormwood, eucalyptus, and cedar shavings.

To discourage bugs entering a house, dip a feather in turpentine and trace window door openings.

AUTUMN HARVEST CALENDAR

SOUTHERN CALIFORNIA[1]

FRUITS AND VEGETABLES
apples, artichokes, Asian pears, avocados, broccoli, cabbage, cantalope, carrots, cauliflower, celery, corn, cucumbers, fennel, figs, grapefruit, grapes, green onions, honeydew melons, kiwis, lettuce and greens, melons, mushrooms, onions, peaches, pears, peppers, persimmons, potatoes, pumpkins, raspberries, spinach, strawberries, sweet corn, sweet potatoes, tomatoes, Valencia oranges, zucchini

OTHER PRODUCTS
beans, dried fruits and nuts, eggs, farm fresh scallops, honey, lobster, macadamia nuts

NEW MEXICO[2]

FRUITS AND VEGETABLES
apples, cabbage, chiles, lettuce, onions, potatoes

OTHER PRODUCTS
peanuts, pecans

ARIZONA[3]

FRUITS AND VEGETABLES
acorn squash, apples, bell peppers, black-eyed peas, butternut squash, cantalope, cassava melon, chile peppers, cucumbers, golden delicious apples, granny smith apples, green beans, green onions, honeydew melon, hubbard squash, lettuce, melons, okra, peaches, pears, pumpkins, red delicious apples, sweet corn, tomatoes, watermelon, white (tamale) corn, yellow squash, zucchini

OTHER PRODUCTS
honey, pecans, pistachios

[1] From the Cooperative Extension Service, University of San Diego, the Produce Marketing Association's Produce Availability andMerchandising Guide, and Western Growers Association's 1992 Export Directory.

[2] From the Cooperative Extension Service, New Mexico State University and the Produce Marketing Association's 1992Produce Availability and Merchandising Guide.

[3] From the Cooperative Extension Service, University of Ariziona, the Produce Marketing Associations's Produce Availability and Merchandising Guide, and Western Growers Association's 1992 Export Directory.

Winter

"...Winter is bluff and hearty and jolly
with his crown of icicles wreathed with holly."

Stater

inter's cold sends us inside to family celebrations, leisurely brunches, and cozy fireside suppers.

Gather armloads of evergreens — holly, ivy, juniper, and pine. Place boughs of evergreen on the mantle with clusters of holly berries, pyracantha, pepper tree berries or pinecones. Entwine ivy around candelabras.

Fireside Dining

ool, crisp weather invites fireside suppers. Winter foods are traditionally hearty and satisfying. If you prefer a lighter menu, select one of the salads and lighter pasta dishes. I usually serve four course menus, but three course meals work equally well. Select different flavors and textures — be certain that your first course isn't so highly seasoned that it overwhelms the courses that follow. Everything should be easy to eat. Pick self-contained courses that don't require a lot of sauces or cutting. Avoid anything that rolls, runs, or is hard to catch and cut. My favorite entrees for the fireside come from my "one dish" recipes — pastas, stews, chilies, or cassoulets. Consider finger foods for your appetizer course. Don't use liners or chargers for any courses. Soups go in handled mugs. Desserts go in goblets, ramekins, or are finger food.

Any of the "One Dish Meal" Menus are perfect for fireside suppers. Select soups that are cream based since they are easier to transport and handle, and they hold their heat longer than broth based soups.

Serving a Fireside Supper

et up a "service stand" in an unobtrusive but nearby place. You can use counter space, card table, or cabinet top. For a group of two to eight, you will probably be serving guests yourself.

Keep serving pieces simple and lighthearted. Trays of any kind work well for transporting food courses. I prefer large, substantial basket trays because they are warmer textured and promote the casual ambiance. Load trays by course in advance in the kitchen so that all you have to do is pick them up as the course arrives, spending as little time away from your guests as possible. Pick trays that have a decorator appeal; the easiest approach is to serve the course item and leave the tray on the hearth to blend with the decor. Use the same trays later to clear. Use handled baskets for any bread of muffins; guests can pass them with ease, and they look good sitting on the floor or on the hearth.

Service Stand Supplies

May Include:

- *Extra Plates*
- *Extra Silver*
- *Extra Napkins*
- *Coffee Mugs*
- *White Wine in Cooler*
- *Red Wine in Server*
- *Pitchers of Beverages or Water*
- *Condiments*
  (sugar, cream, onions, jam, etc.)
- *Finales*

Select your seating as host with an easy access to and from the kitchen.

For lap service, purchase 12 x 18-inch rattan trays. For appetizer or salads, use 9-inch plates that have a slight lip or raised rim. For soups, consider using German beef steins, pewter tankards, glass mugs or pottery goblets. For entrees, use large pasta bowls or shallow bowls that have at least a 1-inch raised rim.

Supply giant sized napkins, at least 20 inches square. If you are serving anything that requires fingers, have a supply of cocktail napkins on hand as well. If the place setting is not on a table to begin with, I always wrap all silver service items, and occasionally a surprise favor, in a napkin. Secure it with a napkin ring, ribbon bow, or raffia, and then place these packets in a basket that can be easily distributed.

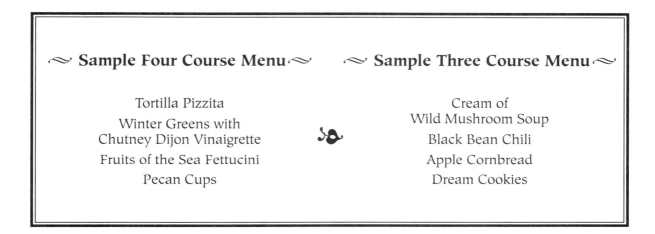

ᔈ Sample Four Course Menu ᔈ

Tortilla Pizzita

Winter Greens with
Chutney Dijon Vinaigrette

Fruits of the Sea Fettucini

Pecan Cups

ᔈ Sample Three Course Menu ᔈ

Cream of
Wild Mushroom Soup

Black Bean Chili

Apple Cornbread

Dream Cookies

The Inviting Setting

Be aware of the light level; enough to see what you are eating, but not enough to diminish the flickering magic of your fire. Play classical or easy listening background music. Make sure you have mastered firemaking. Have fire supplies for the entire evening on hand so that your primary source of atmosphere does not disappear midway through the evening.

Remember guest comfort.

- *Use two 36-inch tables with four chairs each in front of the fire.*

- *Set a large coffee table with place settings and floor cushions. It is always a good idea to test the coffee table and floor cushion layout by using it yourself for an hour of reading or menu planning. If your body parts aren't numb by the end of the hour, your guests should be fine in that setting.*

- *Present individual courses, one by one, using a coffee table or service point for food with seating on couches and comfortable chairs. Guests then dine holding the course in hand or on laps.*

Holiday Magic

The magic of the holiday season offers many opportunities for gathering family and friends together to celebrate. In this section, you will find festive drinks, hors d'oeuvres party ideas, brunches, and some special theme feasts to makes your holidays especially joyous.

Festive Drinks

Keep festive mugs and goblets available for holiday drinks. If you are investing in just one set of mugs or goblets, I recommend clear glass mugs, and pewter goblets for maximum flexibility, since you may wish to use these vessels for first course soups during Fireside Suppers. Decorate these containers with silk ribbon bows, or metallic ribbon streamers. Use cinnamon stick or rock candy swizzle sticks, for added fun.

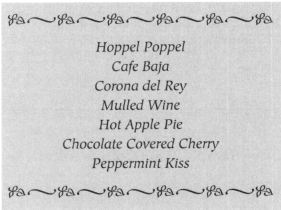

Hoppel Poppel
Cafe Baja
Corona del Rey
Mulled Wine
Hot Apple Pie
Chocolate Covered Cherry
Peppermint Kiss

Bacon Ginger Canapes with Jalapeño Jelly

Spiced Crab on Jicama Rounds

*Meatballs with Cinnamon and Mint
in Ginger Sauce*

*Quesadillas with Piñons and
Sun Dried Tomatoes*

*Sherried Mushrooms
and Garlic Stuffed Mushrooms*

*Chicken Drummettes
with Jalapeño Mustard Glaze*

Scallops Wrapped in Bacon

Hors D'oeuvres

If you are planning a cocktail hour hors d'oeuvre buffet, plan 10 - 12 pieces per person. Include items that take to time to consume like fresh vegetables, a cheese and cracker assortment, and liver patés or salmon mousse, in addition to a balanced assortment of hot and cold canapes that quickly disappear.

During my twenty years of party planning, I discovered that two old favorites "meatballs and drummettes" were continuously requested. I've included unusual versions of these perennial favorites, as well as other personal selections.

Special Holiday Traditions

The holidays are a time for traditions. Celebrate the special customs of your individual heritage. Our family is third generation Californians, descendants from English and French settlers who came to the Southwest as landowners and ranchers. My husband is a Mexican national, and perhaps the true Californian, since California belonged to Spain until 1821, and then to Mexico until 1848. Generations as recent as my great grandparents' lived in California or the Southwest Territories before they became a part of the United States. Their customs and celebrations were tied most closely to their mother countries. For this reason, our family recognizes either our French, Mexican or English heritage by celebrating the holidays with the foods and traditions of one of these countries.

A Toast to Merry Old England

My English forbearers celebrated Christmas Day with an early church service, gift filled stockings, breakfast, and finally the opening of presents. The afternoons were spent sharing traditional English folk carols, followed by dinner which always began with a hot soup, included poultry as the main course and sherry trifle as dessert. Later, paper crackers were popped, and we amused ourselves with hats, fortunes and charms. I have included "Tiddy Dol's Holiday Feast" as a salute to our English heritage.

Tiddy Dol's Holiday Feast

The Legend of Tiddy Dol

English Engraver William Hogarth immortalized an eccentric itinerant gingerbread tradesman in the 17th century with the nickname of Tiddy Dol. "In his person he was tall, well made and his features handsome. He affected to dress like a person of rank; white gold lace suit of clothes, lace ruffled shirt, laced hat and feather, and white silk stockings. The "King of Itinerant Tradesmen" sold his gingerbread by singing out praises of his wares ever finishing his address by singing this chorus end of some popular ballad:

> *"Tid-dy ti, tid-dy ti-ti*
> *Tid-dy ti-dy, dol."*

Hence the nickname of Tiddy Dol. For many years allusions were made to his name by saying: "You are so fine (to a person dressed out of character) you look like Tiddy Dol; you are as tawdry as Tiddy Dol; you are quite Tiddy Dol."

So a favorite holiday tradition in our family is to remember Tiddy Dol by enjoying a traditional 16th century English repast, including gingerbread for dessert, and by dressing "quite Tiddy Dol".

∼ Menu ∼

Elizabethan Mulled Cider

Emerald Soup

Fysshe Pie (Scallops Santiago)

Honeyed Hens

Cauliflower Souffle

Apple and New Potato Cassoulet

Currant Drop Scones

English Trifle

Gingerbread

Christmas Wish Pie

Revellion de Noel

My French great-grandparents traveled from the Bordeaux region to French Quebec and then in 1860, to the Utah territory, bringing with them "Reveillon de Noel", a midnight supper held after midnight mass on Christmas Eve. One or two special presents were opened, and the balance waited until New Year's Day. There were many rules for the foods of Reveillon. Toasts of champagne or a potent liqueur punch opened the celebration. The menu included paté, oysters, partridge pie, roast pork, and thirteen different sweets, recognizing the days between Christmas and January 6, Epiphany, which commemorates the magis' arrival in Bethlehem. I always include a variety of fresh fruits, cookies and sugared nuts in the "thirteen different sweets". This custom is wonderful for utilizing all the remaining holiday sweets from other dinner parties or holiday gift baskets.

This is an excellent meal to serve Buffet Style, but can be served family style at the table as well. Arrange the "thirteen sweets" in a festive display on a sideboard, and let guests serve themselves for dessert.

La Nochebuena Menu

Spanish traditions were brought to Mexico and the American Southwest by early settlers, and richly mixed with the local Indian traditions and foods. A special feast is prepared for La Nochebuena, the Good Night, and enjoyed after mass on December 24th. Gifts are brought by the wisemen, and are opened on The Day of the Kings, January 6th. The mood is one of family warmth and celebration. Traditional foods include turkey and dishes made with ground corn.

Wild turkey, corn, sage, beans, tomatoes, dates, olives and citrus fruits were available and used in abundance. Here is an updated version of "La Nochebuena" using the indigenous ingredients available to the early Southwestern Dons.

∼ Le Reveillon Menu ∼

Champagne
Fresh Oysters
Favorite Chicken Liver Paté
Sherried Mushrooms
Salad of Winter Fruits
Partridge Pie
Roast Pork with Prunes
and Baked Apples
Roasted Potatoes
Carrots with Port
Oranges, Tangerines, Pears, Apples
Sugared Walnuts   Butter Cookies
Macaroons   Walnut Wafers
Cream Puffs   Chocolate Eclairs
Hazelnut Coffee
Lemon Liqueur

∼ La Nochebuena Menu ∼

Dry Sherry
Relish Tray of Black and Green Olives,
Spiced Pickles, Carrot Sticks
and Celery Sticks
Butternut Squash Soup with
Jalapeño Cilantro Salsa
Salad of Root Vegetables
Roasted Turkey with
Apples, Onions and Celery
Sweet Chili Sauce
Candied Yams
Corn Spoon Bread with Sage
Acorn Squash Rings with Ginger
Minted Dates
Bizcochos
Rum Cakes with Almond Cream

Winter

Brunches

A Word About Brunches

Brunches are a favorite entertainment venue. We utilize the garden whenever possible, even on sunny mornings in winter. Brunch offers a great alternative to cocktail receptions or dinner parties. They are informal and carefree. Guests seem to feel more at home and cheerful during the morning hours and are thus more easily entertained.

We usually offer welcoming drinks, hot or cold, as guests are arriving. Flavored coffees and champagne are popular standbys.

For large groups, brunch is served buffet style and guests find seats inside or out and continue their conversations while dining at their own pace. Set up two buffet areas, one for the main course and one for desserts.

For sit-down brunches of twelve or less, we usually serve family-style.

For small family meals, desserts are omitted. The brunch menus at the beginning of this chapter do not include desserts, but select an assortment of cookies or a rich trifle if the time of the event and occasion warrant. If the meal ends after twelve noon, I include one. When entertaining larger groups, I always include one or more desserts, and also include fruit dishes and salads to round out the buffet.

FRUIT IDEAS FOR THE FIRST COURSE

- *Fresh fruit compote utilizing fruit of any season with Créme Fraiche and demara sugar. (See Spring)*

- *Peel and slice fresh oranges; then top with chopped fresh mint and shredded coconut.*

- *Top grapefruit halves with demara sugar and then pop under the oven broiler for three minutes to crystalize the sugar. Garnish with mint or maraschino cherry.*

- *Quarter a fresh pineapple; core, and slice into bit-size piece left in the pineapple shell for a showy presentation. Sprinkle with fresh coconut.*

- *Slice fresh melon. Alternate five thin slices of honeydew and cantaloupe on each plate, and sprinkle with fresh lemon thyme.*

- *Peel and slice fresh papaya; sprinkle with the juice of Mexican limes, and garnish with a lime wheel.*

- *Bake apples stuffed with cinnamon, nuts, and brown sugar (see page 199) or prunes (see page 272).*

- *Slice fresh figs with a dollop of Créme Fraiche, or melted goat cheese.*

- *Prepare fresh grapefruit, orange, and cucumber compote with lime juice and a dash of chile colorado.*

CHILIQUILES

Serve with refried beans and salsa!

SERVES: 6
PREP TIME: Mise en place
COOKING TIME: 55 minutes
MAY BE PREPARED AHEAD: 48 hours

INGREDIENTS:

2 cups shredded chicken
1-1/2 cups Salsa de Chile Rojo (recipe follows)
1 cup green chile salsa
1/2 tsp. oregano
1 tsp. sweet basil
1/4 cup butter
4 tbsp. vegetable oil or bacon fat
8 tortillas, cut into eighths
4 eggs
16 oz. tomato sauce
1 onion, diced
1/2 cup grated parmesan or
monterey jack cheese

PREPARATION: Mise en place

TO COOK:

Put shredded chicken, 1 cup salsa de chile rojo, 1/2 cup green chile salsa, basil, oregano and butter into saucepan. Simmer gently for 30 minutes.

Heat vegetable oil in heavy saucepan. Fry tortillas in hot oil until crispy and golden brown.

Add eggs and mix well; cook until tortillas are coated and eggs are set.

Stir in remainder of green chile salsa and salsa de chile rojo, tomato sauce, and diced onions. Simmer for 10 minutes.

Add to chicken mixture and simmer for 10 minutes more.

If preparing ahead, STOP. Cover and refrigerate for up to 48 hours.

TO SERVE:

Reheat, mixing in 1/4 cup cheese.

Serve on platter garnished with 1/4 cup cheese.

SALSA de CHILI ROJO

SERVES: 12
PREP TIME: 10 minutes
COOKING TIME: 10 minutes
MAY BE PREPARED AHEAD: 2 days

INGREDIENTS:

4 medium tomatoes
3 tbsp. chile powder
1 medium onion, chopped
1 clove garlic, minced
1 tsp. salt
1/4 tsp. sugar
2 tbsp. vegetable oil

PREPARATION:

Put tomatoes in boiling water for 30 seconds and then plunge in cold water. Slip skins off.

Place tomatoes in blender and blend until nearly smooth. Add chile powder, onions, garlic, salt and sugar. Cover and blend until smooth.

TO COOK:

Put tomato sauce in saucepan and add oil. Cook for about 10 minutes.

EGGS - MEXICAN STYLE

SERVES: 6
PREP TIME: 5 minutes
COOKING TIME: 25 minutes
MAY BE PREPARED AHEAD: 4 hours

INGREDIENTS:

12 tbsp. salsa (see page 130)
6 eggs
6 tsp. milk
12 tbsp. cheddar cheese, shredded
6 tbsp. tortilla chips, crumbled

PREPARATION:

Lightly grease 6 custard cups, ramekins, or small baking dishes. Into each cup, measure 2 tbsp. salsa.

Break 1 egg into each container, then top each with 1 tsp. milk, 2 tbsp. shredded cheddar cheese, and 1 tbsp. crumbled tortilla chips.

If preparing ahead, STOP. Cover with plastic and refrigerate for up to 4 hours.

TO COOK:

Place cups or dishes on a baking sheet and bake in a preheated 325 degree oven for 25 minutes.

FIESTA STRATA

I include this volume recipe for large brunch parties. It is easy, satisfying and festive in appearance. For smaller portions, reduce by 1/3 or 1/2.

SERVES: 20-24
PREP TIME: 20 minutes
COOKING TIME: 40 minutes
MAY BE PREPARED AHEAD: 8 hours

INGREDIENTS:

1/2 cup chopped red pepper
1/2 cup chopped green pepper
1/2 cup chopped scallions
1/4 tsp. dried jalapeño
1/4 cup chopped cilantro
Butter as needed
20 slices day-old white bread
1-1/4 lb. thinly sliced ham
1-1/2 lb. grated cheddar cheese
1/4 lb. chopped ham
18 eggs
1 quart milk
1/4 tsp. nutmeg
1 quart half-and-half, or light cream
Salt and pepper to taste

PREPARATION:

Mix together red and green peppers, scallions, dried jalapeño, and cilantro.

In a buttered #100 hotel pan, layer bread, sliced ham, pepper/scallion mix, then grated cheese; top with chopped ham.

Whisk together the eggs, milk, nutmeg, and half-and-half. Season with salt and pepper.

Pour mixture over bread, and let stand briefly until bread absorbs custard.

If preparing ahead, STOP. Cover and refrigerate for up to 8 hours.

TO COOK:

Bake in preheated 350 degree oven until custard is set and well-browned, approximately 35-40 minutes. Serve warm; cut into squares.

SANTA FE QUICHE

SERVES: 6
PREP TIME: 10 minutes
COOKING TIME: 50-55 minutes
MAY BE PREPARED AHEAD: 12 hours

INGREDIENTS:

1 cup sliced scallions
1 cup sliced mushrooms
3 tbsp. olive oil
10 oz. whole baby corn
1/2 cup chicken or ham, optional
1-1/2 cups milk
1/3 stick butter
3 eggs
3/4 cup biscuit mix
1/2 tsp. cajun spice
1/2 cup grated cheddar
1/2 cup grated jack cheese

PREPARATION:

Saute scallions and mushrooms in olive oil until soft.

Arrange baby corn on bottom of 9x14-inch buttered casserole. Spread cooked scallions and mushrooms evenly over corn. If using meat, add now.

Mix milk, butter, eggs, biscuit mix and spice in blender; pour over vegetables. Sprinkle shredded cheeses over top.

TO COOK:

Bake at 350 degrees for 50 to 55 minutes.

If preparing ahead, STOP. Allow to cool, cover and refrigerate. Reheat for 15 to 20 minutes at 325 degrees.

SWEET ONION PIE

SERVES: 6
PREP TIME: 4 - 10 minutes
COOKING TIME: 45 minutes - 1 hour
MAY BE PREPARED AHEAD:
    Not recommended

INGREDIENTS:

3-4 medium sweet onions, chopped
1/4 cup butter or margarine
1 cup light cream or whole milk
1 cup shredded Swiss or cheddar cheese
pepper to taste
2 eggs, beaten
1 unbaked pie crust

PREPARATION:

Saute chopped onion in butter until soft,
approximately 7 minutes. Add cream, cheese
and pepper. Mix well. Add eggs, mixing well.

TO COOK:

Pour into uncooked pie crust and bake
at 350 degrees for 45 minutes to 1 hour
or until firm.

AJOQUESO (MEXICAN RAREBIT)

SERVES: 6
PREP TIME: Mise en place
COOKING TIME: 30 minutes
MAY BE PREPARED AHEAD: 8 hours

INGREDIENTS:

3 sweet red peppers
1 large onion, finely chopped
1 clove garlic, minced
1/4 cup olive oil
1-1/2 cups grated sharp cheddar cheese
Salt and pepper to taste
Dash of hot pepper sauce
1 tbsp butter
2 tsp. flour
1 cup heavy cream
Fried tortillas or toasted English muffins

PREPARATION: Mise en place

TO COOK:

Roast the peppers over a flame; peel
and remove the seeds.

Fry onions and garlic in the oil until
soft, approximately 10 minutes.

Puree peppers, onion, garlic, and oil in a
blender; return to a saucepan and heat
with the cheese. Season to taste with salt,
pepper, and hot pepper sauce.

Blend butter with flour, add little by little
to simmering sauce, and stir until smooth;
add cream and stir until very hot.

*If preparing ahead, STOP. Cover and
refrigerate. Reheat before serving.*

TO SERVE:

Pour over tortillas or toasted muffins.
Garnish with fresh cilantro or sliced olives.

APRICOTS BENEDICT

SERVES: 6
PREP TIME: Mise en place
COOKING TIME: Sauce - 25 minutes;
Eggs/Muffins/Ham - 15 minutes
MAY BE PREPARED AHEAD:
     Sauce - 24 hours

INGREDIENTS:

6 english muffins
12 Canadian ham slices
2 tbsp. butter
6 eggs
18 apricot halves, canned, drained,
     syrup reserved

Apricot Sauce
syrup from apricot halves
1/3 cup light brown sugar, firmly packed
pinch of salt
1/8 tsp. ground nutmeg
1/2 tsp. grated lemon peel
1/4 cup butter

PREPARATION: Mise en place

TO COOK:

Toast English muffins.

Heat Canadian ham slices in microwave
for 3 minutes.

Scramble eggs in butter.

Apricot Sauce
Pour syrup in large saucepan.
Add sugar, salt, nutmeg and lemon peel.

Heat to boiling, stirring frequently.

Lower heat and simmer, stirring until
thickened. Remove from heat.

Add butter and stir until melted. Set aside.

*If preparing sauce ahead, STOP. Cover
and refrigerate. Reheat before serving.*

TO SERVE:

Top English muffins with Canadian
ham slices.

Place 3 apricot halves, skin side up,
in triangle pattern.

Top with scrambled eggs.

Spoon apricot sauce over top.

ORANGE BLOSSOM FRENCH TOAST

What we call "French Toast", the French call Pain Perdu, or lost bread. This recipe was intended to use day old bread that would otherwise be discarded. It is actually better with day old bakery bread that does not have preservatives added, because this bread absorbs the egg better and does not become soggy.

SERVES: 6 (12 slices)
PREP TIME: 10 minutes
COOKING TIME: 10 minutes
MAY BE PREPARED AHEAD: 4 hours

INGREDIENTS:

1 tsp. ground cinnamon
1/2 tsp. ground nutmeg
1 loaf buttermilk bread (ideally
    purchased unsliced from the bakery)
6 eggs
1/4 cup buttermilk
1 tsp. vanilla
1 tbsp. orange flower water
6 tbsp. butter melted
powdered sugar, if desired
6 orange slices and
    six sprigs of mint for garnish

PREPARATION:

Preheat a large griddle to medium high. Mix together cinnamon and nutmeg in a small bowl.

Slice bread in 1/2-inch slices. (Using unsliced bread, allows a thicker slice.)

Whisk together eggs, buttermilk, vanilla, and orange flower water.

If preparing ahead, STOP. Cover egg mixture and store in refrigerator for up to 4 hours.

TO COOK:

Brush griddle with melted butter.

Dip slices of bread in egg batter and place on griddle. Sprinkle with spice mixture.

Turn bread when medium brown shade is reached (about 5 minutes)

Grill on other side. Brush griddle with melted butter as needed so toast does not stick.

TO SERVE:

Dust with powdered sugar, if desired.

Garnish with an orange slice that has a mint spring inserted in center.

Serve with maple syrup, or fruit preserves, and additional melted butter.

MOM'S PANCAKES

These are the lightest you'll ever taste! Mom insists these are "low calorie," but don't bet on it.

SERVES: 4
PREP TIME: 10 minutes
COOKING TIME: 5 minutes
MAY BE PREPARED AHEAD:
    Not recommended

INGREDIENTS:

3 eggs, separated
1/2 tsp. baking soda
2 cups buttermilk
1 cup flour
1/2 tsp. salt
1 tsp. baking powder

PREPARATION:

Mix egg yolks with soda, and stir in buttermilk. Allow mixture to stand while whipping egg whites.

Whip egg whites until fluffy.

Sift together flour, salt and baking powder, and add to buttermilk mixture. Mix well by hand; do not over beat.

Fold in egg whites.

TO COOK:

Drop by spoonful onto greased griddle.

Flip pancakes when brown and bubbles in batter have popped.

TO SERVE:

Serve with Honey Butter (see page 95), Orange Mint Syrup (see page 287) or Banana Jam (see page 206).

SWEET POTATO WAFFLES

SERVES: 16 waffles
PREP TIME: 5 minutes
COOKING TIME: 5 minutes
    per waffle iron use
MAY BE PREPARED AHEAD:
    Not recommended

INGREDIENTS:

1/2 cup sweet butter
3 cups flour
6 tsp. baking powder
2 tsp. salt
1/2 tsp. nutmeg
1/4 tsp. ground cardamon
1/4 tsp. mace
1 tsp. cinnamon
6 eggs, separated
2 cups milk
2 cups mashed sweet potatoes
chopped pecans

PREPARATION:

Melt butter, cool.

Sift together flour, baking powder, salt, nutmeg, cardamon, mace, and cinnamon.

Beat egg yolks, and combine with milk, sweet potatoes and butter. Add to flour mixture.

Beat egg whites until they form soft peaks. Fold into sweet potato mixture.

TO COOK:

Cook on preheated waffle irons.

TO SERVE:

Top with chopped pecans.

Serve with real maple syrup.

STRAWBERRY DUTCH BABY PANCAKES

SERVES: 8
PREP TIME: 5 minutes
COOKING TIME: 15 minutes
MAY BE PREPARED AHEAD:
    Pancakes: NO;
    Strawberry topping: 8 hours

INGREDIENTS:

Pancakes
8 eggs
2 cups flour
2 cups milk
1/8 cup sugar
1 tbsp. vanilla extract
1/2 tsp. ground cinnamon
1/2 cup butter
1 cup sour cream

Strawberry Topping
1 tbsp. cornstarch
2 3/4 cups frozen sliced,
    sweetened strawberries, thawed
1/4 cup light corn syrup
1/8 cup butter

PREPARATION:

Pancakes
Beat eggs.

Whisk in flour and milk; mix smooth.

Whisk in sugar, vanilla and cinnamon;
mix well.

For individual servings: melt 1 tablespoon
butter in 6-inch skillet over medium heat;
pour in 4 ounces (1/2 cup) batter.

TO BAKE:

Bake at 425 degrees for 15 minutes,
until pancake is set and lightly browned.

Gently remove from pan and place on
serving plate. Pour 1/3 cup Strawberry
Topping in cavity.

Garnish with 2 tablespoons sour cream,
if desired.

Strawberry Topping
Blend cornstarch into strawberries
in saucepan.

Stir in corn syrup and butter and bring
mixture to a boil, stirring frequently.

Remove from heat and keep warm.

*If preparing ahead, STOP. Cover and
refrigerate. Reheat before serving.*

FRIED APPLES and ONIONS

Cooked apples and onions are a good side dish at brunch.

SERVES: 4-6
PREP TIME: Mise en place
COOKING TIME: 15 minutes
MAY BE PREPARED AHEAD: 2 hours

INGREDIENTS:

2 cups sliced sweet onions
2 tbsp. butter
2 cups sliced apples
1/2 cup water
1 tsp. salt
1/2 tsp. thyme

TO COOK:

Cook onions slowly in butter until tender, then add apples, water, salt and thyme. Cover and cook until apples are soft.

Remove cover and fry until all water is absorbed and apples and onions are lightly browned.

If preparing ahead, STOP. Place in shallow baking dish, sprinkle lightly with 1 tsp water, cover with foil and hold in warm oven for 2 hours.

BACON and SWEET ONIONS

The bacon and onions have a great taste affinity and are a good contrast to egg dishes.

SERVES: 6
PREP TIME: Mise en place
COOKING TIME: 20 minutes
MAY BE PREPARED AHEAD: 30 minutes

INGREDIENTS:

1 lb. bacon, sliced and cut in half
2 large sweet onions, sliced
1/2 cup fresh parsley, minced

TO COOK:

Cook bacon until just less than crisp; drain excess drippings and place in glass casserole. Keep warm in a 200 degree oven.

Drain excess grease from pan, leaving 4 tbsp. dripping. Add onion slices and saute until transparent (7-10 minutes). Add onions to casserole and mix well.

If preparing ahead, STOP. Keep warm in oven for up to 30 minutes. If excess drippings accumulate, drain off.

SAUSAGE BAKED APPLES

Use as a brunch side dish. This
is especially showy as a buffet item.

SERVES: 6
PREP TIME: 10 minutes
COOKING TIME: 30 minutes
MAY BE PREPARED AHEAD: 24 hours

INGREDIENTS:

6 oz. pork sausage
1/2 tsp. sage
9 tbsp. real maple syrup
6 apples, cored
6 fresh mint leaves as garnish

PREPARATION:

Mix sausage, sage and 3 tbsp. syrup together.

Stuff sausage mixture in center of each
apple and place on foil lined baking pan.

*If preparing ahead, STOP. Cover and
refrigerate for up to 24 hours.*

Drizzle 1 tbsp. maple syrup over each apple.

TO COOK:

Bake for 30 minutes at 350 degrees.

TO SERVE:

Serve warm. Garnish with fresh mint leaves.

BASIC MUFFIN RECIPE and VARIATIONS

SERVES: 12
PREP TIME: 5 minutes
COOKING TIME: 25 minutes
MAY BE PREPARED AHEAD: 4 hours

INGREDIENTS:

2 cups flour
3 tbsp. sugar
1 tbsp. baking powder
1/2 tsp. salt
1 egg
1/4 cup melted butter
1 cup milk

PREPARATION:

Preheat oven to 425 degrees and
grease muffin tins or use paper liners.

Sift together dry ingredients.

In a small bowl, beat egg with butter,
and stir in milk. Make a well in flour
mixture, and add milk mixture, stirring
just enough to moisten.

Halfway through the stirring, add any fruit.
Do not over stir. (Batter will look lumpy.)

TO COOK:

Fill tins two-thirds full and bake for
25 minutes or until well-browned.

*If preparing ahead, STOP. Cover with tea
towel to keep moisture in. Reheat briefly
and serve warm.*

VARIATIONS

Blueberry Muffins
Add 1 cup blueberries, washed and patted dry.

Strawberry Muffins
Add 1 cup strawberries, washed and quartered.

Pumpkin Muffins
Add 1 cup cooked pumpkin, 1/2 cup chopped walnuts, and 1/4 tsp. allspice.

Substitute 3 tbsp. brown sugar for white sugar.

Lemon Poppyseed Muffins
Add 2 tbsp. fresh lemon zest, 1/4 cup fresh lemon juice and 2 tbsp. poppyseeds.

Cranberry Walnut Muffins
Add 1 cup cooked cranberries and 1/2 cup walnuts.

Substitute 3 tbsp. honey for white sugar.

Banana Nut Muffins
Add 1 cup mashed ripe bananas and 1/2 tsp. grated nutmeg.

Substitute 3 tbsp. brown sugar for white sugar.

Oatmeal Raisin Muffins
Add 1 cup raisins and 1/2 tsp. cinnamon.

Substitute 3 tbsp. brown sugar for white sugar and 1/2 cup quick oats for 1/2 cup of the flour.

MAPLE SPOONBREAD with ORANGE BUTTER

SERVES: 12
PREP TIME: 20 minutes
COOKING TIME: 1 hour
MAY BE PREPARED AHEAD:
   No for Maple Spoonbread;
   24 hours for orange butter

INGREDIENTS:

3 cups cornmeal
8 oz. butter
9 cups milk
2 cups maple syrup
12 each large eggs, separated

Orange Butter
1 lb. butter
1/2 cup marmalade
3 tbsp. powdered sugar

PREPARATION:

Combine cornmeal, margarine or butter, and milk in saucepan and boil, stirring constantly, until mixture is thick. Remove from heat and stir in maple syrup and egg yolks. Beat until thoroughly combined.

Whip egg whites until stiff. Fold into cornmeal mixture.

Pour into two well greased springform pans for wedges) or one 12x20-inch pan for squares.

TO BAKE:

Bake at 325 degrees for 60 minutes or until toothpick inserted in the middle comes out clean and top is well browned.

Orange Butter
Whip or beat butter until fluffy. Add marmalade and confectioners sugar and combine thoroughly.

APPLE CORNBREAD

SERVES: 8
PREP TIME: 5 minutes
COOKING TIME: 25 minutes
MAY BE PREPARED AHEAD: 24 hours

INGREDIENTS:

3/4 cup corn meal
3/4 cup flour
3 tsp. baking powder
1/2 tsp. salt
2 tbsp. sugar
1 egg, beaten
3/4 cup sweet milk
2 tbsp. butter, melted
3/4 cup apples, diced

PREPARATION:

Sift corn meal and flour together.
Add baking powder, salt and sugar and
sift entire dry mixture together. Stir in
beaten egg and milk, mixing well.
Add apples and butter.

TO BAKE:

Pour batter into 9-inch square baking
dish or pan and bake in 400 degree oven
for 25 minutes.

APPLE-PUMPKIN CORNBREAD

SERVES: 6-8
PREP TIME: 5 minutes
COOKING TIME: 40 - 50 minutes
MAY BE PREPARED AHEAD: 3 days
    or 2 weeks frozen

INGREDIENTS:

1-1/2 cups flour
3 tsp. baking powder
1-1/2 tsp. salt
1/4 cup sugar
1-1/4 cups cornmeal
1 tsp. cinnamon
1/2 tsp. nutmeg
4 tbsp. butter
2 eggs, beaten
3/4 cup cooked pumpkin
2/3 cup milk
1 cup grated apples
1/2 cup chopped nuts

PREPARATION:

Combine flour, baking powder, salt, sugar,
cornmeal, cinnamon, and nutmeg.

In separate bowl beat together butter, eggs,
pumpkin, apple and milk. Stir in nuts.

TO BAKE:

Pour into square baking pan and bake
in 350 degree oven for 40 - 50 minutes.

*If preparing ahead, STOP. Store in airtight
container for up to three days. Bread may
also be frozen for up to two weeks.*

CHILI CHEESE CORNBREAD

SERVES: 6-8
PREP TIME: 5 minutes
COOKING TIME: 25-35 minutes
MAY BE PREPARED AHEAD: 4 hours

INGREDIENTS:

1 cup creamed corn
2 eggs, beaten
1/3 cup corn oil
3/4 cup milk
1 cup cornmeal
1/2 tsp. salt
1/2 tsp. baking soda
1 4-oz. can green chilies, seeded, diced
1-1/2 cups grated sharp cheddar cheese

PREPARATION:

Preheat oven to 350 degrees. Combine corn, eggs, oil, and milk, mixing well.

Mix together cornmeal, salt and soda. Add to corn mixture; mix until moistened — do not overmix. Fold in chilis and cheese.

TO BAKE:

Pour into rectangular greased baking pan or muffin tins, and bake at 350 degrees for 25-35 minutes, until tester comes out clean.

DILLED SCALLION SCONES

SERVES: 15 scones
PREP TIME: 15 minutes
COOKING TIME: 15 minutes
MAY BE PREPARED AHEAD: 24 hours

INGREDIENTS:

1-1/2 cups all-purpose flour
1/2 cup whole wheat flour
1/2 tsp. baking soda
2 tsp. baking powder
1/2 tsp. salt
1/2 cup sliced scallions
2 tbsp. chopped fresh dill weed
1/4 cup very cold unsalted butter
1/3 cup buttermilk
1 large egg

PREPARATION:

Preheat oven to 400 degrees and lightly butter a baking sheet.

In a large bowl, stir together the flours, baking powder, baking soda and salt. Stir in the scallion and dill. Grate butter over the flour mixture, then stir with fork to blend.

In a small bowl, stir together the buttermilk and egg; add to the flour mixture and knead together until combined.

With lightly floured hands, pat the dough to 1/2 inch thickness on a floured board and cut into rounds with a two-inch cutter.

TO COOK:

Place on the baking sheet and bake for 10 to 15 minutes, or until the scones have risen and are slightly brown.

Removing the baking sheet to a wire rack and cool for five minutes. Using a spatula, transfer the scones to the wire rack to cool.

If preparing ahead, STOP. Cool completely and store in an airtight container.

Reheat and serve warm with cream cheese.

CURRANT DROP SCONES

SERVES: 15
PREP TIME: 15 minutes
COOKING TIME: 15 minutes
MAY BE PREPARED AHEAD: 24 hours

INGREDIENTS:

1 cup fresh currants or
    3/4 cup dried currants,
    rehydrated in 1 cup boiling water
2 cups all purpose flour
2 tbsp. baking powder
1/2 tsp. baking soda
1/2 tsp. salt
1/2 tsp. cinnamon
1/4 tsp. allspice
2 tbsp. brown sugar
1/4 cup cold unsalted butter
1/3 cup buttermilk
1 large egg

PREPARATION:

Rehydrate currants if using dried.
Preheat oven to 400 degrees and lightly
butter a baking sheet.

In a large bowl, stir together flour, baking
powder, baking soda, salt, spices and sugar.
Grate butter over dry mixture and stir
with fork to blend.

In a small bowl, stir together currants,
buttermilk and egg; add to the flour mixture
and knead with hands until well combined.

TO COOK:

Drop by tablespoons onto cookie sheet
and bake 10-15 minutes. Remove to
wire rack and cool 5 minutes.

*If preparing ahead, STOP. Cool completely
and store in airtight container.*

Serve with whipped honey butter.

HEALTHY BREAD

SERVES: 12
PREP TIME: 5 minutes
COOKING TIME: 15 minutes
MAY BE PREPARED AHEAD: 8 hours

INGREDIENTS:

8 oz. margarine
6 oz. wholemeal wheat flour
3 tsp. baking powder
1/2 tsp. salt
water to mix
1 egg beaten

PREPARATION:

Preheat oven to 350 degrees. Grease
a Swiss roll or French roll pan, and line
with greased waxed paper.

Cream the margarine until fluffy. Mix
in the dry ingredients with enough water
to form a stiff dough. Spread in pan and
brush generously with beaten egg.

TO BAKE:

Bake for 15 minutes.

*If preparing ahead, STOP. Cover and
store in cool place for up to 8 hours.*

FOCACCIO with ROSEMARY and SUN-DRIED TOMATOES

SERVES: approximately 2 dozen pieces
PREP TIME: 90 minutes
COOKING TIME: 30 minutes
MAY BE PREPARED AHEAD: 8 hours

INGREDIENTS:

1 pkg. dry yeast
1-1/2 cup warm water
4 cups bread flour
2 tsp. salt
1/4 cup olive oil from sundried tomatoes
1/2 cup sun-dried tomatoes
3 tbsp. fresh rosemary, chopped

PREPARATION:

Preheat oven to 450 degrees.

Dissolve yeast in 1/4 cup warm water and let stand 10-15 minutes until bubbly.

Place flour and salt on floured bread board, stirring with fingers to mix. Make indentation in center, and add yeast mixture and olive oil.

Mix well and knead for 15 minutes until dough is soft and smooth. Add more flour if needed. Add sun-dried tomatoes and 1/2 the rosemary.

Shape into a ball, dust with flour and cover with damp towel. Allow dough to rise in warm draft free place until double in size (about 35 minutes).

Punch dough down and place on greased baking sheet. (If dough is too springy, let it rest 5 minutes.) Spread evenly over baking sheet. Cover with damp towel and let sit for 20 minutes more.

Sprinkle remaining rosemary over top and make rows of dimples in dough with finger.

TO BAKE:

Bake for 30-35 minutes. Cut in 2" x 4" strips and serve with Basil Garlic Oil (see page 285) to dip.

INDIAN FRY BREAD

SERVES: 12
PREP TIME: 45 minutes
COOKING TIME: 4 minutes each roll
MAY BE PREPARED AHEAD:
    Not recommended

INGREDIENTS:

2 cups buttermilk
1 large egg
3 tbsp. vegetable oil
1 tbsp. sugar
1 package active dry yeast
5 - 6 cups unsifted all purpose flour
1-1/4 tsp. salt
3/4 tsp. baking powder
1/4 tsp. baking soda
vegetable oil/shortening for deep frying

PREPARATION:

In small saucepan, heat buttermilk until
it bubbles around the edge of the pan.
Set aside to cool to 110 to 115 degrees.

Stir egg, oil, sugar and yeast into cooled
buttermilk until well combined. Set aside
for 5 minutes to allow the yeast to soften.

In large bowl, stir together 5 cups flour, salt,
baking powder and baking soda. Make well
in center of flour mixture and pour buttermilk mixture into well. Stir until soft dough
forms, adding more flour if needed.

On lightly floured surface, knead dough
8 to 10 times. Invert bowl over dough and
let rest 30 minutes or until double in size.

TO COOK:

In large heavy skillet, heat 1 inch oil until
deep fat thermometer registers 375 degrees.

Shape dough into 1-1/3 inch balls.
On lightly floured surface, roll or stretch
out balls to 3-1/2 inch rounds. Fry rounds
in batches, turning each once to brown
both sides - about 2 minutes each side.

Drain on paper towels and serve warm
with honey butter, if desired.

NAVAJO TACOS

Serve Indian Fry Bread topped with chili,
tomatoes, lettuce and cheese, and salsa,
sour cream and scallions as garnish.

Winter

Festive Drinks

*Warm drinks are a perfect welcoming refreshment
as guests arrive at winter gatherings.
They are also a nice finale to quiet fireside suppers.*

*Mulled wines and ciders date back to the middle ages
and this section includes some recipes from past centuries.
The spiced drinks seem especially appropriate for
the holidays. Their spicy aromas fill the entire house.
In seasonal winter gifts, there is a recipe for mulling spices.*

*Included are cold weather favorites
from the Cafe as well.*

HOPPEL POPPEL

This is a likely forefather of our Tom and Jerry or eggnog. It is a family recipe brought over from Holland to America by one of my great-great-great-great-great-great grandparents, the Brinkerhoffs, in the late 1700s.

SERVES: 6 - 8 drinks
PREP TIME: 10 minutes
COOKING TIME: None
MAY BE PREPARED AHEAD: 1 hour

INGREDIENTS:

4 egg yolks
7 tbsp. sugar
1 tsp. vanilla extract
1 quart hot milk
1 cup rum or cognac
fresh grated nutmeg for garnish

PREPARATION:

Beat egg yolks with sugar until frothy and pale yellow. Stir in vanilla and slowly hot milk, beating constantly.

If preparing ahead, STOP. May reheat before serving.

Mix with rum and pour into heated mugs or punch cups with nutmeg and serve.

MULLED WINE

A 15th century recipe.

SERVES: 12 drinks
PREP TIME: 5 minutes
COOKING TIME: 5 minutes
MAY BE PREPARED AHEAD: No

INGREDIENTS:

1/2 tsp. black peppercorns
1/2 tsp. cloves
2 sticks cinnamon
6 lemon peel twists
1/4 cup sugar
2 bottles red Burgundy wine
1 cup kirsch or cognac
12 cinnamon sticks for "swizzle"
    (optional)

PREPARATION:

Tie spices in cheesecloth.

TO COOK:

Simmer spices, lemon peel, sugar, and wine for 4 to 5 minutes to blend flavors.

Add kirsch or cognac, heat through, and remove spice packet.

Pour into heated mugs and garnish with cinnamon stick.

ELIZABETHAN MULLED CIDER

SERVES: 18 drinks
PREP TIME: 5 minutes
COOKING TIME: 15 minutes
MAY BE PREPARED AHEAD: 24 hours

INGREDIENTS:

12 cups apple cider
1-1/2 tsp. whole cloves
1-1/2 tsp. whole allspice
6 sticks cinnamon
1-1/2 cups brown sugar
1 bottle Calvados or applejack

PREPARATION:

Tie the spices in a cheesecloth.

TO COOK:

Put the cider in a large saucepan and add
the spices and brown sugar. Bring to a boil,
stirring gently to dissolve sugar.

Simmer for 10 minutes to blend flavors.

*If preparing ahead, STOP. Cover and
refrigerate. Reheat to serve.*

Add the Calvados and simmer for 1 minute.
Discard spices.

Serve in heated mugs

CAFE BAJA

SERVES: 1
PREP TIME: 2 minutes
COOKING TIME: None
MAY BE PREPARED AHEAD:
    4 hours - liqueur

INGREDIENTS:

1/2 oz. tequila
1/2 oz. Kahlua
1 cup brewed coffee
whipped cream garnish
shaved chocolate garnish

PREPARATION:

*If preparing ahead, add liqueur to cups;
then add coffee, whipped cream and garnish
as guests arrive.*

Add tequila and Kahlua to coffee. Top with
whipped cream and shaved chocolate

HOT APPLE PIE

A perennial cold month favorite
at the restaurant.

SERVES: 10
PREP TIME: Mise en place
COOKING TIME: 15 minutes
MAY BE PREPARED AHEAD:
    4 hours - liqueur

INGREDIENTS:

2 quarts cider
10 oz. Tuaca
4 sticks cinnamon
optional whipped cream garnish

PREPARATION:

In Volume
Heat cider with cinnamon sticks. Stir in
Tuaca, top with whipped cream, and serve.

One Cup
*If preparing ahead, add liqueur to cups; then
add cider and whipped cream as guests arrive.*

Pour up to 1 oz. Tuaca in mug and
fill with spiced cider.

CHOCOLATE COVERD CHERRY

SERVES: 1
PREP TIME: 2 minutes
COOKING TIME: None
MAY BE PREPARED AHEAD:
    4 hours - liqueur

INGREDIENTS:

1 cup hot chocolate
1 oz. cherry brandy
whipped cream garnish
cherry garnish

PREPARATION:

*If preparing ahead, add liqueur to cups;
then add chocolate, whipped cream
and cherry garnish as guests arrive.*

Add cherry brandy to hot chocolate.

Top with whipped cream and cherry garnish.

HOT BUTTERED RUM

SERVES: 1
PREP TIME: 2 minutes
COOKING TIME: None
MAY BE PREPARED AHEAD:
    8 hours - clove studded lemon wheel

INGREDIENTS:

3/4 cup hot water
1 tsp. brown sugar
1/2 oz. rum
1 tsp. butter
dash ground cinnamon
dash ground nutmeg
1 lemon wheel studded with cloves

PREPARATION:

Dissolve brown sugar in hot water. Add rum.

Add butter and lemon wheel. Stir to dissolve.

Garnish with cinnamon and nutmeg.

PEPPERMINT KISS

SERVES: 1
PREP TIME: 2 minutes
COOKING TIME: None
MAY BE PREPARED AHEAD:
    4 hours - liqueur

INGREDIENTS:

1 cup hot chocolate
1 oz. peppermint schnapps
whipped cream garnish
cinnamon garnish

PREPARATION:

*If preparing ahead, add liqueur to cups;
then add hot chocolate, whipped cream
and cinnamon garnish as guests arrive.*

Add peppermint schnapps to hot chocolate.

Garnish with whipped cream and cinnamon

CORONA DEL REY

This is a cold drink that serves as a nice
finish to a heavy meal. It is served as a
finale in some Baja California restaurants.

SERVES: 4
PREP TIME: 2 minutes
COOKING TIME: None
MAY BE PREPARED AHEAD:
    Not recommended

INGREDIENTS:

1/2 cup vanilla ice cream
1 oz. cream de cacao
1/2 cup cream de noyaux (almond)
ground cinnamon garnish

PREPARATION:

Blend ice cream, cream de cacao and
cream de noyaux until frothy.

Serve in champagne glasses and garnish
with a dash of ground cinnamon.

Winter

Hors D'Oeuvres

A Word About Hors D'Oeuvres

Hors d'oeuvres or tapas are often served as a prelude to dinner, and as such should pique an appetite and not ruin it. Often, the simplest hors d'oeuvres are the best approach. Select salty or crunchy tastes. Avoid any item that is too heavy or too plentiful.

- *Use a selection of fresh baby vegetables with a fresh Dill Dip (see page 42).*
- *Wrap asparagus in the thinnest possible slice of procuitto ham and secure with a decorative pick.*
- *Offer herbed green or black olives.*
- *Pipe cream cheese in a decorative rosette on a cracker and top with jalapeño jelly or chutney.*

When planning a sit-down dinner, you may serve your appetizer course during the cocktail hour. For example, offer a paté or salmon mousse as your first of four courses. Be certain to coordinate this carefully with the balance of your menu. Think of it as part of your meal.

HORS D'OEUVRES RECEPTIONS

Your approach will change when you are entertaining with hors d'oeuvres as your main food course. As mentioned earlier, plan on an average of 12 tastes per person and offer a wide variety of taste, textures and colors. Select from vegetable, carbohydrate, or protein based snacks. Some like to offer fruit kabobs or chunks also; however, for me fruit belongs on the dessert table. Consider the different tastes and texture choices available. Select salty, sour/sweet, smooth, rich, creamy, crunchy, spicy, and bland combinations. In this instance, variety truly is the "spice of life".

Visual Presentation for Hors D'Oeuvres Receptions

Present dishes at different heights. You may use different size serving containers to achieve this effect. One of the simplest ways to introduce height is to place a sturdy box, 12" to 18" in height in the center of your table and cover with your tablecloth or a contrasting drape. The top surface size can vary from square for a centerpiece to a long runner type platform to present many dishes.

Pull the table "together" by scattering rose petals, flowers, or bright colored metallic ribbon curls over the tabletop among the plates.

Conform to a theme in selecting your containers. Is it a Southwestern Buffet? Use colorful Mexican dishes, clay pottery, baskets, large sombreros with chip or cracker filled brims. Is it a country theme? Use copper or iron containers, stoneware, and baskets. Is it fancy? Use crystal and silver.

Because you are presenting many different plates, avoid clutter by visualizing the table as a whole. Use showy centerpieces or a "trail" theme to provide cohesion amid the profusion of dishes. For example, create a "Winter Wonderland". View the entire table as a winter town. Use a white cloth, bunched among the dishes to create a snowy effect. Place a mirrored runner in the center of storybook houses or skating figures. Use clear glass, crystal or silver containers. Scatter metallic silver and iridescent white ribbon curls over the cloth. Create a "trail" to unify the presentation using the snow figures or houses.

Design a "Magic Woodland" by using shades of green or brown linen. Create a forest pool, and feature small fresh plants like ferns or violets packed in moss. Let woodland creatures like bunnies or squirrels wander among the plates. Special rocks or branches with moss may be used. Hollow out breads, gourds or squashes to use for serving containers. Select natural baskets and stoneware.

WINE AND CHEESE

Of course, the quickest and easiest appetizer is cheese and crackers, because you purchase both. Below are tips for excellent wine and cheese combinations. With careful selection, you can turn your "old standby" into a truly gourmet adventure.

In France, cheese is considered a "living" product that changes day by day or even hour by hour as the cheese making organisms react with the milk products. In the US, much of our cheese has stabilizers added. Experiment with fresh young cheese that is still "alive." A reputable deli or charcuterie is a good place to start. In all cases, eat cheese soon after purchase for maximum flavor.

CHEESES	WINES
Cheddars	
New York, Vermont or Wisconsin Cheddar, Cheshire, Caerphilly, Double Gloucester, Colby, Longhorn, Monterey Jack	Ruby Cabernet, California Burgundy, Gamay Beaujolais, California Dry Sherry
Moderately Firm, Mild	
Gouda, Munster, Tilsit, Danbo, Tybo, Edam, Esrom, Bon Bel Fontina	Port du Salut, Bel Paese, Havarti, Pinot Zinfandel, California Gamay, Chardonnay, Johannisberg Reisling
Emmenthal	
American, Austrian or Swiss Swiss, Samsoe, Gruyere, Jarlsberg	French Colombard, California Chablis, Chenin Blanc, Rosé
Blues	
Roquefort, Danish or American Blue, Gorgonzola, Stilton	California Port, Pinot Noir, Barbera
White or Creamy Cheeses	
Boursin, Feta, Boursault, Grape Cheese, Taleggio, Gourmandise	Grey Riesling, Sauvignon or Fume Blanc, Gewurztraminer
Brie, Camembert, Pont L'Eveque	Petite Sirah, Cabernet Sauvignon

- *Mix bland and strong-flavored cheese, familiar and rarer cheeses. Serving all mild cheeses could be boring, and too many full-flavored cheeses might tire the palate.*

- *Serve cheeses at room temperature. Creamy cheeses need be taken from the refrigerator only half an hour ahead; for most others, an hour is about right. White and Rosé wines should, of course, be chilled.*

- *Accompanying crackers or breads should not be salty or too spicy, and there shouldn't be too much of a variety, so as not to mix up the palate, confounding the other flavors.*

TRICOLOR TORTE

The Mexican flag is red, white and green, and this great hors d'oeuvre displays the same colors.

SERVES: 10-12
PREP TIME: 15 minutes + 2 hour chill
COOKING TIME: None
MAY BE PREPARED AHEAD:
    1 week refrigerated;
    3 months frozen

INGREDIENTS:

8 oz. cream cheese
12 oz. montrachet goat cheese
1/2 lb. soft unsalted butter
1 cup minced sun-dried tomatoes
   (see page 209)
1 cup cilantro pecan pesto (see page 102)

PREPARATION:

Blend together cheeses and butter until light and fluffy.

Line a loaf pan with plastic wrap or cheese cloth. Spread sun-dried tomatoes evenly over bottom.

Top with one-third the cheese mixture, spreading evenly. Top with one-half the cilantro pecan pesto, spreading evenly, and follow with one-third the cheese mixture, then the other half cilantro pecan pesto, and the remaining one-third cheese mixture. Cover with plastic wrap and chill for 2 hours.

Unmold and invert to serve.
The plastic wrap will peel off easily, leaving the sun-dried tomatoes intact.
Serve with crackers.

SPICED CRAB on JICAMA ROUNDS

Use jicima rounds or cucumber rounds as the base for seafood canapes. It's a nice fresh change from crackers or toast rounds.

SERVES: 15 - 20 Canapes
PREP TIME: 10 minutes
COOKING TIME: none
MAY BE PREPARED AHEAD:
    Crab - 24 hours

INGREDIENTS:

1 large jicama, peeled, sliced 1/4 in. thick
1/2 lb. shredded crab
3-4 tbsp. mayonnaise
3 scallions, minced
1/4 tsp. Three Chili Mix (see page 129)
salt to taste
cilantro garnish

PREPARATION:

Use 2" round canape or cookie cutter to cut canape base from jicama slices.

Mix crab, mayonnaise, scallions and spices together. Season to taste.

If preparing ahead, STOP. Cover and refrigerate for up to 24 hours.

Place 1 heaping teaspoonful crab mixture in the center of each jicama round.
Garnish with a cilantro trefoil (single leaf).

TORTILLA PIZZITA

Instead of heavy dough and oil drenched toppings, this Southwestern version of a pizza is light and flavorful relying on intensely flavored ingredient combinations for its zing.

SERVES: 8
PREP TIME: 15 minutes
COOKING TIME: 5 minutes
MAY BE PREPARED AHEAD: 4 hours

INGREDIENTS:

8 seven-inch flour tortillas
8 tsp. olive oil
2 hot Italian sausages in casings, or ground
1/4 sweet onion, sliced paper thin
4 large, fresh shitaki mushrooms, sliced thin
3/4 cup grated jack cheese
16 sprigs fresh cilantro (8 for garnish)

PREPARATION:

Place 8 flour tortillas on ungreased cookie sheet. Brush with olive oil.

Place five 1/2-tsp. ball-shaped portions of uncooked sausage meat in an evenly spaced circle, mid-tortilla. If sausage is in casing, remove casing to access ground meat.

Divide sweet onion and shitaki mushroom slices in 8 equal portions evenly over surface of tortillas.

Pull off trefoil leaves from 8 sprigs of cilantro; break each trefoil into thirds and place randomly over tortillas. 1 sprig equals approximately 18 trefoil leaves. Top with grated jack cheese.

If preparing ahead, STOP. Cover with plastic wrap and store in refrigerator.

TO COOK:

Preheat oven to 425 degrees and place cookie sheet in oven and cook for 7 minutes.

TO SERVE:

Garnish pizzita with sprig of fresh cilantro in center and serve hot on 9" plates for sit down, on a platter for buffet style, or cut into 6 wedges with pizza wheel and served as hors d'oeuvres.

VARIATIONS:

Eggplant, grated jack cheese, red onion, cilantro and Italian sausage

Roma tomatoes, summer sausage, grated parmesan, basil, shitake mushrooms, and onions

Grilled duck or chicken, chili sauce, jack cheese, onions, peppers and cilantro

Tomato, eggplant, peppers, onions, shitake mushrooms, romano cheese, and mushrooms

Grilled chicken marinated in rosemary and raspberry vinaigrette, jack cheese and apple chutney

Duck sausage, shitake mushrooms, yellow peppers, grated lite jack, and thyme

GARLIC STUFFED MUSHROOMS

SERVES: 12 appetizers
PREP TIME: 10 minutes
COOKING TIME: 5 minutes
MAY BE PREPARED AHEAD: 8 hours

INGREDIENTS:

1/2 cup chopped onion
1 clove garlic, chopped
12 mushroom stems, chopped
8 tbsp. sweet butter
3 tbsp. parsley, chopped
1 tbsp. basil, chopped
3 tbsp. bread crumbs
12 mushroom caps
3 tbsp. toasted bread crumbs

PREPARATION:

Saute onions, garlic and mushroom stems in butter. Add parsley, basil, and bread crumbs. Cook until thickened.

Put 1 tbsp. stuffing in each mushroom cap and sprinkle with toasted bread crumbs.

If preparing ahead, STOP. Cover and refrigerate for up to 8 hours.

TO COOK:

Brown or broil in 400 degree oven for 5 minutes.

SCALLOPS WRAPPED in BACON

SERVES: 12 appetizers
PREP TIME: 10 minutes
COOKING TIME: 20 minutes
MAY BE PREPARED AHEAD: 8 hours

INGREDIENTS:

12 scallops
6 strips bacon, cut in half
12 toothpicks

PREPARATION:

Wrap bacon around scallops and secure with toothpick.

If preparing ahead, STOP. Cover and refrigerate for up to 8 hours.

Bake in preheated 400 degree oven for 20 minutes until bacon is crisp.

Serve on tray or in chaffer.

BASIL

CHICKEN DRUMMETTES with JALAPEÑO MUSTARD GLAZE

Drummettes are the upper portion of a chicken wing. They are now sold packaged in supermarkets, or ask your butcher to prepare some for you. The are usually served in their original shape of a miniature drumstick. An alternative form is prepared by pushing the meat to the large end of the bone so that you have a handle on one end and a ball of meat on the other.

SERVES: 24 (8 people, 3 each)
PREP TIME: 5 minutes
COOKING TIME: 20 minutes
MAY BE PREPARED AHEAD:
    Not recommended

INGREDIENTS:

24 chicken drummettes
1 cup Jalapeño Mustard Glaze
    (recipe follows)

PREPARATION:

Line a shallow baking pan with foil and place drummettes in a single layer. Top with Jalapeño Mustard Glaze, brushing evenly over all.

TO BAKE:

Bake in a preheated 350 degree oven for 20 minutes. Serve in a chaffing dish.

Alternative Sauce for Chicken Drummettes
Hunter's Sauce (see page 176)

JALAPEÑO MUSTARD GLAZE

SERVES: 2 cups
PREP TIME: Mise en place
COOKING TIME: 20 minutes
MAY BE PREPARED AHEAD:
    1 month refrigerated

INGREDIENTS:

1 cup jalapeño jelly (see page 285)
1 cup dry red wine
2 tbsp. prepared dijon mustard

PREPARATION: Mise en place

TO COOK:

Combine all ingredients in a small heavy saucepan, and bring to a boil. Simmer slowly until slightly thickened.

MEATBALLS with CINNAMON and MINT in GINGER SAUCE

This is an unusual version of the perennial meatball hors d'oeuvre. The spices make it especially nice for holiday entertaining.

SERVES: 24 appetizers
PREP TIME: 10 minutes
COOKING TIME: 1 hour
MAY BE PREPARED AHEAD:
    1 hour stove finish +
    1 hour in warm oven

INGREDIENTS:

Meatballs
3 slices dry bread
1/2 cup hot water
1 lb. ground beef
2 tbsp. minced onions
2 tsp. salt
1 tsp. ground cinnamon
1/2 cup chopped fresh mint
1 egg
2 tbsp. butter or margarine

Ginger Sauce
1-1/2 cups hot water
1/2 cup vinegar
12 whole cloves
1 bay leaf
8 gingersnaps, crumbled coarsely
mint sprig garnish

PREPARATION:

Meatballs
Crumble the bread into bowl and soften in 1/2 cup hot water. Add ground beef, onions, herbs and salt; mix well.

Shape mixture into 24 balls.

TO COOK:

Melt butter in covered saute pan, add meatballs, and brown on both sides.

Ginger Sauce
Combine water, vinegar, cloves, bay leaf and gingersnaps. Pour over meatballs, cover and simmer about 1 hour. Remove bay leaf and cloves.

If preparing ahead, STOP. Cover with foil and hold in a warm oven for up to 1 hour.

TO SERVE:

Serve in chaffing dish or heated casserole. Garnish with mint sprig.

QUESADILLA with PIÑONS and SUN-DRIED TOMATOES

Serve as an appetizer, quick lunch or hors d'oeuvre.

SERVES: 4
PREP TIME: 10 minutes
COOKING TIME: 5 minutes
MAY BE PREPARED AHEAD: 1 hour

INGREDIENTS:

8 tsp. sun-dried tomatoes
4 12" flour tortillas
2 cups chopped spinach
12 oz. grated jack cheese
4 tbsp. piñons (pinenuts)

PREPARATION:

Soak sun-dried tomatoes in hot water for 5 minutes before chopping.

Lay flour tortillas on a large plate, open-faced; top with tomatoes, spinach, cheese and piñons.

If preparing ahead, STOP. Cover with plastic wrap and hold for up to 1 hour.

TO COOK:

Put in 350 degree oven for 5 minutes or until cheese melts. Fold in half and cut in diagonal strips for easy "finger food."

FAVORITE CHICKEN LIVER PATÉ

This is friend's recipe and has become a family favorite. Serve with toast points or crusty french style bread. Make up the recipe to yield four individual patés and save for unexpected guests.

SERVES: 8 portions (2 cups)
PREP TIME: Mise en place
COOKING TIME: 30 minutes
MAY BE PREPARED AHEAD: 1 week

INGREDIENTS:

6 tbsp. sweet butter
1/2 cup finely minced yellow onion
2 garlic cloves, peeled and chopped
1 Tbsp. fresh thyme, minced
1/2 cup celery tops
10 black peppercorns
2 bay leaves
6 cups water
1 lb. chicken livers
2 tbsp. brandy or port
1/2 tsp. salt
1/2 tsp. ground allspice
5 tsp. water packed
    green peppercorns, drained
1/4 cup heavy cream or Créme Fraiche

TO COOK:

Melt butter in a skillet. Add the onion, garlic and thyme and cook, covered, over medium heat for about 25 minutes, or until onion is transparent.

Add celery tops, black peppercorns, and bay leaves to 6 cups of water in a saucepan. Bring to a boil, reduce heat, and simmer for 10 minutes. Add chicken livers to water and simmer for another 10 minutes; then remove and drain.

Process livers, butter, onion and garlic, brandy or port, salt, pepper, allspice, and 4 tsp. of the green peppercorns in a food processor until smooth. Pour in the cream and process again to blend. Transfer to a bowl and stir in remaining teaspoon of green peppercorns.

Pour mixture into four individual paté molds or a 2 cup large mold. Cover and refrigerate for at least 4 hours before serving.

To serve, return pate to room temperature.

If preparing ahead, STOP. Cover and refrigerate for up to 1 week.

Collect decorative gelatin molds for individual patés or mousse. Line individual molds with plastic wrap, and pack with paté. To serve, invert and remove plastic.

SHERRIED MUSHROOMS

SERVES: 6
PREP TIME: Mise en place
COOKING TIME: 20 minutes
MAY BE PREPARED AHEAD: 2 hours

INGREDIENTS:

1-1/2 lbs. fresh mushrooms
1/2 lb. butter
1/4 cup cream sherry
Fresh parsley for garnish

TO COOK:

Place all ingredients in saucepan; cook over low heat for 20 minutes

If preparing ahead, STOP. Cover and allow to remain at room temperature; reheat to serve.

TO SERVE:

Serve as a tapa course in a copper pan with picks or in individual ramikins as a side dish. Garnish with fresh parsley.

BACON-GINGER CANAPES

SERVES: 4
PREP TIME: 15 minutes
MAY BE PREPARED AHEAD: 24 hours

INGREDIENTS:

1 tsp. diced, drained preserved ginger
4 to 5 strips of bacon
2 tbsp. cream cheese, softened
12 melba toast rounds

PREPARATION:

In a medium skillet, cook the bacon over moderate heat until crisp, 5 to 7 minutes. Drain on paper towels and crumble into small bits.

In a small bowl, combine the cream cheese, ginger and bacon pieces. Blend until thoroughly combined.

If preparing ahead, STOP. Cover and store cheese mixture in refrigerator.

Spread about 1 teaspoon of the cheese mixture onto each toast round and arrange on a serving platter.

Winter

One Dish Meals

"One Dish Meals" are great timesavers. In days past,
they were called casseroles and stews. Nowadays, they are
ragouts, rissotos, chiles, cassoulets, sautes and pastas.

They all have the common element of featuring a protein,
vegetable and carbohydrate in a single dish. Some
require only a bread or tortilla to provide a satisfying meal.
With others, a green salad offers good balance.

ALLSPICE and CINNAMON-SCENTED BEEF RAGOUT

SERVES: 6
PREP TIME: 5 minutes + 1 hour soak
COOKING TIME: 1 hour, 20 minutes
MAY BE PREPARED AHEAD: 24 hours

INGREDIENTS:

1/4 lb. dried apricots
1/4 lb. pitted prunes
red wine as needed
4 tbsp. vegetable oil
3 lb. top round, cut in 1-1/2-in. cubes
salt and pepper to taste
1 onion, pared, chopped
1-1/2 cups beef or chicken stock
1/3 cup ground toasted almonds
1 tsp. cinnamon
1 tsp. allspice
1 tsp. ground cumin
1 tsp. ground coriander
1/2 cup toasted almond slivers for garnish

PREPARATION:

Cover dried apricots and prunes with
red wine and soak for 1 hour. Drain
fruit, reserving wine and half the fruit.

Place other half in a food processor
and puree until smooth.

TO COOK:

Heat oil in 4 quart saucepan. Sprinkle beef
with salt and pepper and saute with onions.

Add fruit puree to meat along with reserved
wine, stock, ground almonds and spices.
Heat to boiling.

Reduce heat and simmer, covered, for
about 1 hour or until meat is tender.

Add remaining fruit and cook for 5 minutes.

*If preparing ahead, STOP. Cover and
refrigerate. Reheat to serve.*

TO SERVE:

Sprinkle with toasted almond slivers and serve.

CHICKEN RAGOUT with TARRAGON

SERVES: 8
PREP TIME: 15 minutes
COOKING TIME: 1 hour, 15 minutes
MAY BE PREPARED AHEAD: 1 day

INGREDIENTS:

6 tbsp. unsalted butter, room temperature
3 tbsp. peanut oil
6 chicken breast halves, trimmed
6 chicken thighs, trimmed
salt and pepper to taste
3 leeks, tops chopped
3 large carrots, peeled,
    cut to matchstick-size pieces
3 large garlic cloves, minced
1/2 cup fresh tarragon, chopped
3-1/4 cups dry white wine
1-3/4 cups chicken stock
1-3/4 cups beef stock
1/4 cup all purpose flour
6 oz. snow peas, trimmed
10 oz. package frozen baby peas, thawed
drained tarragon sprigs for garnish

PREPARATION:

Melt 3 tbsp. unsalted butter with 3 tbsp.
peanut oil in heavy large Dutch oven
or casserole over medium-high heat.
Season chicken breasts and thighs with
salt and pepper. Saute in Dutch oven
until golden brown (about 8 minutes).
Transfer chicken to platter.

Saute leeks in Dutch oven for 3 minutes.
Stir in carrots and garlic cloves, and
saute until leeks are almost tender,
another 3 minutes. Add 1/4 cup tarragon.

TO COOK:

Return chicken to Dutch oven. Add dry white wine, chicken stock and beef stock. Bring mixture to boil. Reduce heat to medium-low. Cover and simmer until chicken is tender, about 50 minutes.

If preparing ahead, STOP. Cover and refrigerate. To continue, bring ragout to simmer.

Strain chicken pieces and vegetables, reserving cooking liquid, and place on large platter. Return cooking liquid to Dutch oven. Boil cooking liquid until reduced to 5 cups, about 10 minutes.

Stir remaining 3 tbsp. unsalted butter and flour in small bowl until paste forms. Gradually whisk paste by tablespoonfuls into simmering cooking liquid. Simmer until liquid is thickened to sauce consistency, about 5 minutes.

Return chicken pieces to Dutch oven. Add peas and snow peas and simmer until peas are crisp-tender, about 1 minute.

Arrange chicken pieces and vegetables on serving platter. Spoon some sauce over. Sprinkle with chopped fresh tarragon. Garnish platter with fresh tarragon sprigs. Serve, passing remaining sauce separately.

FAJITAS DE PAVO

SERVES: 4
PREP TIME: 5 minutes + 2 hour marinade
COOKING TIME: 2-4 minutes
MAY BE PREPARED AHEAD:
    may be marinated overnight - 24 hours

INGREDIENTS:

1-3/4 lb. turkey breast
1 tsp. salt and black pepper
dash of crushed red pepper seeds
1 cup lemon juice
1 cup sliced green bell pepper
1 cup sliced red bell pepper
1 cup soybean oil
1 cup sliced onions

PREPARATION:

Slice turkey breast into thin strips, about 4 inches long.

In a bowl, combine turkey, salt, pepper, crushed red pepper, lemon juice and bell pepper slices. Cover and marinate for 2 hours.

If preparing ahead, STOP. Refrigerate for up to 24 hours.

TO COOK:

In a very hot saucepan, add soybean oil and saute turkey mixture and onions for 2 minutes.

TO SERVE:

Serve in a hot pan with flour tortillas and Pico de Gallo.

NAPO'S POSOLE

SERVES: 8
PREP TIME: Mise en place
COOKING TIME: 2 hours 45 minutes
MAY BE PREPARED AHEAD: 3 days

INGREDIENTS:

2 white onions, in chunks
5 cloves garlic,crushed
2 pork soup bones, preferably shoulder hocks
6 quarts water
2 lbs. boneless pork loin, in 3/4-in. cubes
2 lb. boneless chicken breast, in small pieces
2 tbsp. bacon drippings
salt and pepper to taste
20 oz. can prepared hominy

For the Garnish
8 oz. shredded white cabbage
1 cup diced white onion
1 oz. crushed red chile
1 oz crushed dried oregano

PREPARATION: Mise en place

TO COOK:

Boil onion, garlic, soup bones and water
for 2 hours.

Saute pork and chicken in bacon fat for
15 minutes; salt and pepper to taste.

When stock is reduced by half, strain and
remove bones. Add pork, chicken and
hominy. Boil for 30 minutes, or until pork is
entirely cooked. Adjust seasoning if needed.

*If preparing ahead STOP. Soup may be stored
up to three days. Reheat before serving.*

TO SERVE:

Ladle hot soup into bowls.
Serve dishes of garnish on the side.

COUNTRY RISSOTO

SERVES: 4
PREP TIME: 15 minutes
COOKING TIME: 1 hour
MAY BE PREPARED AHEAD: 24 hours

INGREDIENTS:

1/4 cup butter
1 small onion, chopped
1 cup sliced mushrooms
1-1/2 cup chicken or ham
1 cup Italian rice or rissoto
3 cups chicken stock
1/2 tsp. dill (dried)
1 tsp. salt
3 medium chopped tomatoes
3/4 cup grated cheddar cheese
6 sprigs chopped parsley (garnish)

PREPARATION:

Saute onion, mushroom and meat in butter.
Place in casserole, add rissoto, chicken
stock, dill, salt and tomatoes and mix well.

TO COOK:

Bake for 45 minutes at 350 degrees.
If rice needs additional moisture, add
additional stock. Rissoto is able to
absorb great quantities of liquid.

*If preparing ahead, STOP. Rissotto may be
cooled, covered with plastic and stored in
refrigerator. Otherwise proceed with step below.*

Add 1/2 cup cheese and stir. Top with
remaining 1/4 cup cheese and return to
oven for 15 minutes. Dish may require
up to 30 minutes, if rewarming.
Garnish with chopped parsley.

MEXICALI RICE CASSEROLE

SERVES: 10
PREP TIME: 15 minutes
COOKING TIME: 30 minutes
MAY BE PREPARED AHEAD: 24 hours

INGREDIENTS:

16 oz. sour cream
2 tbsp. milk
15 oz. tomato sauce
1/2 lb. smoked sausage, coarsely chopped
8 oz. chopped green chilies, drained
1/2 cup chopped green onions
4 cups cooked long grain white rice
2 cups shredded mozzarella cheese

PREPARATION:

Blend sour cream and milk. Set aside.

In medium saucepan, combine tomato sauce, sausage, chilies and green onions. Simmer 10 minutes, stirring occasionally.

In a 2 quart casserole, layer one-half of the rice, tomato mixture, sour cream mixture and cheese. Repeat all layers.

If preparing ahead, STOP. Cover and refrigerate. Bring to room temperature before baking.

TO COOK:

Bake at 350 degrees for 30 minutes or until cheese melts and casserole is bubbly.

CHILE CHILI

This is our basic down home CHILI from the restaurant. Serve it with cornbread and honey butter. The older it is, the better it gets (to a point). It's a great "do ahead" dish for late night suppers after holiday outings.

SERVES: 6
PREP TIME: Mise en place
COOKING TIME: 30 minutes
MAY BE PREPARED AHEAD: 2 days

INGREDIENTS:

3 lbs. lean ground beef
1 lb. cubed sirloin steak
1 large onion, finely diced
1 large bell pepper, diced
2 tsp. ground black pepper
1 oz. chili powder
2 tsp. oregano leaves
1 fresh garlic clove, chopped
salt to taste
16 oz. red kidney beans, drained
23 ounces tomato juice

PREPARATION: Mise en place

TO COOK:

In a skillet, saute ground beef along with sirloin cubes, onions, and bell pepper. Add spices and kidney beans after beef is cooked, and pour tomato juice over, stirring. Simmer for 15 minutes.

If preparing ahead, STOP. Cover and store in refrigerator. Reheat before serving.

TO SERVE:

Serve with shredded cheddar on top, and chopped onions, if desired. Complement with flour tortillas or corn tortillas.

BLACK BEAN CHILI

This is a meatless, but very filling entree. You may vary the degree of spiciness by increasing or reducing the cayenne or jalapeño.

SERVES: 8
PREP TIME: 1 3/4 hour + overnight soak
    for beans
COOKING TIME: 20 minutes
MAY BE PREPARED AHEAD: 24 hours

INGREDIENTS:

4 cups black beans, uncooked
1 tbsp. ground cumin
1 tbsp. cumin seed
2 tbsp. oregano
1/2 cup finely chopped jalapeño peppers
1-1/2 cups finely chopped green bell peppers
2 cloves garlic, minced
1/2 cup olive oil
1 tsp. cayenne pepper
1-1/2 tbsp. paprika
1 tsp. salt
3 cups canned crushed whole tomatoes
2 large finely chopped yellow onions
1/2 lb. crumbled goat cheese
2/3 cup sour cream
1/2 cup green onions, finely chopped
8 sprigs cilantro

PREPARATION:

Cull beans and soak overnight. Rinse beans well and place in a large pot. Cover with water to several inches above the top of the beans. Cover and bring to a boil.

Reduce heat and cook for 1 3/4 hour or until tender, adding water as needed. Strain; reserve 1 cup cooking water and add back to the beans.

TO COOK:

Saute onions, green peppers, and garlic in oil with ground cumin, cumin seed and oregano, cayenne, paprika and salt for 10 minutes or until onions are soft. Add tomatoes and jalapeño peppers. Add mixture to the beans and stir.

When preparing ahead, STOP. Cover and refrigerate. Reheat before serving.

TO SERVE:

Place 1 ounce crumbled goat cheese, then 1-1/4 cups hot chili in heated bowl. Top with a spoonful of sour cream, sprinkle with 1 tbsp. green onions and place a sprig of cilantro on top.

WHITE BEAN CHILI

SERVES: 8
PREP TIME: Mise en place +
    overnight bean soak
COOKING TIME: 2 hours
MAY BE PREPARED AHEAD: 24 hours

INGREDIENTS:

4 boneless, skinless chicken breasts
1 tsp. Poultry Seasoning (see page 208)
1/4 cup olive oil
1 lb. dried white beans
6 cups water
1-1/2 medium onions, chopped
3 cloves garlic, chopped
1/2 cup (4 oz) canned green chiles, chopped
2 tsp. ground cumin
2 Tbsp. fresh oregano, minced
1 tsp. salt
1/2 tsp. cayenne pepper
4 cups chicken stock
1/2 cup fresh cilantro, chopped
4 green onions, thinly sliced
1/2 cup grated Monterey Jack cheese

PREPARATION: Mise en place

TO COOK:

Combine beans and salt in a large kettle
and bring to a boil. Reduce heat, cover
and simmer for 1-1/2 hours or until beans
are very tender. Drain beans, add chicken
stock and let stand.

Meanwhile, sprinkle chicken breasts with
poultry seasoning and bake at 350 degrees
for 35 minutes. Cool and cut in strips.

Saute chicken strips, onion and garlic
in olive oil until onion is clear. Add
the chopped chilies, cumin, oregano,
and cayenne and mix thoroughly.
Cook for 10 minutes.

Combine the skillet mixture with the
bean mixture. Add the chopped cilantro.
Cook 15 minutes more to mix flavors,
adding additonal chicken broth, if more
sauce is desired.

*If preparing ahead, STOP. Cover
and refrigerate. Reheat before serving.*

TO SERVE:

Sprinkle with the grated cheese
and sliced green onion.

RED HOT VEGETABLE CHILI

A vegetarian friend who knows I collect chile recipes contributed this. It is more of a vegetable stew, than a true chile.

SERVES: 8
PREP TIME: Mise en place
COOKING TIME: 1 hour
MAY BE PREPARED AHEAD: 24 hours

INGREDIENTS:

3/4 cup olive oil
2 medium zucchini, cut into 1/2-in. cubes
2 medium onions, cut into 1/2-in. cubes
4 cloves of garlic, finely chopped
2 large sweet peppers, cored and cut into 1/4-in. dice
1 can (35 oz.) Italian plum tomatoes
1-1/2 lbs. fresh ripe plum tomatoes, cut into 1-in. cubes
2 tbsp. chili powder
1 tbsp. ground cumin
1 tbsp. dried basil
1 tbsp. dried oregano
2 tsp. freshly ground black pepper
1 tsp. salt
1 tsp. fennel seeds
1/2 cup chopped Italian parsley
1 cup canned dark-red kidney beans, drained
1 cup canned garbanzos, drained
1/2 cup chopped fresh dill
2 tbsp. lemon juice

PREPARATION: Mise en place

TO COOK:

Heat 1/2 cup olive oil in a large skillet over medium heat. Add zucchini and saute until just tender. Remove zucchini to a large casserole or dutch oven. Add remaining 1/4 cup oil to skillet over low heat. Add onions, garlic and red pepper. Saute until just wilted, about 10 minutes. Add to casserole with the oil.

Place the casserole over low heat. Add undrained canned tomatoes, fresh tomatoes, chili powder, cumin, basil, oregano, pepper, salt, fennel, and parsley. Cook uncovered, stirring often, for 30 minutes.

Stir in kidney beans, garbanzos, dill and lemon juice; cook for 15 minutes more. Stir well and adjust seasoning to taste. Serve immediately.

If preparing ahead, STOP. Cover and refrigerate. Reheat before serving.

TO SERVE:

Garnish with sour cream, grated Monterey Jack and sliced scallions.

SOUTHWESTERN CASSOULET

SERVES: 6
PREP TIME: 1 hour +
    overnight soak for beans
COOKING TIME: 1-1/2 hours
MAY BE PREPARED AHEAD: 48 hours

INGREDIENTS:

1 lb. black beans
8 cups cold water
1/2 lb. sliced bacon
1-1/2 lbs. boneless lamb leg or
    shoulder cut in 1-in. pieces
2 large smoked chicken breasts, skinned,
    boned, cut into 1-in. pieces
1/2 lb. pork sausage
1/2 tsp. salt
1/4 tsp. pepper
2 large onions, chopped
1 lb., 12 oz. canned whole tomatoes
1/2 cup dry red wine
3 garlic cloves, finely chopped
1/4 cup chopped parsley
1 tsp. thyme
2 tbsp. chopped cilantro
1 bay leaf

PREPARATION:

Wash and pick over beans. Cover with cold water and soak overnight. Drain and rinse soaked beans.

Cover beans with cold water and heat to boiling. Skim as necessary. Simmer slowly for about 1 hour. Drain cooked beans, reserving liquid.

TO COOK:

Fry bacon in large skillet until some of fat is rendered. Remove from skillet.

Brown lamb, chicken, and sausage in bacon fat. Remove from skillet and blot with paper towels. Season with salt and pepper and drain all but 2 tbsp. fat from skillet.

Add onions and saute until translucent.

Add tomatoes, wine, garlic, parsley, thyme and bay leaf. Combine tomato mixture, drained beans and meats.

Spoon into large casserole or into individual casseroles. Pour reserved bean liquid over mixture just to cover.

Bake at 350 degrees for about 1-1/2 hours.

If preparing ahead, STOP. Cover and refrigerate. Reheat before serving.

THYME

ROTELLI with HOT SAUSAGE and FENNEL

SERVES: 4
PREP TIME: Mise en place
COOKING TIME: 20 minutes
MAY BE PREPARED AHEAD: 8 hours

INGREDIENTS:

1 lb. hot Italian sausage,
    casings removed
2 tbsp. olive oil
1 cup onion, finely chopped
2 large garlic cloves, minced
2 large red bell peppers, chopped
2 fennel bulbs, sliced thin (about 4 cups)
2/3 cup dry white wine
1 cup chicken broth
1/2 cup heavy cream
1/2 cup fresh parsley leaves, minced
salt and pepper to taste
1 lb. rotelli
freshly grated parmesan

PREPARATION: Mise en place

TO COOK:

In a heavy skillet, cook the sausage over moderate heat, stirring and breaking up any lumps, until it is cooked through. Transfer with a slotted spoon to paper towels to drain.

Add oil to skillet and cook the onion and garlic over moderately low heat, stirring, until onion is softened.

Add bell pepper and fennel and cook over moderate heat, stirring occasionally, for 5 minutes, or until bell pepper and fennel are softened.

Add wine and broth. Bring to a boil, lower heat, and simmer, covered, for 5 minutes.

Add cream and boil the mixture until it is thickened slightly and reduced by one-third.

Stir the parsley, sausage and salt and pepper to taste into the fennel mixture.

If preparing ahead, STOP. Cover and refrigerate. Reheat carefully, stirring constantly, and do not allow sauce to separate by overheating.

In a kettle of boiling salted water, cook the rotelli until it is al dente. Drain.

TO SERVE:

In a bowl, toss the sauce with the rotelli and sprinkle with parmesan cheese.

PARSLEY

PENNE with WILD MUSHROOMS

SERVES: 4 - 6
PREP TIME: Mise en place
COOKING TIME: 40 minutes
MAY BE PREPARED AHEAD:
    Sauce - 24 hours

INGREDIENTS:

2 celery stalks, diced small
1 peeled carrot, diced small
8 shallots, diced small
8 oz. wild (or domestic) mushroom stems,
    finely ground or finely chopped
    mushroom tops
1 cup chicken stock
12 oz. heavy cream
salt and pepper to taste
1 cup sliced mushrooms
2 cups cooked penne
chopped chives or parsley for garnish

PREPARATION: Mise en place.

TO COOK:

Lightly saute celery and carrots in olive oil.
Add finely ground stems or finely chopped
mushroom tops.

Cover with chicken stock and simmer
for 10 minutes.

Add heavy cream, stir, and simmer about
20 minutes, or until slightly thickened.

Strain sauce and season with salt and pepper.

Heat sauce and add sliced mushrooms.
Cook until mushrooms are slightly wilted,
about 6 minutes.

*If preparing ahead, STOP. Cover and refriger-
ate. Reheat, stirring constantly, to serve.*

Add cooked pasta and heat thoroughly.

TO SERVE:

Use about 4 oz. sauce per person and 4 oz.
cooked pasta per plate as entree.

Garnish with chopped chives or parsley.

FRUITS of the SEA FETTUCINI

SERVES: 4
PREP TIME: Mise en place
COOKING TIME: 7 minutes
MAY BE PREPARED AHEAD:
    Not recommended

INGREDIENTS:

4 oz. sliced eggplant
4 oz. sliced green pepper
4 oz. sliced mushrooms
4 oz. salad oil
4 oz. dry sherry wine
8 oz. scallops
4 oz. crabmeat cooked
4 oz. bay shrimp cooked
20 oz. semolina fettucini, cooked
2 cups heavy cream
salt, pepper and garlic to taste
4 oz. fresh grated parmesan cheese
4 thin lemon slices
4 sprigs fresh parsley

PREPARATION: Mise en place

TO COOK:

In saucepan, saute all the vegetables
in salad oil until halfway cooked.

Add sherry wine and scallops; cook for a
few more seconds, then add crabmeat,
shrimp and fettucini, following with cream.
Cook until it starts bubbling.

TO SERVE:

Serve on a platter topped with parmesan
cheese, thin slice of lemon and sprig
of fresh parsley.

Winter

Side Dishes

CELERIC and CARROT SALAD
(Salad of Root Vegetables)

SERVES: 8
PREP TIME: 10 minutes +
    4 hours marinade time
COOKING TIME: 5 minutes
MAY BE PREPARED AHEAD: 24 hours

INGREDIENTS:

2 cups celaric cut into matchstick size pieces
2 cups carrots cut into matchstick size pieces
1 quart water
1 tsp. salt

Dressing
1/4 cup mayonnaise
2 tbsp. balsamic vinegar
1 tsp. dried tarragon (or 1 tbsp. fresh)
1/4 tbsp. coarsely cracked pepper

PREPARATION:

Bring water to a rolling boil.

Drop vegetables in boiling salted water for 5 minutes. Drain and rinse with cold water.

Place dressing ingredients in small bowl or French jelly jar, and use hand-held blender to mix.

Mix dressing with vegetables.

Allow flavors to marry in refrigerator for 4 hours.

For mixing salad dressings, use covered "French Jelly" jars available in many cooking or import stores. Their wide bottoms allow a hand-held blender to be used if emulsifying. The covers allow you to add all ingredients, then cover and shake to mix. They then go straight to the refrigerator to store extra dressing.

SALAD of WINTER FRUIT

This salad makes a refreshing first course or works equally well on a buffet.

SERVES: 6
PREP TIME: 15 minutes
COOKING TIME: None
MAY BE PREPARED AHEAD: 8 hours

INGREDIENTS:

4 cups cubed red apples
2 tbsp. lemon juice
3/4 cup chopped celery
3/4 cup raisins
3/4 cup chopped walnuts
3 tbsp. mayonnaise
3 tbsp. Créme Fraiche
1/2 tsp. ground nutmeg
6 sprigs mint for garnish (a fresh
    flower garnish works well here)

PREPARATION:

Sprinkle lemon juice over apples and mix well.

Add celery, raisins, walnuts, mayonnaise, Créme Fraiche and nutmeg, and mix well.

Serve on a lettuce leaf cup and garnish with mint sprigs or fresh flowers.

WINTER GREENS with CHUTNEY DIJON VINAGRETTE

Select a variety of winter greens and design your own salad: Endive, radicchio, arugula, mache, spinach, butter lettuce, red leaf lettuce and romaine. Consider adding mint, sorrel or basil cut in strips.

CHUTNEY DIJON VINAIGRETTE

SERVES: 6
PREP TIME: 5 minutes
COOKING TIME: None
MAY BE PREPARED AHEAD: 1 week

INGREDIENTS:

2 tbsp. balsamic vinegar
1 tbsp. prepared chutney
1 tsp. dijon mustard
1 tbsp. fresh parsley
1 tsp. fresh tarragon
1/4 tsp. freshly ground black pepper
1/2 cup olive oil

PREPARATION:

Place all ingredients in jar
and shake until well blended.

LENTIL SALAD with WALNUTS

SERVES: 8
PREP TIME: 10 minutes (dressing)
COOKING TIME: 45 minutes (lentils)
MAY BE PREPARED AHEAD: 24 hours

INGREDIENTS:

1 lb. dried lentils
2 shallots, finely chopped
3 tbsp. fresh parsley
3/4 tsp. salt
3/4 tsp. pepper
3 tbsp. wine vinegar
1/2 cup walnut or vegetable oil
1/4 cup heavy cream or yogurt
2 cups tomatoes, seeded, chopped
    in small pieces
6 large Boston lettuce leaves
1 cup walnuts, finely chopped

PREPARATION:

Cook lentils in boiling water in a large kettle until soft, about 45 minutes. Drain thoroughly.

Squeeze out shallots in a tea towel to extract juices. Combine shallots with parsley, salt, pepper, and vinegar in a large salad bowl. Gradually whisk in the oil. When the oil is incorporated, whisk in cream or yogurt.

Toss lentils and tomatoes in dressing. Do not overmix, or lentils will become mushy.

If preparing ahead, STOP. Cover and refrigerate for up to 24 hours.

TO SERVE:

Serve on lettuce leaves and garnish with chopped walnuts.

APPLE/NEW POTATO CASSOULET

SERVES: 8
PREP TIME: 5 minutes
COOKING TIME: 1 hour
MAY BE PREPARED AHEAD:
    Not Recommended

INGREDIENTS:

6 sliced apples
1/4 cup melted butter
8 sliced new potatoes
1 tsp. cinnamon

PREPARATION:

Mix ingredients well; cover with foil
in casserole.

TO COOK:

Bake at 350 degrees for one hour.

ACORN SQUASH RINGS with GINGER

SERVES: 6
PREP TIME: Mise en place
COOKING TIME: 20 minutes
MAY BE PREPARED AHEAD: 8 hours

INGREDIENTS:

2 acorn squash
salt and pepper to taste
1/2 cup dark brown sugar
1/4 cup butter, melted
2 tbsp. water
1 tbsp. grated ginger

PREPARATION: Mise en place

TO COOK:

Pierce squash with fork several times
and cook in microwave for 8 to 10 minutes
on medium. Let stand for 5 minutes.
Squash should be soft.

Cut crosswise into 1-inch rings and discard
ends and seeds and put in glass baking dish.
Season with salt and pepper.

Combine sugar, melted butter and water
and mix well.

Spoon sugar mixture over rings and top
with grated ginger. Cover with parchment
or wax paper.

If preparing ahead, STOP.
Keep in a cool place for up to 8 hours.

Microwave 3 to 5 minutes on medium,
basting once.

CARROTS with PORT

SERVES: 6
PREP TIME: Mise en place
COOKING TIME: 10 minutes
MAY BE PREPARED AHEAD: 4 hours

INGREDIENTS:

2 lbs. carrots, peeled, cut into
    thin medallions
4 tbsp. olive oil
1 tsp. sugar
salt and pepper to taste
4 tsp. port
2-1/2 cups concentrated beef bouillon

PREPARATION: Mise en place

TO COOK:

Put carrots, oil, sugar, salt and pepper in
heavy saucepan. Cook over high heat,
shaking frequently, until carrots are golden.
Add bouillon and port. Heat to simmer.
Serve very hot.

If preparing ahead, STOP. Cover and
refrigerate for up to 4 hours. Reheat in
microwave for 3 minutes on medium.

CANDIED YAMS

SERVES: 6
PREP TIME: Mise en place
COOKING TIME: 1 hour
MAY BE PREPARED AHEAD: 3 days

INGREDIENTS:

1 lb. fresh yams, peeled and cut in chunks
OR 1 large can of yams
8 oz. dark brown sugar
1/2 cup chopped walnuts
1/4-1/2 cup water (use with fresh yams)

PREPARATION: Mise en place

TO COOK:

Place all ingredients in saucepan
and cook over medium heat, stirring
occasionally, for approximately 1 hour.
(Dish is done when mixture is reduced
to dark brown chutney-like consistency.)

If preparing ahead, STOP. Cover and
refrigerate for up to 3 days. Reheat to
serve, taking care to not burn bottom.
High sugar content makes it easy to burn.

BAKED CAULIFLOWER PUREE

SERVES: 8
PREP TIME: 20 minutes
COOKING TIME: 30 minutes
MAY BE PREPARED AHEAD: 24 hours

INGREDIENTS:

1 large cauliflower,
    separated into flowerets
1 medium onion, chopped
1/2 cup buttermilk
salt and freshly ground pepper to taste
1/4 tsp. ground nutmeg
3 tbsp. butter
chopped parsley for garnish

PREPARATION:

Preheat oven to 350 degrees.

Place cauliflower flowerets in a saucepan with water to cover. Add onion and cook cauliflower for about 15 minutes, or until tender.

Drain water and puree with hand mixer in pan, slowly adding buttermilk. Season with salt, pepper, nutmeg and butter, and then puree for a few seconds more to melt butter. Place in a buttered 1-quart souffle dish.

If preparing ahead, STOP. Cover and refrigerate for up to 24 hours.

TO COOK:

Place in oven for 30 minutes or until thoroughly heated. Garnish with chopped parsley.

QUICK HOLLANDIAISE SAUCE

Use with broccoli or asparagus for a delicious side dish.

SERVES: 1-1/4 cup
PREP TIME: 5 minutes
COOKING TIME: None
MAY BE PREPARED AHEAD: 30 minutes

INGREDIENTS:

3 large egg yolks
4 tsp. fresh lemon juice, or to taste
pinch of cayenne
1/2 tsp. salt
1 cup unsalted butter, (melted and cool)
fresh lemon juice and cayenne to taste

PREPARATION:

In a food processor fitted with the steel blade, put the egg yolks, lemon juice, salt and cayenne. Turn the machine on and immediately off.

With the motor running, add the butter in a stream. Add the additional lemon juice and cayenne to taste.

If preparing ahead, STOP. The sauce may be kept warm in a small bowl, covered with buttered wax paper, in a pan of warm water for up to 30 minutes.

CORN SPOONBREAD with SAGE

SERVES: 6
PREP TIME: Mise en place
COOKING TIME: 15 minutes
MAY BE PREPARED AHEAD: 24 hours

INGREDIENTS:

2 cups water
1-1/2 cup chicken broth
1 cup yellow cornmeal
1 tbsp. minced fresh sage leaves
2 garlic cloves minced
Monterey jack cheese, shredded
1/4 cup freshly grated parmesan
2 tbsp. minced fresh parsley leaves
    (preferably flat leaved)
tabasco and salt to taste

PREPARATION:

In a 3-quart microwave-safe casserole
with a lid, combine the water and the
broth. Whisk in the cornmeal, a little at
a time, whisking to eliminate any lumps,
and stir in the minced sage and garlic.

TO COOK:

Microwave the mixture, covered, at high
power (100%), whisking every 3 minutes,
for 10 to 12 minutes, or until it is thickened
and the liquid is absorbed. Let mixture
stand, covered, for 2 minutes.

Whisk in the Monterey Jack, parmesan,
parsley, tabasco and salt.

Pour the spoonbread into a serving dish or
individual ramekins or molds sprayed with
with olive oil spray. Garnish with sage sprigs.

*If preparing ahead, STOP. Cover with plastic
wrap and refrigerate. Reheat 30 minutes at
300 degrees before serving.*

REFRIED BLACK BEANS

You may also use this recipe with the
more traditional pinto beans. A dollop
of Créme Fraiche or sprig of cilantro is
an excellent garnish.

SERVES: 8-10
PREP TIME: Overnight soak
COOKING TIME: 1 3/4 hour
MAY BE PREPARED AHEAD: 24 hours

INGREDIENTS:

1-1/4 cup black beans
3 cups water
3 cloves garlic, minced
1 large onion, chopped
2 tsp. salt
1 tbsp. chili powder
1/2 cup bacon drippings

PREPARATION:

In a large kettle, soak beans overnight
in water.

TO COOK:

Bring beans to a boil and add the rest of the
ingredients. Simmer, covered, for 1-1/2 hours,
or until beans are tender. Drain off water.

Puree beans, onions, garlic and spices
with handheld processor.

In a large skillet, melt bacon drippings.
When grease is very hot, add beans and
cook for 5 minutes.

*If preparing ahead, STOP. Cover and refriger-
ate for up to 24 hours. Reheat to serve.*

Winter

Holiday Entrees

*For holiday dinners, main course entrees are more festive
and frequently feature fruits, nuts, and special pastries,
as well as herbs. In past times, these food items were often
a rarity and added to the "special holiday" tradition.*

*Here are a few special main recipes to enhance
your holiday tables. Of course, the most traditional fare
at American tables remain nostalgic favorites.*

*Roast a turkey or goose using the instructions on page 177.
Stud a ham with cloves and glaze with a mixture of
1 cup crushed pineapple and 1 cup dark brown sugar.*

ROAST PORK with PRUNES

SERVES: 6
PREP TIME: 10 minutes +
    overnight prune soak
COOKING TIME: 1 hour
MUST BE PREPARED AHEAD: 24 hours

INGREDIENTS:

1 lb. pitted prunes
1 cup marsala or muscat wine
2-1/2 lbs. boned pork loin roast
2-1/2 tbsp. butter, melted
1 tsp. dried rosemary or 3 sprigs fresh
salt and pepper to taste

PREPARATION:

Soak prunes overnight in wine.
(Reserve 6 prunes for apples.)

Make incisions in pork, and insert prunes
to serve as stuffing. Allow stuffed pork
to remain in refrigerator for 4 hours, so
meat will absorb flavor. Baste with butter.

Roast for 1 hour, basting with pan juices.
After 30 minutes, sprinkle with rosemary,
salt and pepper.

BAKED APPLES to COMPLEMENT ROAST PORK

To cook the Roast Pork with Prunes
for the same meal, cook apples first,
and keep warm while cooking roast.

SERVES: 6
PREP TIME: 5 minutes
COOKING TIME: 1 hour
MAY BE PREPARED AHEAD: 4 hours

INGREDIENTS:

6 apples, cored
6 wine soaked prunes (see recipe above)
1 tbsp. butter

PREPARATION:

Insert 1/2 tsp. butter into each prune and
stuff prune into the center of each apple.

If preparing ahead, STOP.
Cover and refrigerate for up to 4 hours.

Bake in a preheated 300 degree oven
for one hour.

"PARTRIDGE PIE"

Partridges are hard to find these days, so I substitute game hen meat, chicken thighs or any dark poultry meat.

SERVES: 12 (24 "Pies")
PREP TIME: 50-60 minutes
COOKING TIME: 15 minutes
MAY BE PREPARED AHEAD: 8 hours

INGREDIENTS:

3 game hens or 9 chicken thighs
2 apples, peeled, cored and thinly sliced
1 onion, sliced
1 onion, minced
4 tbsp. butter
2 tbsp. cinnamon
1 cup chopped walnuts
2 sheets frozen puff pastry

PREPARATION:

Using Game Hens
Stuff game hens with apples and sliced onions.

Bake in preheated 350 degree oven for 45 minutes.

Using Chicken Thighs
Place chicken in a shallow baking dish and cover with sliced onions and apples.

Bake in preheated 350 degree oven for 35 to 40 minutes.

Allow meat to cool slightly and discard sliced onions and apples.

Discard skin and bones and chop meat into bite size pieces.

Saute minced onion in 2 tbsp. butter.

Mix together meat, walnuts, cinnamon and onions.

Cut pastry into 24 squares and place a spoonful of meat mixture on one side of square and fold over to make triangle. Seal edges and place on baking sheet.

Brush with melted butter.

If preparing ahead, STOP. Cover with damp cloth and refrigerate for up to 8 hours.

TO COOK:

Bake at 350 degrees for 15 minutes, or until "Pies" are golden and puffed.

HONEYED HENS with FIGS

SERVES: 4 to 8
PREP TIME: 15 minutes
COOKING TIME: 1 hour
MAY BE PREPARED AHEAD: 24 hours

INGREDIENTS:

4 Cornish game hens
salt and pepper to taste
3/4 cup Worcestershire sauce
1/3 cup honey
1 tbsp. grated fresh ginger
2 cloves garlic, mashed
1 cup melted butter
parsley and figs for garnish

Stuffing
2 cups breadcrumbs
salt and pepper to taste
1 cup chopped mixed fruit
    (figs, pears, pineapple, prunes,
    oranges - all or some)
1/4 cup melted butter
1-1/2 tsp. minced onion
1/4 cup chopped pecans

PREPARATION:

Prepare stuffing by mixing
all ingredients together.

Season hens with salt and freshly ground
pepper. Rub with a little oil and stuff.

If preparing ahead, STOP. Cover and refrigerate.

TO COOK:

Heat together Worcestershire sauce, honey,
ginger, garlic and butter in a small saucepan.

Roast stuffed chicken in a 400 degree
oven for 15 minutes. Remove and baste
with sauce.

Lower heat to 350 degrees. Return chicken
to oven and roast 45 minutes or until
tender, basting often.

Garnish with parsley and figs.

PARSLEY

Winter

Desserts

MEXICAN LIME PIE

SERVES: 6-8
PREP TIME: 25 minutes
BAKING TIME: 20 minutes
MAY BE PREPARED AHEAD:
    2 days refrigerated

INGREDIENTS:

2-1/4 cup granulated sugar
1/2 cup corn starch
1/3 cup cold water
1/4 tsp. salt
1 3/4 cup hot water
1/2 cup lime juice
4 eggs, separated
1-1/2 tbsp. grated lime rind
1 9-inch pie shell (see Pate Brise, page 117)

PREPARATION:

Combine 1 cup sugar, corn starch, salt and cold water. Add hot water, and cook over very low heat, stirring constantly, until mixture thickens. Remove from heat. Stir in lime juice and return to very low heat, stirring constantly, until thickened. Remove from heat.

In a small bowl, beat egg yolks with 1/2 cup sugar. Add egg yolk mixture to lime mixture and cook over very low heat for 2 minutes. Do not overcook. Remove from heat, add lime rind, and stir well. Let cool. You may wish to add a few drops of green food coloring.

Pour mixture in baked pie shell.

Whip together 4 egg whites and 3/4 cup sugar until peaks form. Spread over the top of the pie.

TO BAKE:

Bake for 20 minutes at 350 degrees until meringue is brown.

PECAN CUPS

SERVES: Makes 24 cups
PREP TIME: 20 minutes
COOKING TIME: 25 minutes
MAY BE PREPARED AHEAD:
    1 week; may be frozen 1 month

INGREDIENTS:

1 cup all purpose flour
1/2 cup butter
3 oz. cream cheese
1 egg
1/2 tsp. almond extract
3/4 cup brown sugar
1 tsp. vanilla
1/2 cup flake coconut
1 tsp. melted butter
1/2 cup chopped pecans

PREPARATION:

Mix together flour, butter, and cream cheese. Form into balls and press into small muffin pans with fingers.

Mix remaining ingredients together and spoon into pastry.

TO COOK:

Bake at 350 degrees for 25 minutes.

If preparing ahead, STOP. Place in airtight container and store in cool area for 1 week or wrap well and freeze for 1 month.

ENGLISH TRIFLE

Any fresh berries or juicy fruit may be used including plums, mangos, strawberries, blackberries, and blueberries.

SERVES: 8
PREP TIME: 1 hour
COOKING TIME: 30 minutes
MAY BE PREPARED AHEAD: 24 hours

INGREDIENTS:

1 12 to 14 oz. pound cake
raspberry jam
1/2 cup medium dry sherry
1/4 cup brandy
5 egg yolks
6 tbsp. sugar
1 tsp. cornstarch
pinch of salt
2 cups milk
2 tsp. vanilla extract
1 pint fresh raspberries
2 fresh peaches, peeled & thinly sliced
1-1/2 cups heavy cream
1 tbsp. powdered sugar

PREPARATION:

Trim poundcake and cut into 1 inch slices. Completely coat each slice with raspberry jam and line bottom of crystal serving bowl with slices.

Cut remaining slices into 1 inch cubes and place one layer only on top of slices in the bowl. Pour sherry and brandy over, cover lightly, and let stand at room temperature for 1 hour.

With wire whisk, mix yolks, sugar, cornstarch and salt.

Heat milk, stirring, until almost boiling. Very slowly, pour milk into egg mixture, stirring well. Transfer to heavy saucepan and cook over medium heat, stirring constantly, until custard coats spoon. Remove from heat, stir, and add vanilla. Blend well and let cool. Do not overcook, or custard will separate.

Reserving 10 to 12 firm raspberries for garnish, arrange berries and peach sliceson cake cubes; repeat layers of fruit and cake cubes.

Pour cooled custard over and refrigerate overnight.

TO SERVE:

Whip cream until thick and gradually whip in the powdered sugar. Whip until firm. Reserve 1/2 cup for garnish, and spread remainder on top of custard. Decorate with reserved berries and rosettes of whipped cream.

CHESS PIES
(Or Christmas Wish Pies)

An old custom bakes a bean or charm into one of the pies. Guests make a wish as dessert is served, and the person whose pie contains the surprise is "King of the Evening" and will have his dream come true. Warn guests to bite gingerly, so they don't get a bigger surprise than planned!

SERVES: 12
PREP TIME: 5 minutes
COOKING TIME: 30 minutes
MAY BE PREPARED AHEAD: 24 hours

INGREDIENTS:

12 individual muffin-sized pie crusts*
3 eggs
1 cup sugar
1 cup chopped walnuts
1 cup raisins
1 tsp. vanilla

PREPARATION:

Spray muffin cups with oil spray, press pastry dough in muffin cups, and flute edges.

Beat eggs and sugar together. Add other ingredients and mix well.

TO COOK:

Put mixture in pielet shells and bake in a 400 degree oven until brown, about 1/2 hour.

If preparing ahead, STOP. Cover and refrigerate. Bring to room temperature before serving.

*Use Cream Cheese Pastry dough (see page 276) or Pate Brisée (see page 117).

CREAM PUFFS

Use for dessert shells. For hors d'oeuvres, stuff with a Curried Turkey Salad or Tuna Salad with Tarragon. For a tasty accompaniment to soups or salads, make cheese puffs by sprinkling shredded gruyere cheese over the small puffs before baking.

SERVES: 12 cream puffs or
        36 canape shells or
        cheese puffs
PREP TIME: 20 minutes
BAKING TIME: 50 minutes
MAY BE PREPARED AHEAD: 24 hours;
        day old puffs may be re-crisped for
        5 minutes in a hot oven.

INGREDIENTS:

1 cup water
1/2 cup butter or margarine
1/8 tsp. salt
1 cup sifted all-purpose flour
4 eggs

PREPARATION:

Preheat oven to 400 degrees.

Put water, butter or margarine, and salt in saucepan; bring to boiling over high heat, stirring occasionally. Lower heat and add flour all at once and stir rapidly until mixture forms a ball and follows spoon around the pan; remove from heat and cool slightly.

Add one egg; beat well until mixture is smooth and egg is blended in. Repeat with remaining three eggs, adding them one at a time and beating until each is blended in before adding the next one. (Mixture will be slippery and separated, but the beating will make it smooth)

Drop from spoon onto ungreased cookie sheet in 12 even mounds, about three inches apart; use a rubber spatula to help push the mixture off spoon. For chocolate eclairs, make a 3-inch long by 1-1/2-inch wide oval. Use teaspoon quantities for 36 canapes.

TO BAKE:

Do not delay in placing puffs in oven. If dough cools, puffs will not rise properly.

Bake puffs 45-50 minutes, or until they are puffed and brown and there are no tiny bubbles of moisture on the surface.

Move from oven and transfer puffs from cookie sheet to wire racks with spatula. Cool them, away from drafts, while you make pastry cream.

Cut tops from puffs with a sharp knife. Remove any pieces of soft dough from the centers.

If preparing ahead, STOP. Store in airtight container for 24 hours. Re-crisp in 400 degree oven for 5 minutes before serving.

Chocolate Eclairs
Fill with almond cream (see page 280) and top with chocolate sauce (see page 120).

Variations

Chocolate mousse topped with raspberry cream anglaise.

Fresh fruit and whipped cream topped with powdered sugar.

COMPANY CAKE

This recipe makes two cakes, one to eat and one to keep on hand for company.

SERVES: 8 - each cake
PREP TIME: 5 minutes
COOKING TIME: 35 minutes
MAY BE PREPARED AHEAD: 24 hours;
    frozen 2 months

INGREDIENTS:

2 cups boiling water
1 lb. raisins
1 tbsp. soda
1 cup cold water
1/2 cup shortening
2 cups sugar
4 cups flour
1 tsp. salt
1 tsp. cinnamon
1 tsp. cloves
1 tsp. nutmeg
confectioners sugar garnish

PREPARATION:

Pour boiling water over raisins. Set aside.

Mix soda in cold water. Set aside.

Cream shortening and 2 cups sugar. Add soda/water mixture.

Mix together flour and spices. Add to shortening mixture.

Add raisins and mix well.

Pour into two 9 x 13 x 2 inch pans.

TO BAKE:

Bake for 35 minutes in a 425 degree oven.

Allow to cool. Place paper doily over cake and dust with confectioners sugar. Lift doily carefully and lace design will remain.

If preparing ahead, STOP. Cover and refrigerate for up to 24 hours. Will keep frozen for up to 2 months.

Serve with whipped cream or double cream if desired.

RUM CAKES with ALMOND CREME

SERVES: 24
PREP TIME: 15 minutes
COOKING TIME: 25 minutes
MAY BE PREPARED AHEAD: 24 hours

CAKE

INGREDIENTS:

1-1/2 cups sugar
2 tbsp. heavy cream
2 eggs
1/8 tsp. salt
1 cup + 2 tbsp flour
1-1/2 tsp. baking powder
1 tsp. vanilla
1/2 cup very hot milk
slivered almonds for garnish

PREPARATION:

Preheat oven to 350 degrees.

Mix together sugar, heavy cream, eggs, and salt until smooth.

Sift together flour and baking powder and add to cream mixture, mixing well. Add vanilla and rapidly mix very hot milk with other ingredients.

Immediately pour batter into large greased muffin tins and put into oven. (Any delay after adding hot milk will prevent cake from rising properly.)

TO BAKE:

Bake 20-25 minutes.

Remove cakes from pan and place in larger rectangular pan. When slightly cooled, cover with rum sauce and allow to soak for 24 hours. Pan should be covered and put in refrigerator.

RUM SAUCE

INGREDIENTS:

1-1/2 cups sugar
1 cup water
1/3 cup dark rum or 2 tsp. rum flavoring

PREPARATION:

Place sugar and water in saucepan and bring to boil. Boil for 3 minutes.

Allow to cool. Add dark rum and mix well.

ALMOND CREME

INGREDIENTS:

1/2 pint whipping cream
1/3 cup confectioner's sugar
1-1/2tsp. almond flavoring

PREPARATION:

Just before serving, mix all ingredients and whip until stiff.

TO SERVE:

Place cake on plate, spoon rum sauce over cake, top with Almond Creme and garnish with slivered almonds.

GINGERBREAD

SERVES: 8
PREP TIME: 5 minutes
COOKING TIME: 15-20 minutes
MAY BE PREPARED AHEAD: 12 hours

INGREDIENTS:

1 3/4 cup all purpose flour
1/2 cup buttermilk
1 tsp. ground cinnamon
1/2 cup vegetable oil
2 tsp. ground ginger
1 tsp. vanilla
1 tsp. baking soda
1/2 grated nutmeg
1/2 tsp. ground allspice
3/4 cup unsulfured molasses
double cream, whipped cream,
     ice cream or homemade applesauce
     to serve with gingerbread

PREPARATION:

Preheat oven to 350 degrees, grease a
rectangular baking pan or 8 small decorative
baking molds, and dust with flour.

Whisk together dry ingredients until well mixed.

In another bowl whisk together wet
ingredients until smooth. Make a well in
the center of the dry mixture, and pour
in the wet mixture. Whisk until the batter
is well combined. Do not overmix.

Bake 13-15 minutes for individual molds;
15 -20 minutes for pan; or until tester
comes out clean. Cool in pan.

*If preparing ahead, STOP. Store in cook
place for up to 12 hours.*

DREAM COOKIES

As a child, these rich, chewy bars were
my favorites. They are forever mixed
in my mind with happy times, daydreams
and a magical sense of well being.

SERVES: 16 squares
PREP TIME: 10 minutes
COOKING TIME: 1 hour
MAY BE PREPARED AHEAD:
     1 week; may be frozen for one month

INGREDIENTS:

1/2 cup butter
2 tbsp. powdered sugar
1 cup cake flour
2 eggs
1/4 tsp. salt
1-1/4 cups brown sugar
1-1/2 tsp. baking powder
2 tbsp. flour
1 cup nut meats
1 cup coconut

PREPARATION:

Cream butter, powdered sugar, and
cake flour thoroughly. Spread evenly
in a greased 8 x 8 x 2" pan, and bake in
350 degree oven for 30 minutes.

Beat eggs until thick and lemon colored.

Sift together salt, brown sugar, baking
powder, and 2 tbsp. flour and add to eggs
along with nuts and coconut. Spread
over first mixture.

Bake in 350 degree oven an additional
30 minutes. Cool in pan and cut in squares.

BIZCOCHOS

Traditional holiday cookies
from Spanish settlers.

SERVES: 5 dozen cookies
PREP TIME: 15 minutes
COOKING TIME: 10 minutes
MAY BE PREPARED AHEAD: 1 week

INGREDIENTS:

2 cups vegetable shortening
1 cup sugar
2 eggs
2 tsp. anise seed
2 tbsp. sherry
6 cups all purpose flour
1 tsp. salt
2 tsp. baking powder
3/4 cup water
1/2 cup sugar + 4 tsp. ground cinnamon
      for topping

PREPARATION:

Preheat oven to 350 degrees.

Cream together vegetable shortening,
sugar and eggs until fluffy. Stir in anise
seed and sherry. The fluffier the whipped
shortening, the lighter the cookie.

Sift together flour, salt, baking powder, and
stir into egg/sugar mixture. Add just enough
water to hold mixture together, and mix well.

On a floured board, roll dough in 1/2 inch
thickness. Cut into fancy shapes (my
favorites are chili peppers or evergreens.).
The traditional shape is a fleur de lis,
a remnant of French influence in Mexico.
Sprinkle with cinnamon sugar.

TO COOK:

Bake on ungreased cookie sheet
for about 10 minutes.

*If preparing ahead, STOP. Store in
an airtight container for up to 1 week.*

PECAN BUTTER ROUNDS

SERVES: 48 cookies
PREP TIME: 5 minutes
COOKING TIME: 12 minutes
MAY BE PREPARED AHEAD: 1 week

INGREDIENTS:

1/2 cup softened butter or margarine
3 oz. cream cheese
1 cup sugar
1 cup flour
1/2 cup chopped pecans or walnuts

PREPARATION:

Blend butter and cream cheese in
food processor. Add sugar, flour and
nuts; blend again.

Drop by teaspoon full on highly greased
cookie sheet.

Bake at 350 degrees for 10 - 12 minutes.

Note: Can double or even triple the recipe.

ALMOND MACAROONS

Lighter than air, these cookies are a perfect accompaniment to fresh fruits or sorbets.

SERVES: 48 cookies
PREP TIME: 10 minutes
COOKING TIME: 15 minutes
MAY BE PREPARED AHEAD: 3 days

INGREDIENTS:

4-1/2 oz. ground almonds
4-1/2oz. granulated sugar
3 egg whites
2/3 cup powdered sugar

PREPARATION:

Preheat oven to 350 degrees and line baking sheet with parchment.

Place ground almonds, granulated sugar, and 1 egg white in food processor and process to make an almond paste.

Beat almond paste and sugar, mixing well. Add egg whites to make a smooth batter. Drop by teaspoonful onto baking sheet.

TO BAKE:

Bake for 15 minutes. Cool before serving.

WALNUT ORANGE WAFERS

SERVES: 36 cookies
PREP TIME: 10 minutes
COOKING TIME: 10-12 minutes
MAY BE PREPARED AHEAD: 1 week

INGREDIENTS:

2 eggs
1 cup brown sugar
2/3 cup flour
1/2 tsp. salt
1/2 tsp. baking soda
1/2 tsp. nutmeg
2 tbsp. grated orange zest
1 cup chopped walnuts

PREPARATION:

Preheat oven to 375 degrees.

Cream together eggs and sugar.

Sift together dried ingredients and add to sugar mixture. Add walnuts, orange zest and nutmeg.

Drop by the teaspoonful onto buttered baking sheet.

TO BAKE:

Bake at 375 degrees for 10-12 minutes.

If preparing ahead, STOP. Store in covered container for up to 1 week.

Winter

Seasonal Gifts

JALAPEÑO JELLY

SERVES: approximately six 8-oz. jars
PREP TIME: 15 minutes
COOKING TIME: 40 minutes
MAY BE PREPARED AHEAD: 6 months

INGREDIENTS:

3 cups ripe red bell peppers
5 jalapeño peppers, finely chopped
1-1/2 cups cider vinegar
6-1/2 cups sugar
6 oz. bottled liquid pectin

PREPARATION:

Clean jelly jars, then boil in at least
one inch water while making jelly.

Chop by hand or use a food processor or
blender to process the peppers in to a
medium grind; combine with the vinegar
and sugar in a large, heavy saucepan.

TO COOK:

Bring mixture to a boil and boil for 30 minutes.

Allow to cool for 10 minutes; then stir
in the pectin and boil for 2 minutes.

Check thickness of jelly by dipping a metal
spoon in at right angles to the surface of the
jelly and lifting it about a foot above the
surface. If jelly does not come together and
sheet off, continue boiling and test again.

Remove from the heat, skim, and allow
the jelly to cool. Stir so that the fruit is
evenly dispersed, then ladle into sterilized
jars. When cool seal with paraffin.

BASIL GARLIC OIL

Use as an instant pasta sauce — just mix
with hot pasta — or as a dip for crusty bread
loaves or bolillos. This is also a wonderful
sauce to brush over fresh grilled fish.

SERVES: 1 quart
PREP TIME: 5 minutes + 2 days storing time
COOKING TIME: None
MAY BE PREPARED AHEAD: 1 month

INGREDIENTS:

2 garlic clove, chopped
1/2 cup parsley, chopped
1/2 cup basil, chopped
1/4 cup piñons, chopped
1 shallot
1 quart olive oil

PREPARATION:

Process garlic, parsley, basil, piñons, and
shallot in food processor until rough chopped.

Add to oil and mix well.

Store for 2 days, shaking daily to mix flavors.

Fill sterilized decanters.

SWEET CHILI SAUCE

Serve over baked ham, egg crepes,
or roast pork. As a gift, I often combine
a jar of this sauce with a pretty antique
cut glass serving dish.

SERVES: 8
PREP TIME: Mise en place
COOKING TIME: 1-1/2 hours
MAY BE PREPARED AHEAD: 1 month

INGREDIENTS:

1 can tomatoes
1/2 green pepper, cut fine
1/2 cup vinegar
1 tsp. salt
1 tsp. allspice
1 medium onion
1 cup brown sugar
1 tsp. cinnamon
1 tsp. cloves
1/2 tsp. cayenne pepper

PREPARATION: Mise en place

TO COOK:

Combine all ingredients and simmer
about 1-1/2 hours, stirring as needed.

*If preparing ahead, STOP. Cover and
refrigerate for up to one month.*

Pour in a decorative jar for gift giving.

TO SERVE:

Bring to room temperature,
or reheat in saucepan.

LEMON VERBENA SYRUP

SERVES: 1 quart
PREP TIME: 2-3 hours steeping time
COOKING TIME: 15 minutes
MAY BE PREPARED AHEAD: 3 months

INGREDIENTS:

3 cups water
1 cup fresh lemon verbena
2 cups dark brown sugar

PREPARATION:

Bring water and lemon verbena to boil.
Remove from heat and allow to steep
for 2-3 hours to develop infusion.
Strain out herbs.

Combine water and sugar in
saucepan and heat to dissolve sugar.
Continue cooking for 10-12 minutes,
stirring constantly as syrup thickens.

Fill sterilized decorative bottles.

ORANGE MINT SYRUP

This is a light syrup without the traditional mapley flavors of most breakfast syrups.

SERVES: 1 quart
PREP TIME: 2-3 hours steeping time
COOKING TIME: 15 minutes
MAY BE PREPARED AHEAD: 3 months

INGREDIENTS:

2 cups water
1 cup fresh spearmint
peel of 1 orange with white part removed
2 cups granulated sugar
1 cup orange juice

PREPARATION:

Bring water, mint, and orange peel to boil. Remove from heat and allow to steep for 2-3 hours to develop infusion. Strain out herbs.

Combine water, juice and sugar in saucepan and heat to dissolve sugar. Continue cooking for 10-12 minutes, stirring constantly as syrup thickens.

Fill sterilized decorative bottles.

SPICY GRANADA SEASONING for MEATS and POULTRY

Years ago, a wonderful spice called "Parisienne" was available to flavor meat and poultry. It became increasingly difficult to find. In fact, I was thrilled to inherit two bottles from my grandmother. It hasn't been on store shelves for about 10 years. I finally solved this shortage by experimenting with this recipe. It is perfect with ragouts, chicken breasts and roasts. If a dish needs depth of flavor, this seasoning offers an "exotic touch. Use sparingly — begin with 1 tsp. over a dish that serves 6, adding more as needed.

SERVES: approximately 1 cup
PREP TIME: 5 minutes
COOKING TIME: None
MAY BE PREPARED AHEAD: 6 months

INGREDIENTS:

3 tbsp. ground cinnamon
2-1/2 tbsp. ground nutmeg
1-1/2 tbsp. ground black pepper
2-1/2 tbsp. ground cardamon
1-1/2 tbsp. ground white pepper
2 tbsp. ground cloves
1-1/2 tbsp. ground allspice
2 tbsp. dried thyme

PREPARATION:

Mix all ingredients well, and regrind using electric coffee mill.

Fill sterilized bottles.

A recipe to use Granada Seasoning follows on the next page.

VEAL GRANADA

Here's a quick and easy dish made gourmet with this seasoning. Include it on a recipe card with a gift of Granada Seasoning! Serve with pasta or rice.

SERVES: 4
PREP TIME: Mise en place
COOKING TIME: 15 minutes
MAY BE PREPARED AHEAD: No

INGREDIENTS:

1-1/2 lbs. veal, cut into 1-inch cubes
1 tsp. Spicy Granada Seasoning
1 cup fresh cooked peas

PREPARATION:

Saute veal cubes in oil until done, about 10 minutes. Sprinkle with spicy Granada Seasoning and mix well, cooking another few minutes. Add peas and mix well.

MULLING SPICE

SERVES: 6 bags
PREP TIME: 10 minutes
COOKING TIME: None
MAY BE PREPARED AHEAD: 3 months

INGREDIENTS:

12 cinnamon sticks
1/4 cup whole cloves
1 tbsp. nutmeg
1 tbsp. cardamom
1/4 cup allspice berries
1/4 cup juniper berries
rind of 1 orange, cut into thin strips
rind of 1 lemon, cut into thin strips

PREPARATION:

Mix all ingredients well, then divide into 6 mounds.

Using 6-inch squares of good cheesecloth or 6 mulling bags, fill with the spices. Leave the string long, so packet can be retrieved easily.

TO USE:

Drop 1 bag into 1 quart cider or wine and heat. Do not bring to a boil. If using a wine, try a hearty burgundy or a rosé.

VARIATION:

For sweet mulling spice, add 1 cup dark brown sugar.

LEMON LIQUEUR

This is a nice digestive after a heavy holiday meal. It can be served as a finale with butter cookies, or try a tablespoonful over lemon sorbet or vanilla ice cream.

SERVES: 1 quart - 16 2 oz. liqueur glasses
PREP TIME: 1 month
COOKING TIME: None
MAY BE PREPARED AHEAD: 1 year

INGREDIENTS:

1/2 cup lemon verbena leaves
4 3-inch strip lemon zest with white
    part cut away
4 cups vodka
2 cups sugar

PREPARATION:

Bruise lemon verbena leaves with wooden spoon. Place zest, leaves, and vodka in sealed sterile jar and steep for 2 days.

Add sugar and steep for 2 weeks, shaking twice a day to dissolve sugar. Strain out leaves and zest.

Bottle in sterilized decorative bottle and age for 2 weeks more.

DRIED LEMON and ORANGE ZEST

Never discard orange, tangerine or lemon peelings. Remove and discard as much of the white membrane as possible, as it tends to be bitter.

Wash and dry the peelings.

Place on cookie sheet and dry on the very lowest heat of your oven — 150 degrees for 3 hours, 170 degrees for 2 to 2-1/2 hours.

Grind in a blender and store in small jars. Will keep 3 to 4 months.

ORANGE WALNUT BREAD

SERVES: 1 loaf; 2 guest loaves
PREP TIME: 20 minutes
BAKING TIME: 50-60 minutes
MAY BE PREPARED AHEAD:
    Fresh - 1 week;
    Frozen - 3 months

INGREDIENTS:

peel from 1 large orange, cut very fine
1/2 cup water
1/4 tsp. salt
1/2 cup sugar
milk (about 1 cup)
1 egg, beaten
2 tbsp. melted shortening
3 tsp. baking powder
1 cup flour
1 cup walnuts, chopped

PREPARATION:

Combine peel, water, salt and sugar in saucepan, and cook until peel is tender, about 10 minutes. Cool and add enough milk to measure 1-1/2 cups.

Cream egg and shortening and mix with milk/orange peel mixture.

Sift together baking powder and flour. Add orange peel mixture and 1/2 cup walnuts, mixing well. Allow to stand for 2 minutes.

Pour into a greased 9" x 5" loaf pan. Top with remaining 1/2 cup walnuts.

TO BAKE:

Bake at 350 degrees for 50-60 minutes.

Allow to cool on wire rack for 1 hour, wrap in foil and tie with a ribbon.

PEAR LIME PECAN BREAD

Combine this gift with a crock of fruit or honey butter (see pages 95-96).

SERVES: 2 large loaves or 4 guest loaves
PREP TIME: 5 minutes +
    20 minutes standing time
BAKING TIME: 60-90 minutes
MAY BE PREPARED AHEAD:
    Refrigerated - 1 week;
    Frozen - 3 months

INGREDIENTS:

1 cup sugar
1/2 cup shortening
2 eggs
1 tsp. vanilla
juice of 1 lime
1 cup mashed pears
1 cup flour
2 tsp. baking powder
1 tsp. salt
1-1/2 tsp. cinnamon
2 tsp. lime zest
1-1/2 cup chopped pecans

PREPARATION:

Cream sugar, shortening, eggs, vanilla, lime juice and pears together.

Sift together flour, baking powder, spices and lime zest, and fold into sugar/egg mixture. Allow to stand for 20 minutes.

Fold in pecans and pour into greased loaf pans.

TO BAKE:

Bake at 350 degrees for 60-90 minutes.

Allow to cool on wire rack for 1 hour, wrap in foil and tie with a ribbon.

For a dressy covering for nut breads and baked goods, purchase a roll of embossed florist foil available at florist supply stores.

CHRISTMAS COOKIE ORNAMENTS

Make gingerbread men, toy soldiers, decorated Christmas trees or angels. Use the dough as clay or roll it as you would for sugar cookies and use cutters. Experiment with kitchen utensils to make decorative designs. Make angels' or gingerbread girls' hair with a garlic press. Garnishing knives and tools work especially well to inscribe designs. *This gift item is not edible.*

SERVES: approximately 24
PREP TIME: Varies
COOKING TIME: 1-1/2 hours
MAY BE PREPARED AHEAD:
    will keep permanently in a dry place.

INGREDIENTS:

4 cups flour
1 cup salt
1-1/2 cup water
paper clips
paint with food-colored water

PREPARATION:

Mix flour, salt and water well.

Cut or form into shapes.

Insert a paper clip to hang.

TO COOK:

Bake at 300 degrees for 1-1/2 hours.

Paint with food-colored water or water paints.

Spray with plastic sealer.

WINTER HARVEST CALENDAR

SOUTHERN CALIFORNIA[1]
FRUITS AND VEGETABLES
apples, asparagus, artichokes, avocados, beets, broccoli, cabbage, carrots, cauliflower, celery, grapefruit, grapes, green onions, kiwis, kumquats, lemons, lettuce and greens, mushrooms, navel oranges, onions, pears, peas, potatoes, rhubarb, snow peas, spinach, strawberries, sugar snaps, sweet potatoes, tangelos, tangerines, tomatoes, zucchini

OTHER PRODUCTS
crab, dried fruits and nuts, eggs, farm fresh scallops, honey, macadamia nuts

NEW MEXICO[2]
OTHER PRODUCTS
pecans

ARIZONA[3]
FRUITS AND VEGETABLES
broccoli, green onions, lettuce

OTHER PRODUCTS
pecans

[1]From the Cooperative Extension Service, University of San Diego, the Produce Marketing Association's Produce Availability and Merchandising Guide, and Western Growers Association's 1992 Export Directory.

[2]From the Cooperative Extension Service, New Mexico State University and the Produce Marketing Association's 1992 Produce Availability and Merchandising Guide.

[3]From the Cooperative Extension Service, University of Ariziona, the Produce Marketing Associations's Produce Availability and Merchandising Guide, and Western Growers Association's 1992 Export Directory.

Weights, Measures and the Metric System
(Most convenient approximations)

WEIGHTS

Conversion Formulas:
Ounces into grams, multiply the ounces by 28.3495
Grams into ounces, multiply the grams by 0.35274

Pounds and Ounces	Metric
2.2 lbs	1 kilogram
1 lb. (16 oz.)	464 grams
3-1/2 oz.	100 grams
1 oz.	30 grams

LIQUID MEASUREMENTS

Conversion Formulas:
Quarts into liters, multiply the quarts by 0.94635
Liters into quarts, multiply the liters by 1.056688
Ounces into milliliters, multiply the ounces by 29.573
Milliliters into ounces, multiply the milliliters by 0.0338

Cups and Spoons	Quarts and Ounces	Metric
4 1/3 cups	1 quart 2 oz.	1 liter
1 cup	8 oz.	1/4 liter
1 tbsp.	1/2 oz.	15 milliliters
1 tsp.	1/16 oz.	5 milliliters

Liquid Measure	Volume Equivalent	Liquid Measure	Volume Equivalent
3 tsp.	1 tbsp.	2 cups	1 pint
2 tbsp.	1 fluid oz.	2 pints	1 quart
4 tbsp.	1/4 cup	4 quarts	1 gallon
16 tbsp.	1 cup or 8 fluid oz.		

TEMPERATURES

Conversion Formulas:
Centigrade to Fahrenheit, multiply by 9, divide by 5, add 32
Fahrenheit to Centigrade, subtract 32, multiply by 5, divide by 9

Fahrenheit	Centigrade	Fahrenheit	Centigrade
50 degrees	10 degrees	375 degrees	190 degrees
100	38	400	204.4
212	100	425	218
275	135	450	232
325	163	550	288
350	177		

Index by Recipe Name